PUBLICATIONS OF

THE COLONIAL SOCIETY
OF MASSACHUSETTS

VOLUME LXXVI

PORTRAIT OF A PATRIOT

THE MAJOR POLITICAL AND LEGAL PAPERS
OF JOSIAH QUINCY JUNIOR

PORTRAIT OF A PATRIOT

The Major Political and Legal Papers of
Josiah Quincy Junior

EDITORS

DANIEL R. COQUILLETTE

J. Donald Monan, S.J. University Professor, Boston College
Lester Kissel Visiting Professor, Harvard Law School

NEIL LONGLEY YORK

Karl G. Maeser Professor of General Education
Chair, History Department, Brigham Young University

❦ VOLUME THREE ❧
The Southern Journal (1773)

BOSTON · 2007
The Colonial Society of Massachusetts
Distributed by the University of Virginia Press

ACKNOWLEDGMENTS FOR THE QUINCY PAPERS

This series of volumes represents the tireless and invaluable work of our research and administrative assistants: Brandon Bigelow, Kevin Cox, Jane Downing, Natalia Fekula, Michael Hayden, Elizabeth Kamali, Christina Nolan, Nicole Scimone, Brian Sheppard, Susannah Tobin, and Elisa Underwood, with special recognition to the Editorial Assistants to the Boston College Monan Chair, Brendan Farmer and Patricia Tarabelsi, and to Inge Burgess at Harvard. Their intelligence and enthusiasm are visible on every page. Of course, we are deeply in debt to John W. Tyler, Editor of Publications of the Colonial Society of Massachusetts and the Committee of Publications, without whose guidance and support this project would have been impossible. Finally, special thanks are also due to the guardians of the Quincy heritage: the Massachusetts Historical Society with its enormously helpful Librarian, Peter Drummey, and his staff, the Museum of Fine Arts, Boston, and the Quincy family itself.

FRONTISPIECE:

"View of Mulberry, House and Street, 1805" by Thomas Coram. Oil on paper. The plantation house, built by Thomas Broughton c. 1711, can be seen in the background. In the foreground are the plantation's slave quarters. Quincy had grave reservations about the prevalence of slavery in the South, both for moral reasons and for what he saw as its corrupting influence on Southern landowners. Image courtesy of the Gibbes Museum of Art and the Carolina Art Association.

Printed from the income of the Sarah Louise Edes Fund

JOSIAH QUINCY JR.
Political and Legal Works

VOLUME THREE

THE SOUTHERN JOURNAL
(1773)

CO-EDITORS:
Daniel R. Coquillette
Neil Longley York

VOLUME EDITOR:
Daniel R. Coquillette

"If we act only for ourselves, to neglect the study of history is not prudent. If we are entrusted with the care of others, it is not just."

SAMUEL JOHNSON
[*Rasselas*] *The Prince of Abissinia*,
Chapter 30. (London, 1759)

To Judith

CONTENTS

VOLUME 3

ACKNOWLEDGMENTS
VOLUME THREE

AT THE OUTSET OF VOLUMES ONE AND TWO, and at various points throughout this volume, I have praised the efforts of a wonderful group of students and colleagues who have helped me at every step of the way. Let me repeat a few heartfelt "thank yous" here. Michael H. Hayden not only transcribed the *Southern Journal*, but added copious annotations. Brandon Bigelow, Kevin Cox, Elizabeth Kamali, Christina Nolan, Nicole Scimone, Susannah Tobin and Elisa Underwood provided valuable research assistance. Three Editorial Assistants to the Monan Chair labored long and hard at these complex and difficult manuscripts: Brendan Farmer, Patricia Tarabelsi, and Charles Riordan, together with Inge Burgess at Harvard Law School. Their intelligence and thoroughness marks every page. I have enjoyed library support of the very first order, with particular thanks to Karen Beck and Mark Sullivan at Boston College Law Library and David Warrington at the Harvard Law Library, and David Whitesell at Harvard's Houghton Library. Then there have been my colleagues at the famous Stinehour Press, whose craftsmanship and design skills are self-evident in these volumes. There has also been the invaluable support of two other great institutions: the Colonial Society of Massachusetts, with its distinguished Editor of Publication, John W. Tyler, and the Massachusetts Historical Society and its enormously helpful librarian, Peter Drummey, along with his staff. Finally, I must thank my colleague and co-editor, Neil York, for his constant assistance, encouragement and friendship, my invaluable colleagues at both Boston College and Harvard, and, of course, my family and my wife, Judith, who have truly made all this possible.

DANIEL R. COQUILLETTE
Volume Editor

JOSIAH QUINCY JR.'S
Southern Journal
(1773)

Volume Editor
DANIEL R. COQUILLETTE
J. Donald Monan, S.J. University Professor,
Boston College Law School
Lester Kissel Visiting Professor,
Harvard Law School

Transcribed, and Annotated with the Volume Editor, by
MICHAEL H. HAYDEN, ESQ.
J.D., Boston College Law School, Class of 2004
Member of the Massachusetts Bar

With many thanks for the extraordinary and invaluable assistance of Nicole Scimone, J.D. Boston College Law School Class of 2005, Susannah Tobin, J.D. Harvard Law School Class of 2004, Kevin Cox, J.D. Harvard Law School Class of 2006, Elizabeth Papp Kamali, J.D. Harvard Law School Class of 2007, unparalleled research assistants; and Charles Riordan, Patricia Tarabelsi, and Laurie Tautkas, the simply invaluable Editorial Assistants to the Monan Chair.

Josiah Quincy Jr.'s *Southern Journal*
(1773)
Daniel R. Coquillette

T HIS NEW TRANSCRIPTION AND EDITION of Josiah Quincy Jr.'s extraordinary southern adventure has been an adventure in itself. My fellow travelers have been my exceptional research assistants: Michael H. Hayden, Boston College Law School Class of 2004, Nicole Scimone, Boston College Law School Class of 2005, Susannah B. Tobin, Harvard Law School Class of 2004, and Elizabeth Papp Kamali, Harvard Law School Class of 2007. Michael Hayden also provided the transcription, which is a true labor of love, and many of the annotations. Without all this great effort, the project would have been impossible. All in all, this was a team effort, and it has been a privilege to work with such outstanding young people.

The manuscript of the *Southern Journal* is at the Massachusetts Historical Society in Boston in the Quincy, Wendell, Holmes and Upham Family Papers (hereafter "Quincy Papers") microfilm P-347, Reel 3, Ms. QP-61, JQII. It was first printed in Josiah Quincy, *Memoir of the Life of Josiah Quincy Jun.* (1st ed., Boston, 1825), pp. 73–141 (hereafter "*Memoir*"), a book actually prepared in most part by Quincy's granddaughter, Eliza Susan Quincy (1798–1884), but published under her father's name. Eliza prepared a second edition in 1874, in which the *Southern Journal* appears at pp. 56–111. Both of these versions are unreliable, Eliza having excised important material. As she noted: "Some of his particular observations, from the familiarity of our present intercourse, might appear trite and uninteresting, and will be omitted, as also will be, for the most part, all those particular strictures on the nature of the population of the southern colonies, which was most likely to make the deepest impression on an inhabitant of the northern, and by which a stranger, of his turn of mind, could not fail to be peculiarly affected." See *Memoir, supra,* pp. 72–73. Needless to say, these omissions include particularly interesting material! Eliza also omitted important materials from Quincy's letter to his wife of March 1, 1773, from Charleston. See *Memoir, supra,* pp. 71–73, 2d ed., pp. 73–96. For a full account of Eliza Quincy's literary activity, see Neil L. York's "Prologue" and "The Making of a Patriot: A Life Cut Short" at pp. 10–11, 15 in volume 1 of this series, *Portrait of a Patriot: The Major Political and Legal Papers of Josiah Quincy Jr.* (hereafter *"Quincy Papers"*).

The *Southern Journal* has only been published once before in an unexpurgated version, by the legendary Mark Antony DeWolfe Howe in the *Proceedings of the Massachusetts Historical Society,* vol. XLIX (October 1915–June 1916), pp. 426–481 (hereafter, "Howe, *Proceedings,* 1915–1916"). Howe, who was related to the Quincy family by marriage, also transcribed Quincy's *London Journal,* an account of his voyage to London in 1774–1775, which has been newly edited for these volumes by my co-editor, Neil Longley York, in Volume 1 of the *Quincy Papers, supra.* Professor York has included a compelling short biography of Howe at Volume 1, pp. 219–221, which I will not attempt to repeat here.

This new transcription and edition of the *Southern Journal* was done directly from the manuscript, and is more accurate than the earlier version. Where, however, Howe's annotations proved valuable, they have been retained, with citations to the *Proceedings.*

Such a massive project would have been impossible without the extraordinary efforts of the transcriber, Michael H. Hayden, Esq., Boston College Law School Class of 2004 and Member of the Massachusetts bar. In so many ways, Mr. Hayden was the ideal student, research assistant, and colleague. Enthusiastic, original, and thorough, he has an exceptional historical sense and a taste for grinding hard work. The quality and care of the transcription, which, unlike Howe's, reproduces each page of the manuscript, is a labor of love. Further, Mr. Hayden provided a large number of the annotations and illustrations, with this co-editor taking responsibility for the rest, together with any errors. Mr. Hayden's *Transcriber's Foreword,* which follows, gives only a brief glimpse of his scholarship and dedication.

I should also again acknowledge the loyal and intelligent assistance of Susannah Tobin, Harvard Law School Class of 2004, who provided the Latin translations, Elizabeth Kamali, Harvard Law School Class of 2007, who reviewed them, and Nicole Scimone, Boston College Law School Class of 2005, who labored long and hard to supplement the annotations and to locate the many wonderful illustrations. As always, it has been an exceptional pleasure to work with my co-editor, Neil Longley York, Karl G. Maeser Professor at Brigham Young University and Chair of the History Department, and John W. Tyler, Editor of Publications to the Colonial Society of Massachusetts and Chair of the History Department at Groton. They are both gentlemen and scholars in every sense of the word. Finally, special thanks are due to that great institution and guardian of our nation's history, the Massachusetts Historical Society, its exceptional Librarian, Peter Drummey, and to the Quincy family, who have taken a close interest in this project.

THE TEXT

The text has been reproduced as closely as possible to the manuscript itself, with each page printed as it appears in the manuscript. This is a major improvement on the expurgated, if not censored, version of Eliza Quincy and on Howe's transcription. Thanks to the extraordinary efforts of Michael H. Hayden, we have Quincy's original page numbering, and the important distinction between Quincy's text and the margin notes. Each line corresponds exactly to the lines in the original. See Michael Hayden's *Transcriber's Foreword*, *infra*, for his sensitive treatment of spelling and abbreviations.

Where useful, some of Howe's annotations have been retained, with a citation to "Howe, *Proceedings*, 1915–1916," but the notes have been greatly expanded and brought up-to-date. Howe actually annotated the *Southern Journal* very lightly compared to his edition of the *London Journal*, with 97 notes over 55 pages for the former, and 176 notes over 37 pages for the latter. This new edition has 327 notes and 24 illustrations, plus an index.

The *Transcriber's Foreword* also discusses the mystery of the missing pages 125 and 126, which were cut out by a blade. Quincy also crossed out lines at pages 81 and 92, and left blanks on pages 138 (where he could not recall a name), on page 155 (where he did not wish to enter Benjamin Franklin's name), on page 159 (where he could not recall the first name of a "Dr. Cox"), and on page 164, in the middle of a discussion of Pennsylvania's politics. These blanks are all indicated where they occur in the original manuscript. There are also some most interesting later inserts, ably discussed by Michael Hayden in the *Transcriber's Foreword*, *infra*.

Michael H. Hayden, Esq.
Member of the Massachusetts Bar

THIS TRANSCRIPTION of the journal Josiah Quincy Jr. maintained during his 1773 travels through the southern colonies was inspired, supported and guided by Professor Daniel R. Coquillette.

The transcription adheres as closely to Quincy's original layout as possible; Quincy's pagination is preserved, as are line breaks and spatial layout. Thus, where Quincy started a new page, so does the transcription. Where Quincy started a new line, so does the transcription, where practical. Where impractical, the transcription indicates, through hard parenthetical notation, where Quincy's original layout placed such headings and marginalia.

All pagination is correspondingly indicated by Quincy in the original, as are all dates. Thus, where Quincy skips pages or dates, so does the transcription. Quincy's spellings and abbreviations have been modernized to allow for easier reading, but, as Professor Neil York has done with Quincy's *London Journal*, misspellings of proper names have been preserved to communicate Quincy's attempt at phonetic accuracy in lieu of actual knowledge of the names he encounters.

Of missing pages:

Pages 125 and 126 of Quincy's original journal, a single sheet of paper with writing on both sides, have been removed. The removal appears to have been performed with a blade, as the remains of the page removed reflect a smooth cut along its edge, not the ragged edge of a torn page. The religious scandal described by Quincy might possibly have touched too close to home for some interested party, prompting the removal of the missing page. Here is the context:

The State of Religion here is a little better than to the South; tho I hear the most shocking accounts of the depravity and abominable wickedness of their established Clergy, several of whom keeping public taverns and open gaming houses: Other crimes of which one [of] them (who now officiates) is charged and . . .

[PAGES 125 AND 126 MISSING]

safe-guard from future invasions and oppressions. I am mistaken in my conjecture, if in some approaching day Virginia does not more fully see the capital defects of her constitution of gov:t and rue the bitter consequences of them.

In a momentary lapse, Quincy skipped page number 177. An extra page was also inserted between pages 156–157. This page is a wonderful reflection of the volatility of opinion concerning Benjamin Franklin in the nineteenth century. Quincy was clearly fond of Franklin and is unabashed in communicating his affection. The inserted page, however, reflects a different concern of Quincy's descendants. According to Eliza:

[Quincy, Massachusetts February 12/1878] When the Memoir of J. Quincy Jr. was published in 1825, my father decided not to publish this passage. Some years after, the passage was read to Mr. Sparks, who regretted it was not published, and asked and obtained a copy of it. When I published a 3 Edition in 1874–5, I intended to print it, but my brother, Edmund, told me there was yet a strong dislike of Franklin in some classes in Philadelphia, who said that in some important respects, his conduct had been a great disadvantage to the young men of Philadelphia, and set them a bad example. I therefore concluded to follow my father's opinion and omit it.

Eliza Susan Quincy.

Of currency:

Quincy's reference to currency, rather than by "pounds" or "coin," is most often made using "sterling" or "guineas." For this reason, Quincy probably either carried British sterling, to avoid the necessity of exchanging local currencies throughout the colonies, or he calculated the exchange rates for us and himself, facilitating his own ability to recollect the amounts spent on his travels, without need for later calculations. In either event, the currency equivalencies of today have been calculated based upon the amounts he communicated, taken as British sterling.

ACKNOWLEDGMENTS

With great thanks, this work has been magnificently supplemented by the careful Latin translations of Professor Coquillette's research assistant, Susannah Tobin, Harvard Law School Class of 2004. Equal thanks and appreciation are due to Professor Coquillette's Boston College Law School's research assistant, Nicole Scimone, Boston College Law School Class of 2005, who helped to track down the difficult and historical annotations which Professor Coquillette and I had failed to locate; making this volume a much more thorough and complete reflection and introspection into Quincy's entire journey. Nicole also provided a careful, and much appreciated, editorial eye.

Finally, indelible thanks must again be directed to Professor Coquillette. His patience, guidance, and command of the techniques of historical research made this transcription at once a fluid and rigorous endeavor. In addition, he has added many of the annotations. I hope I am so lucky as to enjoy his company and wisdom again in future works and collaborations.

AN ODYSSEY OF AMERICA ON THE BRINK OF REVOLUTION

Josiah Quincy Jr.'s Voyage to the South (1773)*

Daniel R. Coquillette

I. THE *SOUTHERN JOURNAL*

ALL OF JOSIAH QUINCY JR.'s adventures were those of a young man. The cruel tuberculosis that cut off his life at age 31 in 1775 saw to that. The spirit of youthful daring and exuberance, of titillation and risk, and of new discovery and awakening fill the pages of even his most serious work. But not all was positive. The young Quincy knew that he lived at the edge of divides and violence inconceivable to the generation behind him, and he saw clearly the horrors and dangers as well. To everything, he brought the candor of youth.

No writing of Quincy was more filled with the daring and contradictions of youth than his *Journal* of his journey to the South in 1773. (Hereafter, for convenience, "*Southern Journal*" to distinguish it from his later, and equally fascinating *London Journal* of his voyage to England in 1774–1775, edited by my able colleague Neil L. York and set out in volume 1 of this series, *Quincy Papers*, at pp. 219–269.) The *Southern Journal* recounted a great adventure, which included a near fatal sea voyage, introductions to the beauty and elegance of Southern society—and womanhood—and a political "Grand Tour" of the colonies from South Carolina to Rhode Island, including notes about every conceivable topic, from apple cider to the grim realities of slavery. Quincy

---

*An abbreviated version of this introduction was published as Daniel R. Coquillette, "Sectionalism, Slavery, and the Threat of War in Josiah Quincy Jr.'s 1773 *Southern Journal*," 79 *New England Quarterly* (2006), pp. 181–201.

himself drew the analogy to the "Grand Tour" of Italy that marked the "coming-of-age" of his aristocratic English contemporaries, the trip that replaced, at least in theory, the blinders of childhood with a full appreciation of the "world" as it is.[1]

But Quincy was already no child, and the trip had a most serious agenda. Quincy's family was split politically. His brother Samuel (1734–1789) was made Solicitor General of Massachusetts in 1771 and would be proscribed as a loyalist in 1778.[2] Quincy had firmly allied himself with the patriot cause. Nevertheless, like many of his contemporary patriots, including Benjamin Franklin, Quincy was a moderate.[3] He was fearful of what war would bring, and even more fearful of the fragmented state of the colonies. Could such a "grab bag" of vastly differing societies make a common cause, particularly if the British proved cunning and resourceful? While Quincy was careful of what he would put down in writing, there is no doubt that this "Southern Journey" was, in part, to assist committees of correspondence and to improve communications between likeminded patriots. As will be discussed below, Quincy worked assiduously at this task, and many an elegant dinner party had another, more serious, agenda.

But for Quincy there was an even more profound purpose for this difficult, if exhilarating adventure. Quincy wanted to find out what America was really like. Exceptionally sensitive, particularly given the times, Quincy was interested in different political systems, in geography, in religious differences, in what we today call "gender issues," particularly the role of educated women, in race and in slavery, and in the difference in regional cultures. And, of course, as a young lawyer he was interested in the law. He was an astute and frank observer of all these things, partly because of the deeply troubling questions always at the back of his mind. In particular, there was always the question of whether, from this diversity, Americans could make a true nation. In short, the *Southern Journal* is no simple snapshot of a tourist, but a deeply reflective portrait of the character of America on the brink of the Revolution.

---

1. See the discussion in Bruce Redford, *Venice and the Grand Tour* (New Haven, 1996), pp. 5–25. See also Jeremy Black, *The Grand Tour in the Eighteenth Century* (London, 1999).

2. See biographical sketch in *Law in Colonial Massachusetts* (editors D. R. Coquillette, R. J. Brink, C. S. Menand, Boston, 1984), pp. 350–351. (Hereafter, "*Law in Colonial Massachusetts*.")

3. See Gordon S. Wood's excellent discussion in *The Americanization of Benjamin Franklin* (New York, 2004), pp. 105–151.

This is a complex portrait, and it is not possible to discuss all its aspects with thoroughness. But I have chosen certain categories of particular importance, and of particular interest to Quincy, to discuss below. For the rest of this fascinating and nuanced account, I will let the *Southern Journal* speak for itself.

II. TRAVEL

Quincy's *Southern Journal* was, first and foremost, a travel book. The fact that it was an expression of political and philosophical views on the great subjects of time, including slavery and colonial independence, should not obscure its additional importance as a detailed account of how Americans traveled before the Revolution. Of course, travel, in turn, had direct political and historical consequences in the colonies. When Quincy addressed "[T]hou therefore into Whose hand this Journal, either before or after my death, may chance to fall," he noted that it contained "trifles and impertinencies." *Southern Journal*, p. 1. (All citations to the *Southern Journal* refer to Quincy's original pagination, preserved in this edition.) But it is these very details that make the account so readable; the trip, so human; and the travelogue, so significant.

Class mattered in colonial America, and Quincy saw himself as a gentleman. He was accompanied by a servant, Randall, and was not short of money or, equally important, social connections. And he was not an explorer traveling in the wilderness.[4] His journey lay along the primary communication and trade routes between the major American cities of the day: Charleston, Wilmington, Williamsburg, Baltimore, Philadelphia, New York, Newport and Boston. Further, the timing was designed to be auspicious, a direct voyage to Charleston and then, by horse, through the spring countryside of the Carolinas and Virginia, to Philadelphia. It would be peach blossom time, and the seasonal weather in the South would be mild. The plan was clearly to follow the spring north, avoiding both extreme heat and cold. [A similar idea lay behind Edwin Way Teale's famous journey, chronicled in his *North With the Spring* (New York, 1951).] Nevertheless, despite these careful plans, the travel turned out to be hard.

---

4. Compare the "rough travel" journals set out in *Travels in the American Colonies* (Newton D. Mereness, ed., 1st published 1916, reprinted, 1961, New York).

A. Travel by Sea

Quincy set sail on a "Bristol Packett," a fast boat designed to carry mail.[5] The trip began on February 8, 1773 but he did not enter Charleston harbor until February 28. From the outset he was terribly seasick, and so was his servant, who had originally laughed at Quincy's plight. "But when in calling for my servant I was told he had taken to his bed, my revenge was satisfied, tho' if I would have moved he should have seen my sides shake his turn." *Id.*, p. 7. Even the cabin-boy, who had been at sea for three years, "was exercised with strains and throws more violent than my own." *Id.*, p. 8. Quincy's constitution was weak from tuberculosis, but it was the seasickness that caused "fainting turns" and confined him to a "sultry and hot" cabin. "A more disagreeable time can hardly be conceived, than the season of my first days and nights. Exhausted to the last degree, I was too weak to rise, and in too exquisite pain to lie in bed." *Id.*, p. 9. What food he could eat was foul.

Yet this was normal seafaring. The real trouble began when the ship encountered a major storm off the coast of North Carolina, "in the latitude of the Bermudas," on February 21st, nearly two weeks out. Quincy's eldest brother Edmund had died in a storm in those latitudes in 1768, on a voyage to Barbados, and Quincy could not help but reflect on his brother's fate. "We were now in that latitude in which the remains of my Elder Brother lay deposited in the Ocean; and probably very near the spot where Mr. John Apthorp and lady were foundred." *Id.*, pp. 28–29. Indeed, it is a comment on eighteenth-century sea travel that, eventually, Quincy, and his other older brother, Samuel, would both die on sea voyages. See Neil L. York's fine introduction "The Making of a Patriot" to *Quincy Papers, supra,* vol. 1, p. 13ff. (Hereafter, "York *Introduction.*") It is worth noting that the cause of both these deaths was not shipwreck, but the ordeal of the voyage itself.

But Quincy's ship was nearly wrecked. The captain himself observed that the storm was the worst he had ever seen. "Mr. Q[uincy] come and see here: you may now say you have seen a storm at sea. I never saw so dismal a time in my life." *Id.*, pp. 24–25. Quincy had to tie himself to his bunk, observing, "In short horror was all around Us." *Id.*, p. 26. "I believe every soul on board

---

5. *Southern Journal*, p. 3. Sailing packets rivaled steam craft for speed well into the nineteenth century. See Seymour Dunbar, *A History of Travel in America* (Indianapolis, 1915), vol. 2, pp. 372–392.

expected to perish." *Id.*, p. 28. Navigation was impossible. There was no "sight of the sun" for "upwards of an 100-hour," and no way to calculate longitude astronomically. (A chronometer would have been highly unlikely on Quincy's ship in 1773.)[6] When the ship began to approach land, Quincy observed that "whether this land was off the Barr of Carolina, off Roman Shoals or the Bahama Sands was altogether uncertain to every person on board." *Id.*, p. 34. Finally, after six days, the storm abated, on February 27, and the ship was found to be south of Charleston. After meeting another nearly wrecked ship, it crossed the Charleston-Bar. Even then, because the wind was head on the ship, it took "the whole day beating up" to the port. *Id.*, p. 41.

Despite the danger, by sea was still the fastest way to travel long distances.[7] Charleston was full of shipping, with nearly "350 sail" laying off the port, "far surpassing" what Quincy had seen in Boston. *Id.*, p. 41. The journey, though terrifying, was only half the usual time of a passage to England which, in Quincy's case, would take 41 days each way, while this voyage, even with the storm, was only 20 days.[8]

B. Lodging and Overland Travel

Several commentators have observed that the shortage of decent inns made for a culture of hospitality, particularly among gentlefolk.[9] This was certainly true for Quincy. On arrival in Charleston, he found "very great difficulty" in

---

6. John Harrison (1693–1776) finished his famous chronometer "H-4" in 1759, but he was not acknowledged as solving the longitude "problem" until 1773, the year of Quincy's voyage. Although Captain James Cook tested chronometers successfully between 1772 and 1775, they were not generally deployed on commercial vessels until the nineteenth century. See Derek House, *Greenwich Time and the Discovery of the Longitude* (Oxford, 1980), pp. 71–72. The only usual methods to calculate longitude before the chronometer was the complex "lunar distance" method or "dead reckoning" using a ship's log to calculate speed through the water, a highly inaccurate method. *Id.*, pp. 16, 54, 194–197. Both would have been useless in a storm like the one experienced by Quincy. See also, Rupert T. Gould, *The Marine Chronometer: Its History and Development* (London, 1923), pp. 40–70; *The Quest for Longitude* (ed. William J.H. Andrews, Cambridge, 1996), pp. 235–254; and Dava Sobel, *Longitude* (New York, 1995), pp. 152–164.

7. In 1786, it still took four to six days just to go to New York, from Boston, by road, depending on the weather. Major road improvements took place between 1790 and 1840. See Jack Larkin, *The Reshaping of Everyday Life 1790–1840*, pp. 205–211.

8. See York, *Introduction, Quincy Papers*, vol. 1 at pp. 35, 43.

9. See Alice Morse Earle, *Home Life in Colonial Days* (New York, 1898), pp. 325–363. Gordon S. Wood, *The Radicalism of the American Revolution* (New York, 1992), pp. 24–56. (Hereafter "Wood, *Radicalism*.")

obtaining lodgings.[10] The problem was solved by "Mr. Lavinus Clarkson to whom I had Letters," who in turn "politely attended me to introduce me to those to whom I had Letters of recommendation." *Id.*, p. 42. Though Quincy stayed in lodgings in Charleston, arranged by Clarkson, he more frequently was a guest in private homes, to which he either had letters, or to whom he was introduced by others to whom he had letters. Often Quincy would be invited to dinner, musical soirees, church services, horse races, and other social occasions. When riding north, he was often accompanied by his host to the next destination.

Quincy set out "Northward" on March 20th, 1773, accompanied by Thomas Lynch (1727–1776), who represented South Carolina in the Stamp Act Congress of 1765, staying the night at Lynch's plantation on the Santee River. While the riding and weather "were agreeable," crossing the rivers was difficult. "Had a three hour tedious passage, Santee-river." *Id.*, p. 81. Quincy moved from plantation to plantation, usually with local guides provided by his hosts. "This Gentleman [Joseph Allston] sent his servant as our guide between 30 and 40 miles much to our preservation from very vexation difficulties. Lodged the last night at the Plantation of Mr. Johnston [Allston's brother-in-law]. Mr. Withers . . . [another Allston brother-in-law] . . . came as our guide about 10 miles." *Id.*, p. 83. Sometimes the countryside was filled with blossoming peach trees and lovely weather. Other times, "a most barren, dreary rode; 9 cows and oxen had perish within a week for want of sustenance: great difficulty to get food for man or beast." *Id.*, p. 83.

Quincy's observation confirmed that of other early travelers. Roads varied greatly, with the best being in Pennsylvania.[11] One stretch could be highly difficult, the next a delight. "As soon as you enter Pennsylvania . . ." Quincy observed, "the regularity, goodness, and the strait, advantageous disposition of Public Roads are evidence of the good policy and laws of this well regulated province." *Id.*, p. 143. "My Journey for this several days has not only been delightful from the gratification of the Eye, but the exquisite scent from blooming orchards gave a rich perfume . . ." *Id.*, p. 144. On the other hand, the roads between Boston and New York were notorious. In 1793, Quincy's son

10. *Southern Journal*, p. 42. Note, all footnote citations to the manuscript are to Quincy's original pagination, carefully retained in this edition.

11. See Larkin, *The Reshaping of Everyday Life 1790–1840, supra*, pp. 211–213.

Josiah, the future Mayor of Boston and President of Harvard, observed that it took "a week's hard traveling" to go from Boston to New York.[12] "[W]hether it snowed or rained, the traveler must rise and make ready, by help of a <u>horn lantern and a farthing candle</u>, and proceed on his way over bad roads, sometimes getting out to help the coachman life the coach out of a quagmire . . ."[13] Bridges were frequently in bad repair and dangerous.[14] In 1796, the stage trip from Philadelphia to Baltimore took five days, and Ann Wards, traveling in 1795, observed two overturned stage wagons between Philadelphia and New York.[15]

In any event, Quincy reached New York on May 11, 1773 having traveled 52 days from Charleston. *Id.*, p. 173. His prior experience with Connecticut roads was so bad that he elected to sail "down the Sound for Newport" Rhode Island instead, "with some other polite company." "Was the rather induced to this tour by water than thro' Connecticut, having before gone thro' that Colony and by horses being so fatigued with their journey as to render it doubtful whether they could reach home by Land." Even so, Quincy's ship had to ride out a storm for a day "laying at Anchor." *Id.*, p. 180.

C. Significance

In concluding his *Southern Journal*, Quincy observed, "Where [sic] I to lament any thing, it would be the prevalent and extended ignorance of one colony of the concerns of another." *Id.*, p. 184. He had traveled the most beaten paths between the colonies, by both land and sea. He had no shortage of money or friends. Yet the journey took nearly four months. Most of it was hard traveling, and the sea passage south was terrifying. Charleston was easier to reach than London, but it was still weeks at sea, in dangerous latitudes. The only way to really see the land and converse with the people was to ride for months.

Quincy feared that the great economic and social difference between the colonies, and the difficulty of secure communication between them, would permit the British to divide and manipulate.[16] After all, they controlled the sea

---

12. See Alice Morse Earle, *Home Life in Colonial Days* (New York, 1898), p. 346.

13. *Id.*, p. 346.

14. *Id.*, p. 348. "The traveler Weld, in 1795, gave testimony that the bridges were so poor that the driver had always to stop and arrange the loose planks ere he dared to cross." *Id.*, p. 348.

15. *Id.*, p. 349.

16. See *Southern Journal*, pp. 87–88.

lanes. Quincy's journey to the South had a political agenda, and his member-
ship since November 1772 in the Boston Committee of Correspondence, made
him a good person to establish contact with like-minded patriots in other
colonies.[17] He was deeply interested in the geography of America, and how
easy it was to move and communicate for strategic purposes. In the end, he
discovered some important obstacles, both philosophically and physically.
Yet, typical of Quincy, he was determined to prove they could be overcome.

III. GENTILITY

Quincy was ranked at Harvard College by his social standing, as were all students. He was ranked fifth in a class of forty-one.[18] Quincy believed in gentility. He observed that "[t]aste, like philosophy, falls to the lot of only a small
select number of privileged souls . . ."[19] He saw himself a gentleman, and
expected recognition by his peers and subordinates alike. Those he admired,
such as "the Farmer," John Dickinson (1732–1808), enjoyed "*otium cum dignitate*," "leisure with dignity."[20] Indeed, Quincy's trip itself demonstrated that
the young man had the freedom from mundane cares that marked a gentleman. True, Quincy was a practicing lawyer, but everyone knew the difference
between the gentleman barrister and the solicitor or "pettifogger," and Quincy
was a barrister in spirit, if not in fact.[21]

17. York, *Introduction*, vol. 1, *supra*, pp. 27–28.

18. See Clifford K. Shipton, *Sibley's Harvard Graduates, vol. XV: Biographical Sketches of Those Who Attended Harvard College in the Classes 1761–1763* (Boston, 1970), pp. 348–349 (hereafter, *Sibley's Harvard Graduates*). Quincy's age was listed as "13'14." *Id.*, p. 348. See Neil L. York's excellent biographical introduction to volume 1 of this series, "A Life Cut Short," *Quincy Papers*, vol. 1, pp. 15ff.

19. See *Southern Journal*, p. 132. In this, Quincy would recognize his future collaborator, Ben-jamin Franklin, as a "gentleman" despite his origins in trade. "In 1748, at the age of forty-two, Franklin believed he had acquired sufficient wealth and gentility to retire from active business. This retirement had far more significance in the mid-eighteenth century than it would today. It meant that Franklin could at last become a gentleman, a man of leisure who no longer would have to work for a living." Gordon S. Wood, *The Americanization of Benjamin Franklin* (New York, 2004), p. 55. (Hereafter, "Wood, *Franklin*.") See generally, *Id.*, pp. 17–60, "Becoming a Gentleman."

20. *Southern Journal*, p. 132.

21. Quincy was never formally made a barrister, although he argued cases before the Supe-rior Court of Judicature. "I argued . . . to the Jury, though not admitted to the Gown: ___ The

As a matter of society and travel hospitality, Quincy's class superficially trumped any political differences. As Gordon Wood has observed: "Despite the fact that most of colonial society was vertically organized, there was one great horizontal division that cut through it with a significance we today can scarcely comprehend—that between extraordinary and ordinary people, gentleman and commoners."[22] The difficulties of travel and communication between the colonies, just discussed, provided the vertical divisions. As Richard Beeman has demonstrated, each colony had its own political and social culture, and its own ideologies.[23] Indeed, Quincy remarked constantly throughout his *Southern Journal* how the people of the colonies differed as much as the soil, the vegetation, and the climate. But one thing cut through horizontally: class.

Quincy thought nothing of sitting at dinner with a group of wealthy slaveholders in Charleston, many of loyalist sympathy ("hot sensible flaming tories"), admiring the silver, the china, the wine and the women.[24] He was careful not to be rude, or to interject his own beliefs, even his passionate opposition to slavery, in an inappropriate way.[25] Among Quincy's favorite new friends was the Commander of Fort Johnston, Colonel Robert Howe, "[a] most happy compound of the man of sense, sentiment and dignity, with the man of the world, the sword, the Senate and the Bucks."[26] Although Howe

---

Legality and Propriety of which some have pretended to doubt; but as no Scruples of that kind disturbed me, I proceeded (manger any) at this Court to manage all my Business . . . though unsanctified and uninspired by the Pomp and Magic of—the Long Robe," *Reports*, p. 317. His great-grandson Samuel noted that this was due to "[t]he political course of Mr. Quincy having rendered him obnoxious to the Supreme Court of the Province . . ." *Id.*, p. 317 n. (1), quoting Quincy's *Life of Quincy*, p. 27. The truth of that loyal remark is hard to judge. Certainly the like of John Adams and James Otis Jr. were admitted to the bar, but earlier. See *Reports*, p. 35, Memorandum of 1762 listing the members of the bar.

22. Gordon S. Wood, *The Radicalism of the American Revolution* (New York, 1992), p. 24. (Hereafter "Wood, *Radicalism*.") See also Ronald Schultz, "A Class Society? The Nature of Inequality in Early America," *Inequality in Early America* (Hanover, N.H., 1999), p. 203. Schultz believes that America only became "a true class society" in the 1880s. See *Id.*, p. 216.

23. See Richard R. Beeman, *The Varieties of Political Experience in Eighteenth-Century America* (Philadelphia, 2004), pp. 1–30. (Hereafter, "Beeman.")

24. See *Southern Journal, infra*, p. 53.

25. *Id.*, p. 57. Quincy was horrified by dinner conversation indicating that "to steal a negro was death, but to kill him was only fineable" (emphasis in original). His reaction at the table, however, was to say "Curious laws and policy!" *Id.*, p. 57.

26. *Id.*, p. 98.

was a crown officer, Quincy approved of Howe's "staunch Whig sentiments," and praised Howe's plan "to keep a regular Journal . . . of the Conduct of every Public Character," thus encouraging good governance![27] Likewise, Quincy was greatly taken with Daniel Dulany, Attorney General of Maryland, "a Diamond of the first water:—a gem that may grace the cap of a patriot or the turban of a Sultan," even though Dulany was eventually deprived of his property as a Loyalist.[28] But lack of gentility brought instant criticism. "[T]he middling order in the Capital [Charlestown] are odious characters."[29]

Quincy's respect for Commander Howe and for Daniel Dulany illustrated how gentility merged, in this crucial political period, with what Gordon Wood describes as "classical republican values."[30] As Wood has demonstrated, these values were a direct result of the Enlightenment and, far from necessarily rejecting the monarch, "[m]onarchial and republican values existed sided by side in the culture, and many good monarchists and many good English tories adopted republican ideals and principles without realizing the long-term political implications of what they were doing."[31] Throughout the *Southern Journal*, Quincy critiqued the communities he observed, not in terms of loyalty to, or against, the British Crown, but rather whether the governments were honest and responsible, encouraging individual merit, virtue, and learning, or whether they were corrupt, lazy, and indifferent to the public welfare. As Wood observed, "educated people of varying political persuasions celebrated republicanism for its spirit, its morality, its freedom, its sense of friendship and duty, and its vision of society."[32] "Republicanism as a set of values and a form of life was much too pervasive, comprehensive, and involved with being liberal and enlightened to be seen as subversive or as anti-monarchical."[33]

In the same notebook that contained his *Southern Journal*, Quincy carefully copied down passages from William Shenstone's (1714–1763) *Essays on Men and Manner* (London, 1769). See P347, Reel 4, QPG1 pp. 255–259. There he focused on elements of gentility, labeled "Of reserve," "Of the World," "Of

---

27. *Id.*, pp. 96, 98–99.
28. *Id.*, p. 138. On Dulany's fate as a loyalist, see *Dictionary of American Biography* (New York, 1943), V, p. 499.
29. *Id.*, p. 89.
30. Wood, *Radicalism, supra*, p. 101.
31. *Id.*, p. 99.
32. *Id.*, p. 99.
33. *Id.*, p. 99.

Hypocrisy & a Censorious Temper," "Of Government," "Popularity," "Resistance to Reigning Powers," and "Of Mankind." The emphasis was on patriotic resolve, tempered with concern for the less well off. See M. Drabble, ed., *Oxford Companion to English Literature* (5th ed.) p. 896. See also *Compact Edition, Oxford Dictionary of National Biography* (Oxford, 1975), vol. 2, p. 910.

It was too early for men like Quincy to see themselves as enemies of a British Crown or as something other than English. But Quincy certainly did see himself as a member of an educated colonial gentility, committed to very specific republican values and autonomy of colonial government. He despised corrupt placemen, both English and colonial, and particularly despised colonial elites that failed to meet their civic duties, such as, in his opinion, those of South Carolina. "What will become of Carolinian freedom? The luxury, dissipation, life, sentiments and manners of the leading people naturally tend to make them neglect, dispise, and be careless of the true interests of mankind in general."[34] Republican values reflected a good classical education and a good upbringing, that reflected the model of Cicero (106–43 B.C.) and the other classical heroes.[35] They emphasized advancement through merit, but were also the mark of true gentility.[36] Wealth and leisure were wasted without learning and the resulting sense of civic responsibility. Quincy certainly knew

---

34. *Southern Journal*, p. 88.

35. The Estate Catalogue of Quincy's library indicated a "Cicero Thoughts" as Item 256. *Quincy Estate Catalogue, Quincy Papers*, vol. 5 *(Appendix 9)*. This book was probably the popular English translation *Thoughts of Cicero*. "First published in Latin and French by the Abbé d'Olivet." The translator was Alexander Wishart. It was first published in London in 1751, then in Glasgow in 1754, and again in London in 1773. Thomas Jefferson had the Glasgow edition in his library [7.84]. See *Catalogue of the Library of Thomas Jefferson*, vol. II (Charlottesville, 1983), p. 37. The book consisted of translated extracts from Cicero's most famous letters, tracts, and speeches, including *De Legibus* (begun 52 B.C., not published until after Cicero's death in 43 B.C.), the *Tusculum Disputations* (45–44 B.C.) and his letters to his brother, *Ad Quintum Fratrem* (59–54 B.C.). See *The Oxford Companion to Classical Literature* (2d ed., M. C. Howatson, ed., 1989), pp. 131–134. In his *Political Commonplace*, item 97, Quincy quoted from Cicero's "Oration for Sextius," *Pro Sextus Roscias* (80–79 B.C.). "The Republic is always attacked with greater vigour than it is defended . . . whereas the honest . . . when they would be glad to compound at last for their quiet, at the expence of their honour, they commonly lose them both." See *Political Commonplace, Quincy Papers* (Hereafter, "Political Commonplace"), volume 1, pp. 138–139, 204. See also *The Oxford Companion to Classical Literature* (M. C. Howatson, ed., Oxford, 1989), pp. 128–134. (Hereafter, "Howatson.")

36. Wood quotes Conyers Middleton's popular *Life of Cicero* (1741). "[N]o man, how nobly soever born, could arrive at any dignity, who did not win it by his personal merit." Wood, *Radicalism, supra*, p. 100.

who the "gentlemen" were, wherever he went. He had letters to many of them, but class consciousness brought with it Quincy's sense of the responsibility of class. His greatest condemnation of Carolinian gentry was just this. "Political enquiries and philosophie disquisitions are too laborious for them: they have no great passion to shine and blaze in the forum or Senate." It was a matter of education and merit, and a matter of responsible effort. But it was, in Quincy's mind, a class issue, too.

IV. GENDER

Both Quincy's *Reports* and his *Law Commonplace Book* focused, in key areas, on the rights of women. There were three important issues: 1) whether the male entail, the bane of daughters, would be presumed in the absence of correct wording in the will, even if the intent were clear; 2) how liable married women would be for their husbands' debts; and 3) how readily the harsh statutory punishments would fall on women for gender-based crimes—such as execution for the unexplained death of an infant.[37] The issue of the "entail male" sounds esoteric, but surely not to any readers of Jane Austen.[38] Massachusetts had long rejected the English doctrine of primogeniture, or inheritance of all lands by the eldest son, adopting instead coparcenage, in which all children inherited equally.[39] The Massachusetts courts debated whether wills restricting inheritance to male heirs as an "entail male" under English law were valid if the exact legal wording was not used—despite clear testator

---

37. On entail, see *Dudley* v. *Dudley*, *Reports*, p. 12; *Elwell* v. *Pierson*, *Reports*, p. 42; and *Baker* v. *Mattocks*, *Reports*, p. 69. On extent of liability for a husband's debts, see the famous "naked wife" case, *Hanlon* v. *Thayer*, *Reports*, p. 99. On the harsh threat of execution to the mother of a stillborn child if she could not prove she was married, due to a statutory presumption of murder, see *Dom. Rex* v. *Mangent*, *Reports*, p. 162. There were also cases on the husband's liability to support an abandoned wife and children. See *Brown* v. *Culnan*, *Reports*, p. 66. Interestingly enough, the only woman to feature in *Quincy's Reports* in a business context was indicted for "keeping a bawdy house." See *Dom. Rex* v. *Doaks*, *Reports*, p. 90.

38. See J. H. Baker, *An Introduction to English Legal History* (4th ed., London, 2002), pp. 272–296 (hereafter, "Baker"); Marylynn Salmon, *Women and the Law of Property in Early America* (Chapel Hill, 1986), pp. 81–90. See generally, Susan Stevas, *Married Women's Separate Property in England 1660–1833* (Cambridge, Mass., 1990).

39. See the extensive discussion in the note to *Baker* v. *Mattocks*, *Reports*, p. 69.

intent.[40] Quincy's *Reports* appear to disfavor the male entail. Quincy's *Law Commonplace* was quite concerned with the legal powers of married women, which were sharply curtailed.[41] Finally, his *Reports* recounted the terrifying story of a young woman who could have been executed under a Massachusetts law that presumed that an unmarried mother murdered a stillborn baby —unless there was a witness or she could prove she was in fact married.[42]

Quincy's *Southern Journal* was not as explicit in its interest in gender issues, but it still reveals Quincy as a man whose sensitivity was in advance of his day. When he arrived in Charleston, he had just turned 29. He had been happily married for four years, since 1769, to Abigail, the daughter of William Phillips of Boston. She is referred to as "E" or "Eugenia" in the *Southern Journal* according, as Mark Antony deWolfe Howe would say, to "the affectation of the day."[43] His love and his respect for her lasted to the hour of his death on that ill-fated voyage home from London in 1775. The wrenching letter he dictated to a sailor on his death bed gives eternal testimony to this love .[44] But her love for him lasted far longer, through a long, lonely widowhood. She died and was laid next to him by her son at midnight, on a moonlit night in March 1798, 23 years later.[45] Although she never knew her grandfather, the deep devotion of Quincy's granddaughter and biographer, Eliza Susan Quincy (1798–1884),

40. See the extensive discussion in the notes to *Dudley* v. *Dudley*, *Reports*, p. 12. Virginia, on the other hand, made it particularly difficult to bar entails, even prohibiting the "Common Recovery" fiction for barring entails used in England. See *Baker, supra*, pp. 281–283. Quincy disapproved. "An Artistocratical spirit and principle is very prevalent in the Laws policy and manners of this Colony, and the Law ordaining that Estates—tail shall not be barred by Common Recoveries is not the only instance thereof." *Southern Journal*, p. 128.

41. See also the discussion in the notes to *Elwell* v. *Pierson*, *Reports*, p. 42. See "Baron & Feme," *Law Commonplace*, *Quincy Papers*, vol. 2, pp. 25–28 citing Quincy's pagination. (Hereafter, "*Law Commonplace*.") For a good account of the legal status of colonial women, see Mary Beth Norton, "Either Married or to Bee Married: Women's Inequality in Early America," in *Inequality in Early America* (eds. C. G. Pertand, S. V. Salinger, Hanover, N.H., 1999), pp. 25–45.

42. In this case, the mother's life was saved when the court held that a marriage license by an out-of-state clergy was admissable "without any authentication from any Magistrate." See the extensive notes to *Dom. Rex* v. *Mangent*, *Reports*, p. 162.

43. See *Southern Journal*, p. 1, n. 1.

44. See *London Journal*, *Quincy Papers*, vol. 1, pp. 267–269.

45. See Neil L. York, *Introduction*, vol. 1, pp. 44–45. Five years after her husband's death, Abigail wrote, "I have been after told, that time would wear out the greatest sorrow, but mine I find is still increasing. When it will have reached its summit I know not." *Id.*, p. 44.

provides compelling evidence of how the man was loved by the women of his family.

But Quincy was interested in other women, particularly intelligent women. On arrival in Charleston, he was invited to the St. Cecilia Concert, March 3, 1773.

> Here was upwards of 250 ladies, and it was called no great show. I took a view of them, but I saw no E-. [No women the equal of his wife, "Eugenia" or Abigail.] However I saw 'Beauty in a Brow of Egypt, to be sure not a Helen's.

The last phrase is from Shakespeare's *A Midsummer Night's Dream*, Act V, Sc. 1, line 7. "The lunatic, the lover, and the poet are of imagination all compact: One sees more devils than vast hell can hold, That is, the madman: the lover, all as frantic, see Helen's beauty in a brow of Egypt." This was certainly one of Quincy's more cryptic comments. Was there a racial overtone?[46] Later, he would remark on "[t]he enjoyment of a negro or mulatto woman" as "spoken of as quite a common thing: no reluctance, delicacy or shame is made about the matter."[47]

Quincy noticed women's fashions.

> In loftiness of head-dress these ladies stoop to the daughters of the North: in richness of dress surpass them: in health and floridity of countenance veil to them: in taciturnity during the performances greatly before our ladies; in noise and flirtations after the musick is every pretty much on par.[48]

But, intellectually, Quincy preferred Northern women. "If Our Women have any advantage, it is in White and red, vivacity and fire."[49] Quincy blamed slavery for the degradation of the subordinate classes in South Carolina, and for the laziness and intellectual torpor of the elites.[50] In his view, this doubtless extended to the status of women. "The ladies of Charleston want much of the

---

46. See *Southern Journal*, p. 45, n. 57.

47. *Id.*, at p. 113.

48. *Id.*, at p. 45.

49. *Id.*, at p. 45. Quincy wrote to his brother Samuel on April 6, 1773: "I saw little of that exuberance, hilarity and roar which are so incident to a Northern festival and entertainment: Indeed in point of genuine vivacity and fire the Northern Bells and Sparks surpass those of the South whose spirit and blaze seem exhausted or extinguished by a warmer sun." Dana Mgs. (Massachusetts Historical Society), *Sibley's Harvard Graduate, vol. XV, supra*, p. 484.

50. *Id.*, at pp. 90–95.

fire and vivacity of the North, or I want taste and discernment," he repeated.[51]

Quincy rarely mentioned the women he met by name. Mrs. McKenzie of Charleston was an exception, not because of her personality, but because she was an immensely wealthy widow of only twenty, and a daughter of a prominent man.

> In company dined on Mr. Thomas Bee, a planter of considerable opulence. A gentleman of sense, improvement, and politeness; and one of the members of the house;—just upon the point of marrying Mrs. McKenzie, a young widow of about 20 with 8000 or 9000 guineas independant fortune in specie, and daughter to Mr. Thomas Smith.[52]

Even a happily married man like Quincy would notice Mr. Bee's good fortune. Women could be a source of wealth and lineage, and racial purity, too.

Quincy reflected the paternal views of his day, described by Gordon Wood as "patriarchal dependence."[53] Women were loved and even respected, but their place was narrowly defined, by both law and custom. "Women of the planter class never questioned the traditional notion of female subordination, even as they assumed the crucial task of deputy whenever the need arose."[54] This was not to mean that women did not carry authority, or lacked social, and even political importance, but that this occurred, with very rare exception, in carefully limited ways.[55] As Elizabeth Ann Dexter observed: "The attempt to visualize the work of women in colonial times is somewhat like watching a play by occasional flashes of lightning."[56]

51. *Id.*, at p. 89.

52. *Id.*, at p. 67.

53. See Wood, *Radicalism, supra*, pp. 43–56. See also Ruth H. Bloch, *Gender and Morality in Anglo-American Culture, 1650–1800* (Berkeley, 2003), pp. 1–17.

54. Cara Anzilotti, *In the Affairs of the World: Women, Patriarchy and Power in Colonial South Carolina* (Westport, Conn., 2002), p. 193.

55. See "Editor's Introduction," *Beyond Image and Convention: Explorations in Southern Women's History*, J. L. Coryell, M. H. Swain, S. C. Treadway, E. H. Turner eds. (Columbia, S.C., 1998), pp. 1–9; Mary Beth Norton, *Founding Mothers & Fathers: Gendered Power and the Forming of American Society* (New York, 1996); Patricia Cleary, "She Will Be in the Shop: Women's Sphere of Trade in Eighteenth-Century Philadelphia and New York," 119 *Pennsylvania Magazine of History and Biography* (1995), 181–202; Elizabeth Anthony Dexter, *Colonial Women of Affairs: A Study of Women in Business and the Profession in America Before 1776* (Cambridge, Mass., 1924), pp. 180–194; and Ruth H. Bloch, *Gender and Morality in Anglo-American Culture 1650–1800*, pp. 363–373.

56. *Id., supra*, p. 180.

In the *Southern Journal* there were some flashes of lightning. One was "Mrs. Reed the Daughter of the late Dennis Debert, Esq." of Philadelphia, another rare mention of a woman by name. She greatly impressed Quincy as "an ornament of her own sex, and the Delight of Ours."[57] Quincy was also impressed by actresses, such as Elizabeth Morris (1753–1826),[58] Sarah Hallam, "queen of the American stage,"[59] and Maria Storer, all of whom he saw in New York and carefully noted. Occasionally an amateur, such as Col. William Bayard's daughter, Mrs. Johnson, also deserved special note.

> Dined with Col. William Bayard at his seat on North River. His seat, table, and all around him in the highest elegance and taste. His daughter, Mrs. Johnson sung 3 or 4 songs with more voice, judgment, and execution than I ever heard any lady. Several of the Company who heard the best singers in London said she surpassed them: All agreed she equaled the celebrated Mrs. Brent [Charlotte Brent, d. 1802], but Dr. Middleton said his complaisance did not lead him to say he had never heard better singing in England, but he had met with nothing like it in America.[60]

Far more common, however, was the treatment given to Mrs. John Broome, "Drank tea with Mr. Broom and lady; she appeared in her usual goodness; he is endowed with much civility, understanding and politeness."[61]

Handicrafts were another way for a woman to get noted. Quincy saw slavery as removing the incentive for work and skills by free yeomen and women alike. Those who were nevertheless skilled craftsmen and women earned his admiration, even if they were the wives and sisters of wealthy men like Thomas Loughton Smith (1741–1773).[62]

> Mrs. Smith shewed me a most beautiful White Sattin and very richly embroidered Lady's work bag, designed as a present for a lady in London. Miss Catherine Ingliss, her Sister, a still more finely embroidered festoon (as they called it) of flowers. Both their own work; and surpassing anything of the kind I ever saw.[63]

57. *Southern Journal*, p. 149.
58. *Id.*, p. 174.
59. *Id.*, p. 178.
60. *Id.*, p. 175.
61. *Id.*, p. 176.
62. *Id.*, pp. 49–50.
63. *Id.*, p. 50.

One social ritual particularly impressed Quincy, the toasts given by women as part of the ceremony of dining. This gave women a relatively rare chance to be creative, even daring, and intellectually clever. All this was before the women had to withdraw at the dinner's conclusion. Quincy complimented David Deis' daughters, aged "about 16 and 10," who were "called upon [to give a toast] <u>for a Gentleman</u> and gave one with ease. The ladies withdrew after the first round of [of toasts]—the father seemed displeased at it."[64] Quincy sometimes recorded a woman's toast in full.

> 1st Toast, Our Boston—friends and their Good health Sir:—the Unmarried Lady (of 19) at my right "your good health and best affections Sir!" Miss ____ your toast madam. "Love and friendship and they who <u>feel them</u>!" Toasts called for from the Guests, etc. till Coffee etc.[65]

Quincy was even concerned about where women sat at the table. He observed that, "Very few ladies in Philadelphia head their tables on days of entertainments of several gentlemen."[66] Quincy was uncertain whether this deference was a good thing. "At first I was not pleased with this custom . . ." but on second thought, "on reflection and further consideration, I approve it—However I prophesy that it will be laid aside here in a very few years."[67]

Toasts aside, there was not a single record of what any woman actually <u>said</u> in the entire *Southern Journal*, which is otherwise packed with economic, legal and political discourse. When we recall how much Quincy cared about legal issues affecting women, as evidenced by his *Law Commonplace* and *Reports*,[68] this is a striking testimony to the world of paternalism described by Gordon Wood.[69] Quincy found slavery repellant, described it graphically, and spoke out against it repeatedly in the *Southern Journal*. Gender was different. There

64. *Id.*, p. 47.
65. *Id.*, p. 49. See also, *id.*, p. 66. "Two ladies being called on for toasts, the one gave—'Delicate pleasures to susceptible minds.' The other, 'When passions rise may reason be the guide.'" *Id.*, p. 66.
66. *Id.*, p. 170.
67. *Id.*, p. 170.
68. See note 37, *supra*.
69. See Wood, *Radicalism*, *supra*, pp. 43–56. See also Laurel T. Ulrich, *Good Wives: Image and Reality in the Lives of Women in Northern New England 1650–1750* (New York, 1982), pp. 237–241 (hereafter, "Ulrich"); and Kathleen M. Brown, *Good Wives, Nasty Wenches and Anxious Patriarchs* (Chapel Hill, 1998), pp. 367–373.

were, as Elizabeth Dexter said, "occasional flashes of lightning," but, in general, we are left in the dark.[70] One thing is certain, however. As Laurel Ulrich observed, referring to the study of early New England, "gender is as important a category as race, wealth, geography, or religion."[71] There were many sociological barriers to communication evidenced by Quincy's *Journal*, but gender could have been the biggest one of all.

V. RACE AND SLAVERY

Slavery was common in Quincy's Massachusetts, and Quincy's *Reports* contained two slave cases, a dispute about the sale of two mulattoes as slaves in *Oliver* v. *Sale*[72] and "Trover for a Negro" ["trover" being the cause of action to recover the value of goods against another] in *Allison* v. *Cockran*.[73] In addition, the brigantine *Peggy* involved in *Scollay* v. *Dunn*[74] may have been a slaver. The actions of the court in all of these cases assumed the legality of slavery.[75] Quincy did add a marginal note to the report of *Allison* v. *Cockran*, "Qu. [querie] If this Action is well brought, for Trover lies not for a Negro," citing English authorities.[76] But as his great-grandson, Samuel, observed in a

70. See note 56, *supra*.

71. See Ulrich, *supra*, pp. 237–241.

72. See the annotations at *Reports*, p. 29.

73. See the annotations at *Reports*, p. 94.

74. See the annotations at *Reports*, p. 74.

75. See Oscar Reiss, *Blacks in Colonial America* (Jefferson, N.C., 1997), pp. 65–72. (Hereafter "Reiss.")

76. See the discussion at *Reports*, p. 95. Quincy cited to *Smith* v. *Brown and Cooper*, 2 *Salkeld's Reports* 666 (1706) and *Smith* v. *Gould*, 2 *Salkeld's Reports*, pp. 666–667 (1706). See also 2 *Lord Raymond's Reports*, pp. 1274–1275, for another report of *Smith* v. *Gould* with the head note "Trover does not lie for a negroe." *Id.*, p. 1274. [Trover was the general cause of action for recovering the value of goods against another.] In the former case, Chief Justice Holt held "that as soon as a negro comes into England, he becomes free one may be a villein in England, but not a slave." *Smith* v. *Brown and Cooper*, 2 *Salkeld's Reports* (1706) at p. 666. But he added this advice to the plaintiff, who sought to recover £20 "for a negro sold by the plaintiff to the defendant," by the contractual action of *indebitatus assumpsit*

> Holt, C.J. You should have averred in the declaration, that the sale was in Virginia, and, by the laws of that country, negroes are saleable: for the laws of England do not extend to Virginia, being a conquered country in their law is what the King pleases; and we cannot take notice of it but as set forth; therefore he directed the plaintiff should amend, and

lengthy note, the English authorities did not apply to colonial cases. "At the time of the trial of the case [1764] here reported by Quincy, negro slaves were held and sold as property in Massachusetts."[77]

Thus the institution of slavery itself could not have been strange to Quincy, and his family may well have held slaves.[78] In addition, by nature Quincy was a relatively calm and factual observer. As we shall see in the next section, he was quite tolerant in the case of religious differences, and always respectful to his hosts. But his reaction to the slavery he saw in South Carolina was passionate. "Slavery may truly be said to be the peculiar curse of this land . . ."[79] "There is much among this people of what the world call hospitality and

---

the declaration should be made, that the defendant was indebted to the plaintiff for a negro sold here at London, but that the said negro at the time of sale was in Virginia, and that negroes, by the laws and statutes of Virginia, are saleable as chattels. *Id.*, pp. 666–667.

The report in *Smith* v. *Gould*, *supra*, was even more ambiguous. This also involved "trover," an action for recovery of the value of goods.

Lastly, it was insisted, that the Court ought to take notice that they were merchandize, and cited 2 Cro. 262. The case of monkeys, 2 Lev. 201. 3 Keb. 785. 1 Inst. 112. If I imprison my negro, a *habeas corpus* will not lie to deliver him, for by *Magna Charta* he must be *liber homo*. 2 Inst. 45. *Sed Curia contra*, Men may be the owners, and therefore cannot be the subject of property. Villenage arose from captivity, and a man may have trespass *quare captivum suum cepit*, but cannot have trover *de gallico suo*. And the Court seemed to think that in trespass *quare captivum suum cepit*, the plaintiff might give in evidence that the party was his negro, and he bought him. *Id.*, p. 667.

The head note reads "Trover lies not for a negro; but in trespass *quare captivum suum cepit*, plaintiff may give in evidence that he was his negro." *Id.*, p. 667.

Given Quincy's personal opposition to slavery, so strongly reflected by the *Southern Journal*, the marginal note may reflect his view of what the law should be in Massachusetts, rather than what it was.

77. *Reports*, p. 98. As Samuel Quincy noted, the Massachusetts Superior Court of Judicature upheld a trover action for a negro in 1763. *Id.*, p. 98. See *Goodspeed* v. *Gay*, Barnstable, *Records* 1763, Vol. 47. Slavery was finally abolished in Massachusetts by Quok Walker and Nathaniel Jennison case between 1781–1783. See Reiss, *supra*, pp. 71–72, William O'Brien, "Did the Jennison Case Outlaw Slavery in Massachusetts?" 17 (3d series) *William and Mary Quarterly* (April 1960), pp. 224–233; and Robert M. Spector, "The Quok Walker Case (1781–1783): The Abolition of Slavery and Negro Citizenship in Early Massachusetts," 52 *Journal of Negro History* (1968), pp. 12–16.

78. Reiss reports that "[i]n Boston . . . a runaway named Josiah Quincy was saved when a mob beat a marshal trying to do his duty." Reiss, *supra*, p. 194.

79. *Southern Journal*, p. 91.

politeness, it may be questioned what proportion there is of true humanity, Christian charity and love."[80]

Quincy's views on slavery set him apart from many of his "enlightened" contemporaries. Today, we are so familiar with the passion of abolitionism that we take strong words for granted in confronting such an evil. But as Gordon Wood has observed:

> By the middle of the eighteenth century black slavery had existed in the colonies for several generations or more without substantial questioning or criticism. The few conscience-stricken Quakers who issued isolated outcries against the institution hardly represented general colonial opinion.[81]

In addition, Quincy was very familiar with indentured servitude, which could be so cruel that Thomas Hutchinson saw little to distinguish it, in moral terms, from slavery.[82]

> By modern standards it was a cruel and brutal age, and the life of the lowly seemed cheap. Slavery could be regarded, therefore, as merely the most base and degraded status in a society of several degrees of unfreedom, and most colonies felt little need as yet either to attack or defend slavery in any more than other forms of dependency and debasement.[83]

But, without disagreeing with Gordon Wood's characterization, Quincy's *Southern Voyage* either tells a different story or, more likely, reflects a very different kind of man. Here was no "conscience-stricken Quaker." Quincy was a mainstream, entitled aristocrat, yet he hated slavery, and feared its long-term consequences.

It is useful to divide his account into three categories: 1) his factual observations of slavery and racism as a social and economic force, 2) his ideological reasons for opposing slavery, and 3) his concerns about the political impact of slavery and racism on the future of the American colonies.

---

80. *Id.*, p. 95.

81. Wood, *Radicalism, supra*, p. 54.

82. See *Law Commonplace, supra*, "Of Apprentices & Servant," pp. 19–21, and the annotations. Hutchinson vetoed a bill in 1771 barring the importation of slaves into Massachusetts, pointing out that "a slave was in no worse position than 'a servant would be who had bound himself for a term of years exceeding the ordinary term of human life.'" See Bernard Bailyn, *The Ordeal of Thomas Hutchinson* (Cambridge, Mass., 1974), p. 378. (Hereafter, "Bailyn, *Ordeal*.")

83. Wood, *Radicalism, supra*, p. 55.

A. Slavery and Racism as Facts

Quincy was a close factual observer. "Having blended with every order of men as much as was possible and convenient I had considerable opportunity to learn their manners, genius, taste, etc."[84] Nowhere was this more true than his careful attention to the lives of blacks in the colonial South. He was interested in everything. How many slaves were there on a large plantation? ("Mr. Joseph Allston had 5 plantations with 100 slaves on each.")[85] What games did blacks play? ("pawpaw, huzzle-cap, push penny.")[86] What did blacks wear? ("their kind of breeches, scarce sufficient for covering.")[87] What did blacks do on Sunday when they were free from labor for their masters? ("[A]ll kinds of work for themselves on hire.")[88] What laws affected blacks?[89] What were the sexual relations between the races?[90] What were the cultural and linguistic cross-influences?[91] Quincy asked all the questions, both easy and hard.

Quincy's careful observation led him to hate the slavery that he witnessed. More importantly, it led him to the realization that slavery was not a "property" or a "contract" issue, such as indentured servitude or even marriage, but was based on an unmitigated evil, racism. This clear recognition, in itself, set Quincy apart from most of his contemporaries.

Quincy also observed that free blacks suffered severe restrictions on their rights in a predominantly slave society, and that the habits of slavery made the life of all blacks worse. When he referred to the "herds of Negroes and tawny slaves"[92] and the "enjoyment of a negro or mulatto woman,"[93] he did not distinguish between the hardship of free blacks and slaves, and when he attacked the summary execution law of South Carolina he observed that "[t]his law too was for <u>free</u> as well as <u>slave</u>—Negroes and mulattos."[94] While many arguments

---

84. *Southern Journal*, p. 84.
85. *Id.*, p. 82. For a typical large plantation of the area, see *Illustration 2*.
86. *Id.*, p. 89.
87. *Id.*, p. 80.
88. *Id.*, p. 89.
89. *Id.*, pp. 56–57.
90. *Id.*, pp. 113–114.
91. *Id.*, pp. 92–93.
92. *Id.*, p. 110.
93. *Id.*, p. 114.
94. *Id.*, p. 57. (Italics in original.)

for slavery used ownership and property rights language, Quincy saw the underlying issue of race clearly.[95]

Quincy did not believe some of what he was told in South Carolina, and did his own assessments. To start, he did not believe the numbers reported to him.

> A few years ago; it is allowed, that the Blacks exceeded the Whites as 17 to 1. There are those who now tell you, that the Slave are not more than 3 to 1, some pretend not so many. But they who talk thus are afraid that the Slaves should by some means discover their superiority: many people express great fears of an insurrection, others treat the idea as chimerical. I took great pains finding much contrariety of opinion to find out the true proportion the best information I could obtain fixes it at about 7 to 1, my own observation leads me to think it much greater.[96]

Modern scholarship has confirmed Quincy's view. "[T]he low-country South Carolina planters [were] surrounded and outnumbered by slaves—in some regions by as much as seven or eight to one . . . "[97]

Quincy was one of the first to observe that slavery had a bad effect on the white population.[98] Where there were fewer slaves, and they were better treated—as in North Carolina—they "are of consequence better servants." The effect was also beneficial to the entire economy, with direct improvements in agriculture and a better work ethic for laborers of both races.[99]

95. Quincy thus anticipated the central issue of *Dred Scott* v. *John F. A. Sandford*, 60 U.S. (19 Howard) 393 (1857). As Chief Justice Roger Taney put it, it was not an issue of property law, but whether any person "of that class of persons . . . whose ancestors were negros of the African race, and imported into this country, and sold and held as slaves" could ever be citizens "when they are emancipated, or who are born of parents who had become free before their birth." *Id.*, p. 403. "The question is simply this: Can a negro, whose ancestors were imported into this country, and sold as slaves, become a member of the political community formed and brought into existence by the Constitution of the United States." *Id.*, p. 403. Free black or not, the answer was "no." The issue was race, not property rights.

96. *Southern Journal*, pp. 91–92.

97. Beeman, *supra*, p. 135. See also Reiss, *supra*, pp. 108–114. The ratio of whites to blacks in North Carolina was 4 to 1, *Id.*, p. 115. The 1790 census, the first official census, gave the total white population of South Carolina as 140,178 with 107,094 slaves and only 1,801 free blacks. This, of course, included the back country, where slaves were less numerous than in the plantations on the rivers. By comparison, there were only 948 slaves in a population of 68,825 in Rhode Island. Slavery was already abolished in Massachusetts, although those who owned slaves were allowed to keep them even after 1780. Courtesy U.S. Census Bureau.

98. See *infra*, p. 34, fn. 105.

99. In this observation, too, Quincy was in the vanguard of shifting opinion. As Michael

The number of Negroes and slaves are vastly less in No[rth] than So[uth] C[arolina]. Their staple-commodity is not so valuable, being not in so great demand, as the Rice, Indigo, etc. of the South. Hence labor becomes more necessary, and he who has <u>an interest of his own to serve</u> is laborer in the field. Husbandmen and agriculture increase in number and improvement. Industry is up in the woods, at tar, pitch, and turpentine—in the fields plowing, planting, or clearing and fencing the land. Herds and flocks become more numerous, and they resemble not Pharoah's lean kine, so much as thos of the Prov[ince] I had just left. You see husbandmen, yeomen and white laborers scattered thro' country, instead of herds of Negroes and tawny slaves. Healthful countenances and numerous families become more common as you advance North.[100]

Quincy was also one of the first to recognize that cultural and linguistic influences went both ways, that black culture and language had a direct influence on whites—in part because many white children were raised by black nannies and household servants. He was not, however, advanced enough to see that this could be a cultural enrichment.

By reason of this Slavery; the children are early impressed with infamous and destructive ideas, and become extremely vitiated in their manners—they contract a negroish kind of accent, pronunciation, and dialect, as well as ridiculous kind of behavior:—even many of the grown people, and especially the women, are vastly infected with the same disorder. Parents instead of talking to their very young children in the unmeaning way with us, converse to them as tho' they were speaking—to a new imported African.[101]

Quincy also made the link between slavery and the status of women. Abuse of power relationships between white masters and black slaves exploited both inequalities, and the ban on interracial marriage produced corrosive results.[102]

Greenberg has demonstrated, "[c]riticism of the morality of slaveholding increased as more and more people realized that slave labor was incompatible with the ethical and material basis of a market society." Michael Greenberg, "Of Men and Markets: Slavery and the Development of the Virginia Planter Class," in *Essays on Eighteenth Century Race Relations in the Americas*, J. S. Saeger, ed. (Bethlehem, Pa., 1987), p. 73.

100. *Southern Journal*, pp. 109–110.

101. *Id.*, pp. 92–93.

102. See A. Leon Higginbotham, Jr., Barbara K. Kopytoff, "Racial Purity and Interracial Sex in the Law of Colonial and Antebellum Virginia," 77 *Geo. L.J.* 1967 (1989) at pp. 1989–2007; Brown, *Good Wives, Nasty Wenches and Anxious Patriarchs*, pp. 194–211.

"The enjoyment of a negro or mulatto woman is spoken of as quite a common thing; no reluctance, delicacy or shame is made about the matter."[103]

But Quincy's most perceptive observation was how slavery generally brutalized the master class. "Applicable indeed to this people and their slaves are the words of Our Milton — 'Too perfect in their misery, Not one perceive their foul disfigurement.'"[104]

> The brutality used towards the slaves has a very bad tendency with reference to the manners of the people, but a much worse with regard to the youth. They will plead in their excuse — "this severity is necessary." But whence did or does this necessity arise? From the necessity of having vast multitudes sunk in barbarism, ignorance and the basest and most servile employ![105]

The sophistication, wealth, and outward gentility of the Southern elite did not, in the end, escape this vicious and degrading influence.

> In Charlestown and so thro' the Southern prov[inces] I saw much apparent hospitality, much of what is called good-breeding and politeness, and great barbarity. In Brunswick, Willmington, Newbern Edenton, and so thro' the North prov[inces] there is real hospitality, less of what is called politeness and good-breeding and less inhumanity.[106]

B. The Ideology of Quincy's Opposition to Slavery

Quincy's opposition to slavery could have been based on what, today, we would call utilitarian grounds. He had observed that slavery, while "generally thought and called by the people its [this land's] blessing," actually had severe economic drawbacks, and also, in Quincy's view, degraded the quality of life for both races in demonstrable and objective ways.[107] But this was not the primary basis for Quincy's passionate objection. His primary objection grew from his political and legal ideology.

First, Quincy rejected the doctrine of racial inferiority. "The Africans are said to be inferior in point of sense and understanding, sentiment and feeling,

---

103. *Southern Journal*, p. 113.
104. *Id.*, p. 91.
105. *Id.*, p. 92.
106. *Id.*, p. 110.
107. *Id.*, pp. 91–93.

to the Europeans and other white nations. Hence the one infer a right to enslave the other."[108] But this was a "contradiction of human character" that violated the will of God.[109] "[T]hey would do well to remember that no laws of the (little) creature supercede the laws of the (great) creator. Can the institutions of man make void the decree of GOD!"[110] This natural law argument was supplemented by a practical observation, which convinced Quincy that claims of racial superiority were manifestly bogus. There was so much "intercourse between the whites and blacks," specifically between white male masters and black slaves, that racial distinctions were becoming a myth anyway. The "inferior" race could be the master's own children! Indeed, on two occasions Quincy was shocked to see that the master's son was waiting on table, as a slave!

> A mischief incident to both these prov[inces] [South and North Carolina] is very observable, and very natural to be expected:—the intercourse between the whites and blacks . . . It is far from being uncommon to see a gentleman at dinner, and his reputed off-spring a slave to the master of the table. I myself saw two instances of this, and the company very facetiously would trace the lines, Lineaments and features of the father and mother in the Child, and very accurately point out the more characteristick resemblances. The fathers of neither of them blushed or seem disconcerted.[111]

Since this interracial "intercourse" was widely the fact, Quincy asked how—by any reasoning—slavery could be justified. It meant seeing your own offspring "in bondage and misery."

> An African Black labors night and day to collect a small pittance to purchase the freedom of his child: the American or European White man begets his likeness, and with much indifference and dignity of soul sees his progeny in bondage and misery, and makes not one effort to redeem his own blood.—Choice food for Satire—wide field for burlesque—and noble game for wit!—unless the enkindled blood inflame resentment, wrath and rage; and vent itself in execrations.[112]

108. *Id.*, p. 114.
109. *Id.*, p. 93.
110. *Id.*, p. 94.
111. *Id.*, p. 113.
112. *Id.*, p. 114.

Slavery not only violated natural law—God's will and the fundamental human law binding you to your children—but it had an invidious effect on the regular legal system and the "English Constitution."

> From the same cause have their Legislators enacted laws touching negroes, mulattoes and masters which savor more of the policy of Pandemonium than the English constitution:—laws which will stand eternal records of the depravity and contradiction of the human character: laws which would disgrace the tribunal of Scythian, Aral, Hottentot and Barbarian are appealed to in decisions upon life limb and liberty by those who assume the name of Englishmen, freemen and Christians:—the place of trial no doubt is called a Court of Justice and equity—but the Judges have forgot a maxim of English law—Jura naturalia sunt immutabilia[113] ["The laws of nature are unchangeable."]

The worst example, in Quincy's view, was the harsh summary laws of execution for both free blacks and slaves, without the guarantees of due process and jury trial afforded even the lowest person by English Common law.[114] This

---

113. *Id.*, pp. 93–94, notes omitted. See annotations at text. Quincy frequently used Latin maxims to store and convey legal ideas. See the discussion at "Introduction to the *Law Commonplace*," *Quincy Papers*, vol. 2. As to slavery, Quincy once again anticipated modern scholarship, which has described the vicious effect of slavery and racism on colonial jurisprudence. See A. Leon Higginbotham, Jr., Anne F. Jacobs, "The 'Law Only as an Enemy': The Legitimization of Racial Powerlessness through the Colonial and Antebellum Criminal Laws of Virginia," 70 *N.C.L. Rev.* 969 (1992), 984–1016. (Hereafter, "Higginbotham, Jacobs.") "Under this legalized system of 'stripes and death,' blacks had the worst of both worlds: they received almost no protection from cruelty and slaughter and were punished far more severely than whites. They were treated as less than human whenever it benefited the economic interests of the white master or the white power structure. Yet, when it came to punishing them, blacks were held to a more rigorous standard than whites. Not only were they punished more harshly for the same offenses whites committed, but they also risked execution and dismemberment for conduct that was legal for whites. Referred to as ignorant, immoral, and savage, they were expected to conform to a system of laws that legitimized cruelty and rendered them powerless." *Id.*, p. 1068, (notes deleted). See also Sally Hadden's excellent *Slave Patrols: Law and Violence in Virginia and the Carolinas* (Cambridge, Mass., 2001) and C.W.A. David, "The Fugitive Slave Law of 1739," 9:1 *Journal of Negro History* (Jan. 1924), p. 18, at pp. 21–23; David Meaders, "South Carolina Fugitives," 60:2 *Journal of Negro History* (April 1973), p. 291.

114. The classic statement of "The Absolute Rights of Individuals" at common law had just been published by William Blackstone in the first volume of his *Commentaries on the Laws of England* (Oxford, 1765), pp. 117–141. These include "a person's legal and uninterrupted enjoyment of his life, his limbs, his body, his health, and his reputation," *Id.*, p. 125, as guaranteed by the Magna Carta, The 1628 Petition of Right, The 1689 Bill of Rights and other key English constitutional documents. *Id.*, pp. 123–125. Blackstone proudly proclaimed that "[T]his spirit of

was despite the London legal education, in the Inns of Court, enjoyed by several of the South Carolina bar.

> A young lawyer Mr. Pinckney, a gentleman educated at the temple [Inner or Middle Temple of the Inns of Court] and of eminence dined with us. From him and the rest of the Company I was assured, that by the provincial laws of the place any two justices and 3 freeholders might and very often did <u>instanter</u> ["immediately"] upon view or complaint try a negro for any crime, and might and did often award execution of death—issue their warrant and it was done forthwith. Two Gentlemen present said they had issued each warrants several times. This law too was for <u>free</u> as well as <u>slave</u>—Negroes and molattoes. They further informed me, that neither Negroes or molattoes could have a Jury;—that for killing a negro, ever so wantonly, as without any provocation; they gave a late instance of this; that (further) to <u>steal</u> a negro was death, but to <u>kill him</u> was only fineable. Curious laws and policy! I exclaimed. Very true cried the Company but this is the case.[115]

Quincy did not expect that the law would ensure equality. His *Law Commonplace* carefully described a legal system where women, apprentices, and indentured servants, as well as slaves, enjoyed only limited rights.[116] But there were some rights, both procedural and substantive, that were fundamental to the unwritten English constitution, and these attached to every human being.

---

liberty is so deeply implanted in our Constitution, and rooted even in our very soil, that a slave or a negro, the moment he lands in England, falls under the protection of the laws, and with regard to all natural rights becomes *eo instanti* a free man." *Id.*, 123. This doctrine was, of course, not applied in the colonies or even, as a practical matter, in England. Lord Mansfield, as late as 1772, "employed every technical device to evade a declaration upon the legality of slavery." C.H.S. Fifoot, *Lord Mansfield* (Oxford, 1936), p. 41. As to Mansfield's final and famous resolution of the issue in *Sommersett's Case*, 20 St. Tr. 1 (1772), see Steven M. Wise's fine book, *Though the Heavens May Fall: The Landmark Trial that Led to the End of Human Slavery* (Cambridge, Mass., 2005). For a full discussion of the English constitutional documents, see Daniel R. Coquillette, *The Anglo-American Legal Heritage* (2d ed., 2003, Durham, N.C.), pp. 59–63, 311–326, 366–368.

115. *Southern Journey*, pp. 56–57. For an excellent account of "plantation and extrajudicial justice" and how "the law actually sanctioned the master's private law-enforcement authority over the slaves," see Higginbotham, Jacobs, *supra*, pp. 1062–1067. For context, see George C. Rogers Jr., *Charleston in the Age of the Pinckneys* (Columbia, S.C., 1980), pp. 26–88; Weir, *Colonial South Carolina*, pp. 173–203; Robert Bosen, *A Short History of Charleston* (2nd edition, Charleston, 1992), pp. 67–79.

116. See the *Law Commonplace*, "Apprentices & Servants," pp. 19–21; and "Baron & Feme," pp. 25–29.

Quincy, as a good common lawyer, could not abide the laws of slavery, "laws which will stand eternal records of the depravity and contradiction of the human character."[117] And as a natural lawyer and a Christian, he could not abide what slavery did to corrupt our common humanity.

> Mr. Lynch told me, that he knew several Negroes who had refused to implore a forgiveness when under sentence of death, tho' a pardon was insured on this easy term. Preferring death to their deplorable state, they died with a temper deserving a better fate. There is much among this people of what the world call hospitality and politeness, it may be questioned what proportion there is of true humanity, Christian charity and love.[118]

C. The Politics of Slavery

Quincy did not oppose slavery because of its politics. He hated it for core ideological reasons that were quite independent of its political significance. But he understood that slavery also presented both immediate and long-term problems for his political agenda. As discussed before, Quincy was a product of the republican sentiment of the Enlightenment, so well described by Gordon Wood.[119] This did not, in itself, make him a revolutionary, or even opposed to the monarchy, but it did establish ideals of civic virtue.[120] It was these ideals that justified resistance to British colonial policies that encouraged cronyism and corruption in government, while evading political accountability.

Quincy was no egalitarian, but he understood that some inequalities directly influenced the political character of civil societies. While comparing North and South Carolina, Quincy observed that, "[p]roperty is much more equally diffused in one prov[ince] than the other, and this may account, for some, if not all, the differences of Character of the inhabitants."[121] Of course, slavery existed in both North and South Carolina. Indeed, it existed in Massachusetts.[122] But in South Carolina the extent and invasive influence of slavery had changed the character of the people for the worse, even compared to North Carolina.

---

117. *Southern Journal*, p. 93.
118. *Id.*, pp. 94–95.
119. See "III. Gentility," p. 18 *supra*. Wood, *Radicalism, supra*, pp. 95–109.
120. *Id.*, pp. 100–101.
121. *Id.*, p. 110.
122. See text at notes 72–77, *supra*.

For this, and other reasons of concentrated wealth and agricultural eco-
nomics, South Carolina's leaders might be more vulnerable to manipulation
by the British, at least in the short term. As Quincy observed:

> The planter (like the fox) prides himself in saying the grapes are sower [sour]:
> his fortune inclines and makes him look with contempt on the official
> grandee.—Thus the rights and liberties of the State are in some measure
> safe—but from a very unstable cause. This government is composed of two
> aristocratic parts and one monarchical body: the aristocratic parts mutually
> dislike each other.—Let us suppose a change in British policy. Compose the
> Council of the first planters, fill all the Public offices with them—give them
> the honour of the State, and tho' they don't want them, give them it and emol-
> uments also:—introduce Baronies and Lordships—their enormous estates will
> bear it. What will become of Carolinian freedom? The luxury, disipation, life,
> sentiments and manners, of the leading people naturally tend to make them
> neglect, dispise, and be careless of the true interests of mankind in gen-
> eral.—Hence we may suppose, that when a different policy is gone into with
> regard to this people, there will be a very calamitous alteration in the views and
> conduct of the Planters and therefore also with regard to the true interests of
> the province. State, magnificence and ostentation, the natural attendants of
> riches, are conspicuous among this people: the number and subjection of their
> slaves tend this way.[123]

And this was not just Quincy's intuition. Political opponents to Quincy's
vision of a unified colonial resistance to British abuses seized on these differences to promote distrust of other colonies, Massachusetts in particular.[124]
Thus Thomas Shirley, "a hot sensible flaming tory . . . (a native of Britain),"

> —Strongly urged that the Massachusetts were aiming at sovereignty over the
> other provinces; that they now took the lead, were assuming, dictatorial etc.
> "You may depend upon it (added he) that if G[reat]B[ritain] should renounce
> the Sovereignty of this Continent or if the Colonies shake themselves clear of
> her authority that you all (meaning the Carolinas and the other provinces) will
> have Governors sent you from Boston; Boston aims at Nothing less than the
> sovereignty of the whole continent; I know it."[125]

---

123. *Southern Journal*, pp. 87–88.
124. Exploiting distrust of Massachusetts and its leaders has a long and continuing history,
as Presidential candidates Governor Dukakis and Senator Kerry can attest.
125. *Southern Journal*, p. 54.

When Quincy smoothly replied that Massachusetts "paid a very great respect to all the Sister provinces, that she revered, almost, the leaders in Virginia and much respected those of Carolina,"[126] Shirley was unconvinced.

> Mr. Shirley replied, when it comes to the test Boston will give the other provinces the shell and the shadow and keep the substance. Take away the power and superintendency of Britain, and the Colonies must submit to the next power. Boston would soon have that—power rules all things—they might allow the other a paltry representation, but that would be all.[127]

It would have been unfair to ask Quincy to look beyond the immediate threats that slavery presented to his mission of correspondence and unity, to the greater threat slavery would pose to a young republic after independence. As we will see in the section on Quincy's politics, he—like Benjamin Franklin and most colonial advocates—was still seeking a political solution to colonial autonomy. But Quincy saw clearly the fault lines that slavery created between North and South. And he understood the terrible danger slavery presented in any long-term future for America. Having recounted the serious evils of slavery for the present, he uttered deeply prophetic words for the future. "These are but a small part of the mischief of Slavery—new ones are every day arising—futurity will produce more and greater."[128]

VI. RELIGION

Quincy had a great interest in different colonial religions and religious practices. Both Charleston and Philadelphia had a policy of toleration, including toward Jews and Catholics, but Quincy also encountered some bitter religious controversies, particularly in Maryland.[129] Part of Quincy's interest was the natural curiosity of an orthodox New England Congregationalist. He was

126. *Id.*, p. 55.

127. *Id.*, p. 55.

128. *Id.*, p. 94.

129. *Southern Journal*, pp. 134–135. On religious practices in the colonies, see Patricia U. Bonomi, *Under the Cope of Heaven: Religion, Society, and Politics in Colonial America* (New York, 1986); Richard Pointer, *Protestant Pluralism and the New York Experience: A Study of Eighteenth Century Religious Diversity* (Bloomington, Ind., 1988). See also Sally Schwartz, *"A Mixed Multitude": The Struggle for Toleration in Colonial Pennsylvania* (New York, 1987); Jon Butler, *Awash in a Sea of Faith: Christianizing the American People* (Cambridge, Mass., 1992); and Roger Finke and Rodney Stark, *The Churching of America, 1776–1990* (New Brunswick, N.J., 1992). (Hereafter, "Finke and Stark.")

genuinely interested in the practices of Anglicans, Catholics, Moravians, and Quakers, all of whose services he visited.[130] But, as a son of the Enlightenment, Quincy was also well aware of the potential for divisiveness. The differences between the colonies were not just about the religions represented, but, perhaps more importantly, about the proper relationship between the state and religion. These differences could threaten colonial unity, as anyone with a sense of history would understand. As Frank Lambert observed:

> Before the War of Independence, predictions abounded on both sides of the Atlantic that Americans could not form a lasting union. Among the reasons for the gloomy prognosis was the region's religious diversity. The centrifugal forces of myriad sectarian interests, it was feared, would render futile any attempt at defining a common faith.[131]

Quincy understood this risk perfectly well. He was interested in religious differences for the same reason that he was interested in slavery, partly as a matter of principle, partly as matter of curiosity and partly as the basis for a hard-headed assessment about the likelihood of a united colonial front on key issues. Quincy had a low opinion of British cleverness in exploiting the differences between the colonies, but feared "a change in British policy" that would make it more effective.[132]

> At present, the house of Assembly are staunch Colonists. But what is it owing to? Bad policy on the other side of the water.[133]

Slavery and religion were the sociological fault lines dividing the colonies, areas of dangerous practical vulnerability. So were the differing economic interests, and different standards of civic virtue. The lax state of the establishment religion in Charleston, mixed with slavery and an aristocracy of planters, made it subject to British bribery and manipulation.[134] On the other hand, the god-fearing Quaker leadership of Philadelphia had high civic standards, but was unreliable on defense.[135] These were not just theoretical issues to Quincy in 1773.

---

130. See Section "A," p. 42 *infra*.

131. Frank Lambert, *The Founding Fathers and the Place of Religion in America* (Princeton, 2003), p. 206. (Hereafter "Lambert.")

132. *Southern Journal*, p. 88.

133. *Id.*, p. 86.

134. *Id.*, pp. 87–88.

135. *Id.*, pp. 165–166.

A. Religion as Fact

Quincy had a fine analytical mind, but the value of the *Southern Journal* always begins with his keen eye for detail and for the facts. When Quincy visits St. Phillip's Church in Charleston, the famous Anglican citadel of the Rev. Robert Smith, he misses nothing. How was attendance? ("[V]ery few . . .")[136] How were the prayers read? ("[W]ith the most gay, indifferent and gallant air imaginable.")[137] Does the congregation bother to stand while singing hymns? ("[v]ery few men and no women . . .")[138] How long was the sermon? (Very short for Quincy's time, 17 ½ minutes, on Job 22.21). And "it was very common in prayer as well as sermon-time to see gentlemen conversing together."[139] There were a lot of marble monuments and "a majority of both sexes . . . appear in mourning."[140] "I have seen and have been told, that mourning apparel at funerals is greatly in fashion."[141]

Quincy had a low opinion of the established Anglican church in the South. This was partly due to the casual attitude of the congregation, "I could not help remarking the time of it, that here was not, certainly 'solemn mockery,'"[142] and also to the superficial content of the sermons.

> This divine after shewing that avocations, business etc. precluded a certain species of acquaintance with GOD, very sagely said "I come now to show that there is a certain allowable acquaintance with GOD." Qu. What kind of acquaintance can the Creature have with the Creator which is not allowable? [left margin, ll. 5–16][143]

Observation of the Sabbath, a tenet of good Congregationalism strictly observed even by the grandmother of this author, was in sad disarray.

> The Sabbath is a day of visiting & mirth with the Rich, and of license, pastime and frolic for the negroes. The blacks I saw in great numbers playing pawpaw, huzzle-cap, push penny, and quarrelling round the doors of the Churches in service time—and as to their priests—Voltaire says—"always speak well of the

136. *Id.*, p. 51.
137. *Id.*, p. 51.
138. *Id.*, p. 51.
139. *Id.*, p. 52.
140. *Id.*, p. 52.
141. *Id.*, p. 52.
142. *Id.*, p. 52.
143. *Id.*, p. 52.

prior."—The slaves who don't frolic on the Sabbath, do all kinds of work for themselves on hire.[144]

The bottom line was that the state of religion was, to Quincy, a farce in South Carolina, and hardly better in North Carolina. In general, Quincy preferred the moral climate of North Carolina, something he attributed to it having fewer slaves.[145] But there was no "Great Awakening" of religion there, either.

> However, in one respect, I find a pretty near resemblance between the two Colonies: I mean the State of Religion. At a low ebb indeed in both Provinces. 'Tis certainly high time to repeal the Laws relative to religion and the observation of the Sabbath, or to see them better executed.[146]

Quincy, as a good lawyer, hated to see a law that was honored in the breach and would rather repeal the Sabbath laws than have them mocked. As to the religious differences between Congregationalism and Anglicanism, these concerned him far less than secular indifference to any religious values.

The situation in Virginia was hardly better. The missing pages 125 and 126 in the *Southern Journal* occur when Quincy begins to describe crimes with which an active clergyman was charged.[147]

> The State of Religion here is a little better than to the South; tho I hear the most shocking accounts of the depravity and abominable wickedness of their established Clergy, several of whom keeping public taverns and open gaming houses: Other crimes of which one them (who now officiates) is charged and
>
> [PAGES 125 AND 126 ARE CUT OUT][148]

But it was the situation in Maryland that really interested Quincy.

> The clergy and people of this prov:[ince] are ingaged in a very bitter, important contest, and if we may judge by their public papers 'tis like to prove a very wordy war. Til this controversy begun, which is not of very long standing, the clergy received from all taxables, which are all men, black and white, and all women, except white women, from sixteen to sixty, unless exempted for age or infirmity by the County-Court according to positive law, forty pounds of

---

144. *Id.*, p. 89.

145. See discussion at Sec. V, "Race and Slavery," *supra.*

146. *Southern Journal*, p. 111.

147. Did Eliza S. Quincy, in shock, cut these out? Or was it her father, Josiah the Mayor? It is a mystery. See the discussion in the *Editor's Foreword* and the *Transcriber's Foreword, supra.*

148. *Southern Journal*, p. 124.

tobacco a year: and this tax is payable by all Religious sects and denominations without exception.[149]

If there was one thing that concerned Quincy more than religious indifference, it was an unreasonable sponsorship by the state of religion, backed by the taxing power of the state. Of course, Massachusetts certainly had, by today's standards, an established religion.[150] But the Maryland tax went too far. Quincy exclaimed:

> Curious Craft!—Jesuitical policy! Rare sport for the genius of Voltaire! The clergy tell us with immaculate truth and still more unhypocritical solemnity, "the religion and kingdom of CHRIST and his followers are not of this world." 'Tis certainly happy for mankind, that these assay-masters of religion and the faithful are inducted into their office by nothing more than temporary State-power, and their commissions are only durante hâc vita: ["during this life"] 'tis well well for the Cloth, that no express positive institution is in force and use, limiting their authority, revenue and office quam diu se bene & christianâ fide gesserint. ["As long as they shall behave themselves with Christian loyalty"][151]

Despite the history of established Congregationalism in his native province, Quincy linked religious indifference to established religion. His concern was not about too much religion, but about degraded religion. Ironically, this led Quincy to admire a political order that protected religious diversity.

Thus, it was religion in Pennsylvania that most fascinated Quincy. It was almost like Quincy's experience with the theater in New York, where he protested that he would never support such a thing in his colony, while attending performances almost every night![152] During his time in Philadelphia,

---

149. *Id.*, pp. 134–135.

150. See Lambert, *supra*, pp. 73–99. Massachusetts only discontinued tax support for religion in 1833. *Id.*, p. 223.

151. *Southern Journal*, pp. 135–136. Quincy noted that "[t]here are upwards of 5000 Roman Catholicks in this province," *id.*, p. 140, but the Calvert proprietors had renounced Catholicism in 1715 for Anglicanism. By 1773, Catholics were still tolerated, but were a distinct minority. They had never been a majority. As Roger Finke and Rodney Stark observed, "Founded by Lord Baltimore as a haven for Roman Catholics, Maryland was the most Catholic colony in 1776. But that wasn't very Catholic—about three people in a hundred." Finke and Stark, *supra*, p. 30. Anglicanism was the established religion. See *Id.*, p. 140, note 222.

152. "I was however upon the whole much gratified, (and believe if I had stayed in town a month should go to the Theatre every acting night.) But as a citizen and friend to the morals

Quincy attended Catholic masses, Episcopalian services, Quaker meetings and even received accounts "of Bethlem and it's Inhabitants, who are all Moravians, . . . truly singular and surprising."[153] Nothing escaped him.

Of particular interest to Quincy was Catholicism. Philadelphia sheltered one of the oldest Catholic parishes in the English colonies, St. Joseph's. It dated from 1733. St. Mary's Church, across the street, was completed in 1763. They formed one parish.[154] The parish was protected by William Penn's 1701 Charter of Privileges, as were all Christian religions in Pennsylvania (Jews were also tolerated). At the time of Quincy's visit the pastor was Father Robert Molyneux (1738–1808), a Jesuit, who, despite the official suppression of the order in 1773, continued his allegiance to the order.[155]

Quincy was fascinated. Nevertheless, he resisted, as a good Congregationalist "should," "the force of superstition and priestcraft."[156]

> Went to the Public worship of a Romish Church. Such ceremony, pomp, and solemnity were surprising, entertaining and instructive. The Devotion of priest and people were evidences of the force of superstition and priestcraft. The deepest solemnity of worship and musick: the greatest sanctity of countenance and gesture.
>
> While external forms and appearances made a deep impression on my own mind, I could easily conceive how much deeper they must impress others. While attention held me mute, reason lost part of her influence, and left subsequent reflection to lead me to a better judgment.
>
> In the words of the NEW England psalms—"In me the fire enkindled is."[157]

Quincy later visited both Father Molineux and another Jesuit, Father Ferdinand Farmer (1720–1786). His description of the visit remains one of the most important accounts of a Jesuit mission during the suppression. Father Farmer was from a Swabian family. He ministered to the German-Catholic

---

and happiness of society I should strive hard against the admission and much more the Establishment of a Playhouse in any state of which I was a member." *Id.*, pp. 174–175.

153. *Id.*, p. 150. Quincy attended a Moravian service, with mixed results. See p. 46 and note 160, *supra*.

154. See *Id.*, p. 151, note 254. See also the *New Catholic Encyclopedia* (Palatine, Ill., 1981 reprint), vol. 9, pp. 972–973. Arguably, the Catholic chapels in Maryland were older. See *Id.*, vol. 9, pp. 971–972, 1016.

155. See *Southern Journal*, p. 157.

156. *Id.*, p. 151.

157. *Id.*, p. 151.

congregation in Philadelphia, and founded the first Catholic congregation in New York in 1778. He also ministered to the Hessian regiments, but bravely refused to assist the British effort to raise a company of Catholic "volunteers" in 1777.[158] Quincy described every detail of the visit, including the paintings in the Old Chapel at St. Joseph's.

> Mr. Molineux told us very freely that he and Mr. Farmer were both of the order of the Jesuits. He and the Sexton (a Dutchman) on entering the Chapel sprinkled themselves with holy water and crossed themselves: on approaching the Communion-table bowed the knee very low, and on entering within performed the same ceremony, and the like at their departure.[159]

Quincy then sought out a Moravian worship, and was less impressed.

> Attended the Moravian—worship: the softest kind of vocal and instrumental musick made some compensation to the Ear for the gross affronts offered the understanding. (More incoherent, fulsome, absurd and almost impious nonsense I never heard.) The prayers, addresses and worship of this sect seem very much confined to the 2d person in the Trinity.[160]

Freedom of religion for both Moravians and Quakers presented a practical problem, as Quincy clearly recognized. Both groups had pacifist principles, and Benjamin Franklin had already experienced great difficulty in defending the colony against the French and Indians.[161] Quincy was hopeful that they could be persuaded to support a defensive war.

> There is no militia in the prov:[ince] and of course no seeking after petty commissions, etc.—The advantages and disadvantages of this is a topick of doubtful disputation:—we shall never all think alike on this head.—Many of the Quakers and all of the Moravians hold defensive war lawful; offensive otherwise.[162]

The Quakers were politically powerful, and nursed an "antipathy against New England" because of "severities used toward their ancestors in that province."[163] Quincy regarded these stories as "exaggerated," although four

---

158. See *id.*, p. 158, n. 271.

159. *Id.*, p. 158. Quincy, was, however, rude about the communion, referring to "nick nacks," slang for appetizers. "We were not asked to come within the Communion, nor presented with a sight of the Nick nacks I had seen at a distance." *Id.*, p. 158.

160. *Id.*, p. 152. See, on the Moravians, *id.*, p. 150, n. 253. It was a "Christ-centered" worship, as Quincy noted.

161. See Wood, *Franklin, supra*, p. 69.

162. See *Southern Journal*, p. 166.

163. *Id.*, p. 167.

Quakers had been executed in Massachusetts, including Mary Dyer.[164] Despite their commitment to toleration, Quaker political power could be a threat to real religious diversity as well. "[B]y their union they defeat the operation of all other sects in question which any way relate to or may in the end affect religious concerns."[165] Quincy respected Quakers, "they are very public spirited," but he clearly worried about this influence in the centrally important colony of Pennsylvania.[166]

Despite these daring experiments with what to Quincy were exotic religions, he did not neglect the more mainline churches in Philadelphia. There were detailed observations about St. Peter's, the Episcopalian parish, and its Loyalist rector, Thomas Coombe (1744–1822). Quincy found Coombe "a little affected." He used "look and gesture . . . not conformable to his subject, station and language."[167]

Philadelphia, despite or perhaps because of its extraordinary religious diversity, had a remarkably secular leadership. Franklin, for example, was affiliated with no religious group.[168] Quincy found him typical:

> All sects of religionists compose this city; and the most influential, opulent and first characters scarce ever attend Public worship anywhere. This is amazingly general and arises partly from policy, partly from other causes. A man is sure to be less exceptionable to the many, more likely to carry his point in this prov:[ince] by neglecting all religious parties in general, than adhering to any on[e] in particular. And they who call themselves Christians much sooner encourage and vote for a deist or an Infidel, than one who appears under a religious persuasion different from their own. "Tantum religio potuit suadere." ["To such (evils) could religion urge people."][169]

B. Religion as Politics

Quincy's descriptions of the diverse religious practices in the colonies were written on the eve of one of the great religious settlements in world history, the federal constitutional guarantees of 1787. As Frank Lambert has pointed

---

164. See *id.*, p. 167, n. 288.
165. *Id.*, p. 165.
166. *Id.*, p. 165.
167. *Id.*, p. 145.
168. See Edmund S. Morgan, *Benjamin Franklin* (New Haven, 2002), pp. 15–22, 59. (Hereafter "Morgan, *Franklin*.")
169. *Id.*, p. 163.

out, all of the colonies, with the exception of those founded by William Penn and Roger Williams, "had organized church-state relations around the central idea of religious uniformity."[170] Yet, within a few years, a new political order would be established "believing that a free, competitive religious market would both ensure religious vitality and prevent religious wars."[171]

But it was years before the first amendment would apply to the states. As Richard Beeman has observed, "[even] after the Revolution, the course . . . toward liberal democracy did not run straight and true."[172] This was so even in Quincy's own Massachusetts. "Remaining true to the vision of a republican society founded upon the virtue of its citizens, Massachusetts also continued to endorse the connection between church and state, proclaiming in its constitution that "the happiness of a people and the good order and preservation of civil government essentially depend upon piety, religion and morality."[173]

Quincy was a good enlightened republican, but at no point in his travels did he condemn a province for imposing piety by law. The only challenge was to South Carolina's Sabbath laws, not because they were imposed, but because they were not enforced.[174] Yet he saw clearly, as a policy matter, the evil of an established religion, particularly one that was imposed as a major financial burden on all sects, as in Maryland.[175] In Quincy's eyes, the evil of establishment was hardly too much piety, but too little, as a population became resentful and the leadership unobservant, cynical, or both. This Quincy found to be the case in South Carolina and Virginia.[176]

Pennsylvania offered another model, under the umbrella of Penn's 1701 Charter of Privileges. But it was no utopia. How much risk did powerful pacifist sects, like the Quakers and the Moravians, present to state security? More importantly, given a proliferation of competing sects, the ruling elites "scarce ever attend Public worship anywhere" because "[a] man is sure to be less exceptionable to the many, more likely to carry his point in this province,

---

170. Lambert, *supra*, p. 205. See also Finke and Stark, *supra*, pp. 22–53.
171. Lambert, *supra*, p. 206.
172. Beeman, *supra*, p. 94.
173. *Id.*, p. 93.
174. *Southern Journal*, p. 111.
175. *Id.*, pp. 134–135.
176. *Id.*, p. 111.

by neglecting all religious parties in general, than adhering to any one in particular."[177] Benjamin Franklin saw little wrong in this "nonsectarian virtue," and it was his life-long political strategy in Pennsylvania.[178] Quincy valued piety more, as part of republican civil virtue. He did not welcome its atrophy among the elites for any reason.

Yet the need to unite the colonies certainly spoke against the extension of established religion, and its inherent evils, to anything bigger than a province. While Quincy could, in 1773, hardly envision a true United States, he clearly opposed a continental religion. The model of tolerance, which he found both fascinating and problematic as a state policy in Pennsylvania, could be the only choice for any power beyond the colony itself. Thus Quincy balanced his "Enlightenment belief in liberty of conscience,"[179] his suspicion of "superstition and priestcraft,"[180] with his conviction that civic virtue included piety. As Gordon Wood has pointed out, the next generation of American leaders would learn the wisdom of this compromise. "Although some of the enlightened gentry remained immune to what was happening and like Jefferson and young John C. Calhoun . . . enthusiastically predicted that the whole country was rapidly on its way to believing Jesus was just a good man without any divinity, other liberal gentry knew better: Some of them, rational and enlightened as they had been, even came to find in old-fashioned supernatural Christianity a source of salvation for both their own despairing souls and the shattered soul of the country."[181]

VII. LAWS AND LAWYERS

Quincy defined himself as a gentleman, a lawyer, and a patriot. He saw all three as, not only consistent, but corollaries. When those who defined themselves as lawyers did not behave as gentlemen, Quincy's disapproval was evident, and a lawyer who did not love civic virtue and his country was a men-

177. *Id.*, p. 163.
178. See Morgan, *Franklin, supra*, pp. 15–22, 59.
179. See Wood, *Radicalism*, p. 331.
180. *Southern Journal*, p. 151.
181. Wood, *Radicalism*, pp. 329–330.

ace.[182] Quincy was not as great a snob as John Adams when it came to professional elites, but Quincy did believe in an elite legal profession.[183]

Many of Quincy's views on law and lawyers are to be found in other sections of this series, most obviously his *Law Commonplace* and his *Reports*. There are also some revealing letters, such as his famous reply to his father as to why he was representing British defendants, including Captain Preston, in the Boston Massacre case.[184] But the *Southern Journal* offers us yet another perspective on Quincy's professionalism, a comparative perspective.

Quincy and his contemporary "brethren" at the bar defined their professionalism by three criteria. First there was education. The law was a "learned" profession defined by both the general liberal knowledge expected of any gentleman and a specialized, or "artificial," knowledge expected of an elite lawyer. The *Southern Journal* predated by eleven years the founding of America's first professional law school, the celebrated Litchfield Law School in Litchfield, Connecticut,[185] and by a generation the founding of the oldest surviving American law school, the Harvard Law School, in 1817, a school in which Quincy's son would play a major role. In Quincy's day, the specialized knowledge required by lawyers was taught by apprenticeship and building commonplace books.[186] But this did not excuse technical sloppiness, or ignorance of

182. See *Southern Journal*, pp. 86–87.

183. Adams observed, "Looking about me in the Country, I found the practice of Law was grasped into the hands of Deputy Sheriffs, Petty-foggers and even Constables . . . I mentioned these Things to some of the Gentlemen in Boston, who disapproved and even resented them very highly. I asked them whether some measurer might not be agreed upon at the Bar and sanctioned by the Court, which might remedy the Evil?" *Diary and Autobiography of John Adams*, L. H. Butterfield ed., Vol. III, p. 274. See, Daniel R. Coquillette, "Justinian in Braintree: John Adams, Civilian Learning, and Legal Elitism, 1758–1775," *Law in Colonial Massachusetts*, pp. 359–418. (Hereafter, "Coquillette, *Justinian in Braintree*.")

184. See Josiah Quincy, *Memoir of the Life of Josiah Quincy* (2d ed., Eliza L. Quincy, Boston, 1874), pp. 27–28. (Hereafter, "*Memoir*.")

185. See John H. Langbein, "Blackstone, Litchfield, and Yale: The Founding of the Yale Law School," in *History of the Yale Law School* (New Haven, 2004), pp. 23–32. (Hereafter, "Langbein.")

186. Quincy's legal training is discussed at length in the "The Legal Education of a Patriot: Josiah Quincy Jr.'s *Law Commonplace*," *Quincy Papers*, vol. 2 (Hereafter "Introduction, *Law Commonplace*.") His tutor, from 1763 to 1765, was Oxenbridge Thacher (1719–1765) "one of the most eminent lawyers of the period." See *Memoir*, supra, pp. 6–7 and *Appendix 6* to the *Reports*, *Quincy Papers*, vol. 5, for a brief biography. See also Langbein, supra, pp. 19–20; Charles R.

the English and the Roman legal heritage, at least not in Quincy's view. Quincy, together with John Adams, James Otis Jr., Robert Treat Paine, Thomas Jefferson, John Marshall, Joseph Story, and many others went to no formal law school, but they saw themselves as lawyers with a serious legal education.[187]

Quincy also took seriously the formal organization of the Massachusetts bar, and he studied the structure, or lack thereof, in other colonies. Although Quincy himself was never formally admitted as a barrister, he certainly regarded himself as one.[188] The bench, curiously enough, was not legally trained in Massachusetts, at least not until the appointment of Edmund Trowbridge (1709–1793) in 1765.[189] (Chief Justice Thomas Hutchinson [1711–1780] regarded himself as a merchant.) But Quincy had strong ideas of professional structure here, as well. Judges should be appointed for life, pending good behavior, and should be independent from outside influence. They should be free of British salaries and not be British placeholders. They should also not mix being a judge with other political offices—particularly executive ones.[190] Hutchinson was Chief Justice and Lieutenant Governor simultaneously. In Quincy's view, this would lead to serious trouble.[191]

Quincy also recognized that a true professional culture required a professional literature. This was not just a question of education, but of authority. To what could lawyers, litigants, and judges look for guidance if there were no

---

McKindy, "The Lawyers as Apprentice: Legal Education in Eighteenth Century Massachusetts," 28 *J. Legal Educ.* 124, 127–136 (1976) and Steve Sheppard, "Casebooks, Commentaries, and Curmudgeons," 82 *Iowa L. Rev.* 547, 553–556 (1997).

187. See the "Introduction, *Law Commonplace*," *Quincy Papers*, vol. 2. Thomas Jefferson had the benefit of legal training by George Wythe (1726–1806), but before Jefferson himself established a legal program at William and Mary in 1779, John Marshall was one of Wythe's students there in 1780. Marshall only attended a brief course of lectures in that year. See generally Paul D. Carrington's excellent "The Revolutionary Idea of University Legal Education," 31 *William and Mary L. Rev.* 527 (1990).

188. See *Reports*, p. 317. ". . . I proceed (maugre any) at this court to manage all my own Business. . . though unsanitified and uninspired by the Pomp and Magic of the Long Robe." *Id.*

189. See *Reports*, *supra*, *Appendix 10*, "Composition of the Superior Court of Judicature, 1745–1775."

190. See *Southern Journal*, pp. 68–71, as to South Carolina, where the judges did not serve *quam se bene gesserint* ("as long as they shall behave themselves").

191. See *Reports*, p. 215, pp. 265–272, p. 316. See Bernard Bailyn, *The Ordeal of Thomas Hutchinson* (Cambridge, Mass., 1974), pp. 117–118. (Hereafter, "Bailyn.") Hutchinson was accused of "accumulating offices and functions totally incompatible with each other." *Id.*, p. 117.

law reports, no treatises, or no printed colonial statutes? If the only published authorities were English reports and statutes, the American Courts were being bound by the law they did not make or, worse, by no legal authority.[192] Wherever he went, Quincy tried to buy law books, and asked about sources of law. While in South Carolina, he painstakingly copied a set of law reports.[193] While in Virginia, he took care to obtain the latest treatise.[194] He constantly re-supplied his own library.[195]

Finally, and most importantly, Quincy defined legal professionalism with a belief in a rule of law. Resort to illegal conduct, whether in the Stamp Act riots, the Boston Massacre, or the Tea Party, could rarely be justified, even given extreme provocation.[196] Quincy defined his patriotism as a defense of the rights of Englishmen against tyranny, or law against corruption.

A. South Carolina

As discussed before, Quincy was appalled by the slavery laws of South Carolina, which he saw as antithetical to true rule of law, and also by the corrosive effect of planter society on civic virtue.[197] This did not stop him from enjoying the gilded life of this society, with particular appreciation of the wine, silver, and china, or from making careful inquiry about the legal community in Charleston.[198] He "[r]eceived complimentary visits" from several of the leading "Gentlemen of the Bar." Several of these, such as Charles Cotesworth Pinckney, Esq., had been educated in the Inns of Court in London. Pinckney had matriculated at Christ Church College, Oxford, and the Middle Temple,

192. See Quincy's scathing comments on the lack of published statutes in South Carolina, *Southern Journal*, p. 61, and of "no laws in force" in North Carolina, *id.*, p. 108 (emphasis in original).

193. *Id.*, pp. 74, 77. These had been compiled by Edward Rutledge (1749–1800). Quincy's copy remains in the Massachusetts Historical Society, Quincy Family Papers, No. 60 (Micro. Reel 4). See James Haw, *John & Edward Rutledge of South Carolina* (Athens, Georgia, 1997), pp. 19–21, 179.

194. *Id.*, p. 119.

195. See Introduction, *Law Commonplace, Quincy Papers*, vol. 2. See also *Reports, Quincy Papers*, vol. 5, *Appendix 9*, "Catalogue of Books Belonging to the Estate of Josiah Quincy jun: Esq: Deceas'd."

196. See Quincy's emotional reaction, "I pray GOD give me better hearts," to the looting of Chief Justice Hutchinson's house. *Reports*, pp. 168–173.

197. See *Southern Journal*, pp. 56–61, 87–88.

198. *Id.*, p. 57.

which was a favorite with young men from South Carolina.[199] Quincy said that he "[w]as much entertained by Mr. Pinckney's conversation, who appeared a man of bright natural power, and impressed by a British education at the Temple."[200]

Unlike Quincy's Boston, it was common for young gentlemen in Charleston to have an English education. "[F]ew of the prosperous inhabitants . . . of Charleston had not crossed the Atlantic before the American Revolution and . . . sons of successful planters, merchants and professional men were sent to England for their education and general culture."[201] But "general culture" was a good term for the educational environment in the Inns of Court at the time, where serious legal study was ignored by many of the students, who instead enjoyed the good life of London.

Quincy quickly learned that Charleston legal culture was actually not very sophisticated, despite these English sojourns. Charles Cotesworth Pinckney presented him with "the only digest of the laws of the province," William Simpson's *The Practical Justice of the Peace, and Parish-officer of . . . South Carolina* (Charleston, printed by Robert Wells, 1761), which was already 12 years out of date.[202] What was worse, there were no up-to-date printed collections of the statutes. "[T]here is no collections of the Laws of this Province in a book to be had . . ."[203] This absence of any serious legal literature was outrageous. "No wonder their lawyers make from £2000 to £3000 sterling a year!"[204]

---

199. *Id.*, p. 61, and accompanying notes.

200. *Id.*, p. 61, and accompanying notes.

201. *Id.*, p. 61, and accompanying notes.

202. William Simpson was "One of the assistant-judges of the Court of General Sessions of the Peace, Assize, etc., of the said Province." See Morris L. Cohen, *Bibliography of Early American Law* (Buffalo, 1998), vol. III, p. 25, Item 8001.

203. *Southern Journal*, p. 61. Quincy may have been a bit unkind to South Carolina's legal culture. In 1736 Nicholas Trott, "Chief Justice of the Province of South Carolina," had published *The Laws of the Province of South Carolina* (Charleston, 1736), in two parts, including the "Two Charters granted by Charles II to the Lord Proprietors of South Carolina" and the Act of Parliament in which these proprietors surrendered "their Title and Interest to His Majesty." Earlier, in 1721, Trott had published *The Laws of the British Plantations in America Relating to the Church and the Clergy, Religion and Learning* (London, 1731). But there was no regular publication of the statutory law, as in Massachusetts. See Daniel R. Coquillette, "Radical Lawmakers in Colonial Massachusetts: The 'Countenance of Authoritie' and the *Lawes and Libertyes*" 67 *New England Quarterly* (1994), p. 179 at pp. 194–206. Special thanks to Mark Sullivan.

204. *Id.*, p. 61.

The bar seemed ignorant of even the most fundamental principles of the common law, the forms of action.[205] These traditional categories, based on the old system of writs, defined wrongs that had legal remedies in the king's courts, and remained a dominant force in American legal theory until the establishment of the Federal Rules of Civil Procedure, which abolished the traditional causes of action on September 16, 1938.[206] But, as Quincy observed, "[t]he rule of Action altogether unknown to the people" in South Carolina.[207]

Modern scholarship has confirmed Quincy's observation. According to Gordon Wood, "[L]ocal social superiority, and not any professional legal expertise, was what gave the justices the extraordinary discretionary authority they exercised.[208]

> Law at times seemed to be pretty much what they said it was. For their judgments they scarcely worried about English practices or collections of ancient cases; they instead relied on their own untrained but ritualized sense of justice. Sometimes they even interpreted provincial Statutes to fit their local needs.[209]

It was easy to do that where, as Quincy discovered, the statutes were often unpublished!

Quincy was convinced of the need of a professional literature that was uniquely colonial, if not American, hence his *Reports*.[210] While in South Carolina, he sought to buy any printed colonial sources, and also spent several days transcribing the manuscript law reports of Edward Rutledge (1749–1800).[211] His own legal training, as represented by the *Law Commonplace*, focused on exactly the "collections of ancient cases" and "English practices" that Wood described as ignored in South Carolina.[212]

---

205. See J. H. Baker, *An Introduction to English Legal History* (4th ed., London, 2002), pp. 53–69. (Hereafter, "Baker.") See also Daniel R. Coquillette, *The Anglo-American Legal Heritage* (2d ed., Durham, N.C., 2004), pp. 147–164. (Hereafter, "Coquillette.")

206. See *Federal Rules of Civil Procedure*, Rule 2 "There shall be one form of action to be known as 'civic action'."

207. *Southern Journal*, p. 61.

208. Wood, *Radicalism, supra*, p. 72.

209. *Id.*, p. 72.

210. See Daniel R. Coquillette, "First Flower—The Earliest American Law Reports and the Extraordinary Josiah Quincy, Jr. (1744–1775)," 30 *Suffolk University Law Review* (1996), pp. 1–34.

211. See *Southern Journal*, pp. 74, 77 and accompanying notes.

212. See Introduction, Law Commonplace.

Of course, even the Massachusetts judges were, until Edmund Trowbridge's appointment in 1767, laymen. But they were obsessed with legal
precedents, both English and colonial, often asking the lawyers to find "more
authority."[213] While Quincy's *Reports* reveal a bench that was often "results
driven," men like Chief Justice Hutchinson were alert to precedent and
authority, perhaps worrying even more than the lawyers about legal technical-
ities.[214] In the *Southern Journal*, Quincy told an entertaining tale about Lord
Mansfield and a wine glass. "[T]wo gentlemen being at a tavern. One of them
gave the Pretender's heath, the other refused to drink it, upon which he who
gave the toast threw his glass of wine in the refuser's face. For this an action
of trepass was brôt . . ." Mansfield took a characteristically pragmatic
approach, throwing out the case as "a most trifling affair," to the horror of the
plaintiff's barrister—who exclaimed "[I]f the Jury don't hear law from the
Court, they shall from the Bar."[215] Quincy thought this a most instructive
episode, and asked Pinckney "several times to repeat that I might be the better able to relate it,"[216] comparing Mansfield's action "with some maneuvers of
the little GODS of the North."[217]

One of Quincy's greatest objections to the South Carolina legal establishment was appointment of judges by the Crown. This he blamed on the legislature's foolishness in passing judicial salaries without ensuring life tenure for
the native judges, "men of abilities, fortune and good fame."[218]

> Mark the sequel. No Assistant Judges had ever before been nominated in Eng-
> land. Immediately upon the king's approving this last act, Lord Hillsborough
> in his zeal for American good forthwith sends over, one Chief Justice, and two
> assistant Justices, Irishmen, the other two, was the one a Scotchman, and the
> other a Welshman. How long will the simple love their simplicity? And ye,

---

213. See, for example, *Dudley* v. *Dudley* (1762), *Reports*, pp. 15–25; *Banister* v. *Henderson* (1765),
Reports, pp. 130–155.

214. See the discussion in *Bailyn*, *supra*, pp. 49–51. Governor Bernard was correct in being
able to "count on Hutchinson's diligence in perfecting his knowledge of the law." *Id.*, p. 50. See
Hanlon v. *Thayer*, *Reports*, p. 99, where Hutchinson admonished the lawyers for insufficient use
of authority. *Id.*, p. 102.

215. *Southern Journal*, p. 64. (Emphasis in the original.)

216. *Id.*, p. 62.

217. *Id.*, p. 65. A reference to John Stuart, 3rd Earl of Bute, 1713–1799, see p. 182, n. 91, *infra*.

218. *Id.*, p. 67.

who assume the guileful name, the venerable pretext of <u>friends to Government</u>, how long will ye deceive and <u>be deceived</u>.[219]

Compensation and appointment of the judiciary was to become a major issue in Massachusetts, as well. Quincy could work with a lay judiciary that had the security of a <u>quam diu se bene gesserint</u> (good behavior) tenure, but a judiciary of placemen was an insult to his professionalism.[220]

Quincy was no egalitarian, and he respected the elitist hierarchy of the South Carolina bar, at least "the three first-lawyers in the Province; James Parsons, John Rutledge "and Old Charles Pinckney,"[221] although he thought the bar overpaid.[222] But he also deeply distrusted the lack of learning and professional literature in the colony. In his view, the lack of judicial tenure was a result of this culture of patronage and power.

> The Gentlemen (planters and merchants) are mostly men of the turff and gamesters. Political enquiries and philosophie disquisitions are too laborious for them: they have no great passion for to shine and blaze in the forum or Senate.[223]

But part of the problem was slavery itself. Quincy's outrage at the summary execution laws, "for <u>free</u> as well as <u>slave</u> — Negroes and molattoes . . . Curious laws and policy!," reflected his conviction that no common law system was secure without an underpinning of fundamental rights.[224] An elegant and wealthy legal profession aside, this precondition, of a rule of law in colonial South Carolina, was the hostage of racism. "[B]ut the Judges have forgot a maxim of English law — <u>Jura naturalia sunt immutabilia</u> ["the laws of nature are unchangeable"] and they would <u>do</u> well to remember that no laws of the (little) creature supercede the laws of the (great) creator."[225]

---

219. *Id.*, pp. 68–69. Quincy noted that two of the existing provincial judges had pushed the salary bill through the legislature, only to see their positions assigned to British placemen. "They are now knawing their tongues in rage." *Id.*, p. 73.

220. *Id.*, pp. 68–69.

221. *Id.*, p. 79.

222. See *id.*, pp. 61, 71.

223. *Id.*, p. 88. See also Wood, *Radicalism, supra*, pp. 57–77.

224. See *Southern Journal*, pp. 92–95.

225. *Id.*, p. 94.

B. North Carolina

South Carolina represented a flawed legal system to Quincy, but North Carolina represented <u>no</u> legal system, "no C[our]ts of any kind sitting or even <u>being in the province</u>."[226] Ravaged by the Regulator campaign of 1771 and the retaliation of the Tryonists after the Battle of Alamance on May 16, 1771, the colony was, legally, in terrible shape. Quincy carefully copied a royal decree of February 4, 1772, directed to the Governor of North Carolina prohibiting collection of debts from those outside the colony "otherwise than is allowed by law in Cases of a like nature within our kingdom of Great Britain."[227] He found the premise questionable, and the decree pointless.

> The present state of No[rth] C[arolina] is really envious: there are but 5 laws in force thro' the Colony, and no Courts at all in being. None can recover their debts except before a single magistrate where the sums are within his jurisdiction, and offenders escape with impunity. The people are in great consternation about the matter: What will be the consequences are problematical: many people, as Lord Bottetourt says "augur ill" on the occasion.[228]

Assuming the "5 laws" were the "Six Confirmed Laws" of 1715, Quincy was being a little unfair, as these were "really a codification of all statutes prior to that year."[229] But Quincy was diligently looking for a legal culture, and found a vacuum. "There being no C:[our]ts of any kind in this province and <u>no laws in force</u> by which any could be held, I found little inclination or incitement to stay long in Edenton, tho' a pleasant town."[230] The formal presence of laws on the books was irrelevant without such a culture. As Quincy observed of both Carolinas, "'Tis certainly to the last degree false politicks to have laws in force which the legislators, judges and executive officers not only break themselves, but practically and too often openly and avowedly deride. Avowed impunity to all offenders is one sign at least that the Law wants amendment or abrogation."[231] Quincy enjoyed riding through the North Carolina countryside in the Spring ("[e]xcellent farms and charming large cleared tracts . . . Peach-

---

226. *Id.*, p. 106.
227. *Id.*, pp. 101–102.
228. *Id.*, p. 116.
229. *Id.*, p. 116, note 188.
230. *Id.*, p. 108.
231. *Id.*, pp. 111–112.

trees . . . I had them all-along in their proudest bloom.").[232] But legally, the province was a desert.

C. Virginia

Quincy's visit to Virginia would seem particularly exciting, both to him and to historians today. After all, this was the colony that could, with the most justification, rival the North. The College of William and Mary, with a royal charter of 1693, was second only to Harvard in seniority. It would be there, in 1779, that George Wythe (1726–1806) would be appointed "professor of law and police," the first "law professor" in America.[233] And it would be Wythe who would be "law preceptor" to Thomas Jefferson.[234] But, in 1773, it was a disappointment to Quincy, "'Tis inferior much to my expectation."[235]

Williamsburg was, in general, not impressive. "Nothing of the population of the North, or the magnificence and splendor of the South."[236] The College itself was a true disappointment. "The College in this place is in a very declined state."[237] The architecture was handsome, "but in the rear it is scandalously out of repair."[238]

Quincy, nevertheless, immediately set about seeking law books, and was successful in obtaining *The Acts of Assembly* published in Williamsburg in 1769, "a very handsome Edition."[239] In addition, he was greatly impressed by the law library of the State House Council Chamber, "a large, well chosen, valuable collection of Books; chiefly of law."[240] He also, as was his custom, attended the courts.

These were also unimpressive. Like a good common lawyer, Quincy was wary of the equity jurisdictions, and other special jurisdictions, particularly

232. *Id.*, p. 117.

233. Robert Stevens, *Law School: Legal Education in America from the 1850s to the 1980s* (Chapel Hill, 1983), p. 4. (Hereafter, "Stevens, *Law School: Legal Education in America*.") See Paul D. Carrington's excellent "The Revolutionary Idea of University Legal Education," 31 *William and Mary L. Rev.* 527 (1990).

234. *Id.*, p. 4.

235. *Southern Journal*, p. 118.

236. *Id.*, p. 118.

237. *Id.*, p. 119.

238. *Id.*, p. 118.

239. *Id.*, p. 119.

240. *Id.*, p. 120.

those that combined executive with judicial power.[241] In Massachusetts, the Superior Court of Judicature had jealously defended its jurisdiction against the Vice-Admiralty Court, and colonial lawyers well knew that the Crown preferred the latter, which evaded local juries.[242] The situation in Virginia was far worse.

> The Constitution of the Courts of Justice and equity in this colony is amazingly defective, inconvenient and dangerous, not to say absurd and mischievous. This motley kind of Court called the Gen:l Court is composed of the Governor and Council, who are appointed and created by mandamus [direct prerogative order] from the Crown, and hold bene placito [as long as it "pleased" the Crown]. I am told that it is no uncommon thing for this Court to set one hour and hear a cause as a Court of Law; and the next hour, perhaps minute, to set and audit the same matter as a Court of Chancery and equity: and if my information is good, they very frequently give directly contrary decisions.[243]

As Quincy well knew, equity jurisdiction should be barred where there was an adequate remedy at Law. Concurrent equity jurisdictions undercut common law authority, and replaced it with the discretion of judges appointed at royal discretion.[244]

> It was a matter of speculation with me how such a constitution and form of judicial administration could be tolerable: I conversed with divers who seemed to have experienced no inconvenience and of course to apprehend no danger from this quarter; yet they readily gave into my sentiments upon the subject, when I endeavored to show the political defects and solecism of this constitution. However I saw none who gave me any satisfactory account of the true reason that more mischievous consequences had not flowed from this source.[245]

Quincy wished to learn more about what, to him, was a dangerous system. But in Virginia, Quincy's "web of gentility," his system of introductory letters, failed him.

---

241. See Coquillette, *supra*, pp. 183–188, 205–212, 311–325; Baker, *supra*, pp. 97–125.
242. For John Adams's experience in the colonial vice-admiralty courts, see Coquillette, *Justinian in Braintree*, pp. 382–395.
243. *Southern Journal*, pp. 121–122.
244. See *id.*, p. 121, and accompanying note.
245. *Id.*, pp. 122–123.

Perhaps it was owing to my misfortune in having no Letters to any of the Bar, and but one to any Gentlemen within many miles of Williamsburgh, tho' I had many to persons of distinction expected in town next week. I could only regret, but many circumstances deprived me of remedying, this inconvenience.[246]

Even so, Quincy "spent the Evening with two of the Councils of the Province," and was obliged to decline an introduction to the Governor, the Earl of Dunmore, the next day.[247]

It has been mentioned before that Quincy was alert to gender issues. He was particularly concerned about the effect of the entail, which tended to limit inheritance to issue of the blood and prevent free alienability.[248] Many entails created an interest "in tail male," restricting the estate to male heirs of the blood; this could effectively bar women from holding property. Massachusetts had, by colonial law, replaced primogeniture, which favored the eldest male, with coparcenage, which gave women equality of inheritance, and the Superior Court of Judicature had looked cautiously on efforts to replace this relatively egalitarian jurisprudence by leaving property entailed. Even in England, free alienation had been encouraged by a judicial fiction, the "Common Recovery," which permitted a tenant in tail in possession to bar the entail and sell a free title.[249] But Virginia, to Quincy's dismay, was even more conservative than the home country. "An Aristocratical spirit and principle is very prevalent in the Laws policy and manners of this Colony, and the Law ordaining that Estates-tail shall not be barred by Common Recoveries is not the only instance thereof."[250] All in all, Virginia had not lived up to its reputation.

D. Maryland and Pennsylvania

Quincy was deeply interested in Maryland agriculture, particularly tobacco. He was also deeply interested in Pennsylvania politics. But his comments on the law became sparse, even though he "spent about 3 hours in company with

---

246. *Id.*, p. 123.
247. *Id.*, pp. 123–124.
248. See *Dudley* v. *Dudley* (1762), *Reports*, p. 12 ff., and accompanying notes, and *Baker* v. *Mattocks* (1763), *Reports*, p. 69 ff., and accompanying notes. See also Earl Jowitt, *The Dictionary of English Law* (London, 1959), pp. 715–716.
249. See *Baker*, *supra*, p. 282; Coquillette, *supra*, pp. 113–114.
250. *Southern Journal*, p. 128.

the famous Daniel Dulany, Esq. [1722–1797, educated at Eton, Cambridge, and the Middle Temple] the Attorney General of the province [Maryland] and several others of the Bar, and Gentlemen of the province."[251] In particular, his efforts to observe Maryland courts were disappointing.

> I attended the Supreme (called the Provincial) Court on two Days, but no one cause or motion was argued, and I had therefore no good opportunity to judge of the talents of the Bar, but from some little specimens and appearances I conjecture here is not much of the superlative.[252]

In Pennsylvania, he "[f]easted with the Superior Court Judges and all the Bar on Turtle etc.," and had a letter of introduction to Joseph Reed (1741–1785), another leader of the bar educated at the Middle Temple in London.[253] He was "waited upon . . . for about an hour by Chief Justice [William] Allen [1704–1780] and his sons."[254] He even attended the Superior Court for three days, of which he had a low opinion.[255]

> I attended 3 several days the setting of the Superior Court, (which is as contemptible a one as I ever saw.) Without learning, dignity and order a Court will soon loose much of it's authority and more of it's repute.[256]

But except for a few summary remarks, "[t]he Bar are a very Respectable body."[257] Quincy's Pennsylvania interests had switched from law to politics and religion.[258] What interested him about Chief Justice Allen was Allen's

251. *Id.*, p. 138.
252. *Id.*, p. 140.
253. *Id.*, p. 147.
254. *Id.*, p. 149.
255. *Id.*, p. 162.
256. *Id.*, p. 162.
257. *Id.*, p. 162. Quincy did have a few rude words for another rival of Harvard, the "College" of Philadelphia. "To the South and North of this province we have much too exalted an idea of it." *Id.*, p. 149. This was to become the vestigial University of Pennsylvania, first chartered as an academy in 1751, and then as a college in 1765. In 1790, James Wilson would be appointed professor of law here, and would deliver his famous lectures from 1790–1791. See Stevens, *Law School: Legal Education in America*, pp. 11–12, n. 15, 15, n. 47.
258. Despite the distinction of Pennsylvania, we still know relatively little about its colonial legal system, at least compared to Massachusetts. As George L. Harkins observed in 1983, "[T]here have been few studies of the foundation of Pennsylvania's legal system." See George L. Harkins, "Influences of New England Law on the Middle Colonies," 1 *Law & Hist. Rev.* 238 (1983), at 238, and sources cited. But there are exceptions. See, for example, Paul Lermack, "The Law of Recognizances in Colonial Pennsylvania," 50 *Temp. L. G.* 475 (1977).

attack on Franklin, including the Chief Justice's outrageous accusation that "Dr. Franklin was the first proposer of the Stamp Act."[259] Quincy's interest in New York would run more to the theater than the law, and he would have nothing to say about the Rhode Island legal system either.

VIII. POLITICS

Quincy was an American Whig. As Bernard Bailyn has observed, "The ultimate origins of this distinctive ideological strain lay in the radical social and political thought of the English Civil War and of the Commonwealth period; but its permanent form had been acquired at the turn of the seventeenth century and in the early eighteenth century, in the writings of a group of prolific opposition theorists, "country" politicians and publicists.[260] Excerpts from these writers filled Quincy's *Political Commonplace Book* of 1770–1774, and their vocabulary of civic responsibility and public virtue filled the pages of the *Southern Journal*.[261]

One way to define Quincy's politics is to compare him to Benjamin Franklin (1706–1790), with whom Quincy's life was to become closely linked. Quincy was initially very suspicious of Benjamin Franklin, "a very trimmer—a very courtier,"[262] and recorded negative reports about him from Chief Justice Allen and others in Pennsylvania. "I find men who are very great foes to each other in this province, unite in their doubts, insinuations and revilings of Franklin."[263] But in two years, Quincy would be working in close cooperation with Franklin on the mission that would end Quincy's life. In the margin of

---

259. *Southern Journal*, p. 156. This was a blatant lie, as Quincy later recognized. *Id.*, p. 156. See Morgan, *Franklin*, pp. 149–158.

260. Bernard Bailyn, *The Ideological Origins of the American Revolution* (enlarged ed., Cambridge, Mass., 1992), p. 34. (Hereafter, "Bailyn, *Ideological Origins*.") See also John C. Miller, *Origins of the American Revolution* (Stanford, 1959), pp. 144–145, 304 ("Whig gentry" as opposed to the radicals); Beeman, *Radicalism, supra*, pp. 95–109 ("Classical republican virtue").

261. See York, "The Making of a Patriot," Introduction, *Quincy Papers*, vol. 1.

262. *Southern Journal*, p. 155.

263. *Id.*, p. 156.

the *Southern Journal*, next to his original notes, Quincy added, "I am now fully convinced [Franklin] is one of the wisest and best of men upon Earth."[264]

This switch is hardly surprising, because, at the core, Quincy and Franklin shared a closely matched politics—a pragmatic politics that sought to avoid risk and conflict, when possible, and to get things done by emphasizing common ground and building coalitions.[265] They also came to see the relative strengths and weaknesses of the colonies in the same way, and developed a similar strategy in how to confront British claims. Only very late in the day did they both become convinced that conflict was inevitable and then they faced very real danger with a patriotic courage.[266]

With "twenty-twenty" historical hindsight it is easy to overlook or belittle the efforts of those on both sides of the Atlantic who sought a negotiated political solution. Indeed, such a solution today almost seems unpatriotic. But Franklin and Quincy were both men of cold courage—they stayed in England long after it was safe to do so—and were devoted with all their hearts to the colonial cause. As my co-editor, Neil L. York, has powerfully demonstrated, there was no structural reason why the Revolution was inevitable. Speaking of Lord Dartmouth, a man of "conscience"[267] who sought a "solid, honourable, and lasting" reconciliation,[268] York observes, "[t]hat a solution eluded him had much more to do with practical than theoretical concerns, with the breakdown of political trust rather than with constitutional impossibility."[269] "Anglo-

---

264. *Id.*, p. 155.

265. See Neil L. York, *Turning the World Upside Down: The War of American Independence and the Problem of Empire* (Westport, Conn., 2003), pp. 83–84, 87, 111–114. See also Neil L. York, "Federalism and the Failure of Imperial Reform, 1774–1775," *History*, 86:282 (2001), 155, 160–164 (hereafter, "York, *Federalism*"); Bernhard Knollenberg, *Growth of the American Revolution 1766–1775*, pp. 81–211.

266. See Morgan, *Franklin*, pp. 145–188; Wood, *The Americanization of Benjamin Franklin*, pp. 105–151. The political realities of the American Revolution dawned slowly on the British officials. See the excellent account in Stanley Weintraub's recent *Iron Tears: America's Battle for Freedom, Britain's Quagmire: 1775–1783* (New York, 2005). This book has led Gordon Wood to comment "[I]f history teaches anything, it teaches humility." See Gordon S. Wood, "The Makings of a Disaster," a review of the Weintraub book in *The New York Review of Books*, vol. 52, no. 7 (April 28, 2005), pp. 32–34.

267. York, *Federalism*, p. 170.

268. *Id.*, p. 168.

269. *Id.*, p. 172.

American relations lacked what Hans Kelsen has called a <u>grundnorm</u>, a complementary set of interests and a shared identity."[270] All this, of course, was only obvious after the fact, while the dangers of war were only too apparent.

In addition, Quincy had some of his own concerns about "political trust" and "<u>grundnorm</u>"—on the colonial side. It was clear that his Southern journey had its own political agenda. Quincy was a member of the Boston Committee of Correspondence, and almost certainly delivered more letters than he noted in the *Southern Journal*.[271] "The plan of Continental correspondence highly relished, much wished for and resolved upon, as proper to be pursued."[272] But more importantly, Quincy was concerned about whether, as a practical matter, the colonies had enough shared interests and trust to work together.[273] And, like Franklin, he was well aware of the danger to the colonial cause if the British became more skilled in exploiting mutual suspicion between the colonies. Even at the end of his Southern journey, Quincy lamented, "the prevalent and extended ignorance of one colony of the concerns of another."[274]

A. Hunter, the Dishonest Purser

The first major discussion of politics in the *Southern Journal* took place under very odd conditions. One of Quincy's shipmates was John Alexander Hunter, the former "purser on board his majesty's 20 gun ship of war lying in Boston,"[275] who had been caught stealing. Quincy, quoting a well-known poem of Sir Samuel Garth, observed, rather kindly, "see Little villains hung by great."[276] Quincy was very seasick, but could not resist a political debate.

---

270. *Id.*, p. 178, n. 91. As Neil York has also demonstrated, even the opposition Rockingham Whigs, such as William Dowdeswell, had great difficulty identifying with the colonists' concerns. See Neil York, "William Dowdeswell and the American Crisis, 1763–1775," 90 *History* (2005), 507. "Dowdeswell was the quintessential English country gentleman who could not truly empathize with protesting Americans." *Id.*, p. 507.

271. *Southern Journal*, pp. 96, 107.

272. *Id.*, p. 104.

273. *Id.*, pp. 53–54.

274. *Id.*, p. 184.

275. *Id.*, p. 18.

276. "Where little villains must submit to fate, The great ones may enjoy the World in state," Sir Samuel Garth, *The Dispensary: A Poem in Six Cantos* (London, 1699), first canto. Many thanks to extraordinary diligence of Michael Hayden and Mark Sullivan in identifying this citation.

At one point, Hunter had exclaimed:

> Good GOD! . . . why do I complain? What reason had I to expect any thing
> better. <u>A government that is arbitrary is always unjust: a tyranny in one or
> more is always cruel and unrighteous.</u>[277]

Quincy could not resist the opportunity to test Hunter's enlightenment.

> Hunter was a man of good natural powers; considerably acquainted with
> essays and the Belles Lettres, tho' not learned or conversant with the severer
> studies. I took this opportunity to start the controversy between G[reat]
> B[ritain] and the Colonies. I spoke of the conduct of both; of present measures
> and of the probable consequences. I hoped hence to draw the general opinions
> of his Core and also what must have frequently transpired in his company for
> the last 7 years.[278]

Hunter rose to the challenge

> Very true, said he, Mr. Q[uincy] we all know this. Great Britain has no right
> to tax you. The ministry know it as well as you, but money must be had some
> where. Every thing is strained to the utmost at home. The people of England
> see, as well as you, that N[orth] America must one day be independent, and
> tis her interest and most certainly of the present administration to prevent this
> as much as possible: And they will prevent it for a much longer time than you
> imagine. For you can't contend with the powers of Britain, whose navy con-
> quers the World; and your first men are all bought off and will be more and
> more so in proportion as the ministry are wise and well informed. And who
> can blame them for it, they are in the right of it to do it, and you are in the
> right of it to make opposition, but all will not do. You must submit for a great
> while yet to come. Why all the world are slaves, and N[orth] America can't
> hope to be free.[279]

This, of course, really aggravated the good Whig in Quincy and his inherent
belief in civic virtue. "I almost stormed. The agitation did my health good, if
nothing more; for I wanted my blood to circulate."[280]

> Upon my telling him, that the present steps of the British government were to
> the last degree iniquitous, repugnant to the first notions of right and
> wrong:—"Oh (Mr. Q[uincy] (he replied) what do you tell of that for, there can

---

277. *Southern Journal*, pp. 18–19 (emphasis in original).
278. *Id.*, pp. 19–20. See, on "enlightenment," Wood, *Radicalism, supra*, pp. 146–147, 189–196.
279. *Id.*, pp. 20–21.
280. *Id.*, p. 21.

be no government without fraud and injustice!—All government is *founded* in corruption. The British government is so. There is no doing without it in State-affairs."[281]

Now Quincy was really furious, observing that "this was a clencher."[282] He replied:

> "Well I hope Mr. H[unter] you will never more complain of arbitrary proceedings and wrong and cruelty seeing such is the government you have served and are now raging to be employed by. 'Yes, yes, when it touches one's-self, we have rights to complain. Damn it, was ever any one served as I have been? Admiral M. has himself to my knowledge done ten times as bad, and yet the rascal, the scoundrel persecuted me with unrelenting, brutal cruelty.'"[283]

Quincy then "let matters drop,"[284] but concluded with an observation which would prove deeply troubling in retrospect. "How little variant is this Gentleman from those Zealots for Liberty, who are the Enslavers of Negroes?"[285] Of course, Quincy was on his way to see exactly such people in South Carolina. The matter came up again, in England when Colonel Isaac Barré observed that two-thirds of the English thought, "Americans were all negroes."[286] Quincy replied, "I did not the least doubt it, for if I was to judge by the late acts of Parliament, I should suppose that a majority of the people of Great Britain still thought so, for I found that their representatives still treated them as such."[287] Quincy's exchange with Hunter demonstrated the deep sources of Quincy's political culture, his enlightenment Whiggism, and his profound belief in the triumph of civic virtue over special interests.[288] But it also revealed the greatest challenge to that political faith, slavery. As Richard Beeman has observed, slavery shaped the attitude of colonists, particularly in the South "toward power and authority."[289] As a future age would say, there was the potential for a "train wreck."

---

281. *Id.*, pp. 21–22 (emphasis in original).
282. *Id.*, p. 22.
283. *Id.*, p. 22.
284. *Id.*, p. 23.
285. *Id.*, p. 23.
286. *The London Journal*, 1774–1775, *supra*, p. [248].
287. *Id.*, p. [248].
288. Wood, *Radicalism*, *supra*, pp. 51–55.
289. Beeman, *supra*, pp. 147–151.

B. The Carolinas: "Flaming Tories," "Sensible Tryonists," and Problematic Allies

South Carolina would repeat Hunter's challenge to Quincy's political faith in immediate and harsh terms. On the one hand, British policies—particularly the dumping of placemen like Hunter on the colony—had created resentment.[290] But there was also deep suspicion of the North.[291]

To begin, there was a stronger British presence. Quincy met a number of British "natives," as he called them. "Nothing that I now saw raised my conceptions of the mental abilities of this people: but my wrath enkindled when I considered a King's Gov[ernment]."[292] Some of these also took Quincy on directly in political debate, such as Mr. Thomas Shirley, "a hot sensible flaming tory."

> Politicks started before dinner: a hot sensible flaming tory, one Mr. Thomas Shirley (a native of Britain) present: he had advanced that G[reat] B[ritain] had better be without any of the Colonies; that she committed a most capital political blunder in not ceeding Canada to France: that all the Northern Colonies to the Colony of New York and even NY also were now working the Bane of G[reat] B[ritain]: that GB would do wisely to renounce the Colonies to the North and leave them a prey to their continental neighbors or foreign powers: that none of the political writings or Conducts of the Colonies would bear any examination but Virginia and none could lay any claim to [e]ncomium but that province etc.[293]

Regional suspicions and jealousies were exploited.

> [Shirley] [s]trongly urged that the Massachusetts were aiming at sovereignty over the other provinces; that they now took the lead, were assuming, dictatorial etc. "You may depend upon it (added he) that if G[reat]B[ritain] should renounce the Sovereignty of this Continent or if the Colonies shake themselves clear of her Authority that you all (meaning the Carolinas and the other provinces) will have Governors sent you from Boston; Boston aims at Nothing less than the sovereignty of the whole continent; I know it."[294]

---

290. They offended Quincy, too. "In company were two of the late appointed assistant Justices from G[reat] B[retain]. Their behavior by no means abated my zeal against the British." *Southern Journal*, p. 65.

291. *Id.*, pp. 70–71.

292. *Id.*, p. 46.

293. *Id.*, pp. 53–54.

294. *Id.*, p. 54.

But Quincy was a model diplomat for colonial union.

> It was easy to see the drift of this discourse: I remarked that all this was new
> to me; that if it was true, it was a great and good ground of distrust and dis-
> union between the colonies; that I could not say what the other provinces had
> in view or thôt but I was sure that the Inhabitants of the Massachusetts paid a
> very great respect to all the Sister provinces, that she revered, almost, the lead-
> ers in Virginia and much respected those of Carolina.[295]

This, of course, was tactful fabrication. As we have seen, Quincy's view of
Carolina leadership was far from respectful.[296] And Quincy's response certainly did not thwart Shirley.

> Mr. Shirley replied, when it comes to the test Boston will give the other
> provinces the shell and the shadow and keep the substance. Take away the
> power and superintendency of Britain, and the Colonies must submit to the
> next power. Boston would soon have that—power rules all things—they might
> allow the other a paltry representation, but that would be all.[297]

"The Company seemed attentive—and incredulous" and "were taking sides"
when dinner was called.[298] Quincy believed that Shirley suspected him. "From
his singular looks, and behavior I suspected he knew my political path."[299]

Quincy carefully observed the South Carolina House of Assembly. Like the
British Parliament, there was a mace laid before the speaker to begin the sessions, and the Speaker was "robed in black and has a very large Wigg of State,
when he goes to attend the Chair (with the Mace borne before him) on Delivery of speeches etc."[300] But the conduct of the members was less impressive.
They used "singular expressions for a member of parliament" and were sloppy.

> The members conversed, lolled, and chatted much like a friendly jovial soci-
> ety, when nothing of importance was before the house:—nay once or twice
> while the Speaker and clerk were busy in writing the members spoke quite
> loud across the room to one another.—A very unparliamentary appearance.[301]

295. *Id.*, pp. 54–55.
296. See *id.*, pp. 87–88. "Political enquiries and philosophie disputations are too laborious for
them: they have no great passion to shine and blaze in the forums or Senate." *Id.*, p. 88.
297. *Id.*, p. 55.
298. *Id.*, pp. 55–56.
299. *Id.*, p. 56.
300. *Id.*, p. 78.
301. *Id.*, p. 79.

More importantly, Quincy's Whig politics distrusted any society that relied on a paternal aristocracy, described by Richard Beeman as "complacent oligarchs."[302] Despite Quincy's own consciousness of gentility, and of his <u>own</u> gentility, his was a profoundly middle-class politics. Civic virtue required education, diligence, and a responsible "yeomanry."[303] In South Carolina, "[t]he inhabitants may well be divided into opulent and lordly planters, poor and spiritless peasants and vile slaves."[304] The legislature was dominated by the planter aristocracy, almost all of whom actually lived in Charleston "during the sickly months."[305]

> 'Tis true they have a house of assembly: but who do they represent? The laborer, the mechanic, the tradesman, the farmer, husbandman or yeoman? No. The representatives are almost if not wholly rich planters:—the Planting interest is therefore represented but I conceive nothing else (as <u>it ought to be</u>.)[306]

While many of the Assembly were "staunch Colonists," they were vulnerable.[307] Their allegiance was based on "bad policy on the other side of the water."[308] That could change. At the moment the British were packing the "Council Judges and other great officers" with placemen "disconnected and obnoxious to the people."[309]

> Let us suppose a change in British policy. Compose the Council of the first planters, fill all the Public offices with them—give them the honour of the State, and tho' they don't want them, give them it and emoluments also:—introduce Baronies and Lordships—their enormous estates will bear it What will become of Carolinian freedom?[310]

In short, these could be unreliable allies.

> The whole body almost of this people seem averse to the claims and assumptions of the British Legislature over the Colonies; but you will seldom hear

302. See Beeman, *supra*, pp. 126–156.
303. *Southern Journal*, p. 89.
304. *Id.*, p. 84.
305. *Id.*, p. 86.
306. *Id.*, pp. 85–86. (Emphasis in the orginal.)
307. *Id.*, p. 86.
308. *Id.*, p. 86.
309. *Id.*, p. 86.
310. *Id.*, pp. 87–88.

even in political conversations any warm or animated expressions against the measures of administration. Their fiercer passions seem to be employed upon their slaves . . .[311]

North Carolina was initially more reassuring to Quincy, despite a dearth of laws and almost no functioning legal system.[312] There were fewer slaves and "[y]ou see husbandmen, yeomen, and white laborers scattered thro' the country instead of herds of Negroes and tawny slaves."[313] "Healthful countenances and numerous families become more common as you advance North."[314] "Property much more equally diffused,"[315] and the people seemed better educated. "Arts and sciences are certainly better understood . . ."[316]

But Quincy was unable to make much sense of the colony's recent political troubles. In coastal South Carolina, he had heard accounts of the back-country "Regulator" uprising. These accounts favored, naturally enough, Governor Tryon and the coastal forces of "law and order."[317] Now he encountered both "sensible Tryonists"[318] and others of a very different opinion, those who supported the Regulators.[319]

Quincy stayed with William Hill, Esq., one of the men interested in the Committee of Correspondence. He was a curious mix of Crown officer and "staunch whig and colonist." "Hot and zealous in the Cause of America he relished the proposed Continental correspondence, promised to promote it and write me by the first opportunity."[320]

Hill gave Quincy a "Tryonist" account of the uprising.

> This Gentleman gave me at night a 3 hours minute relation of the motives, views and proceedings of the Regulators, with a particular account of the battle of Allamanze [Alamance, May 16, 1771], and the proceedings of both par-

---

311. *Id.*, pp. 84–85.
312. See VII, *supra*, "Laws and Lawyers," Part B "North Carolina," pp. 57–58, *supra*.
313. *Southern Journal*, p. 110.
314. *Id.*, p. 110.
315. *Id.*, p. 110.
316. *Id.*, p. 111.
317. *Id.*, p. 74 and extensive description of the "Regulators" in note 114.
318. *Id.*, p. 107. Quincy used "sensible" to mean "convinced, persuaded." See *Johnson's Dictionary*, *supra*, n.p. "sensible."
319. *Southern Journal*, p. 97.
320. *Id.*, p. 96.

ties before and after the action. Being on the field he was able to give me a good account. I begun to change my opinion of the Regulators and Governor Tryon.[321]

The Whig in Quincy had sided with the back countrymen who had resisted the royal governor and his corruption. But he was also hostile to mob violence and disruption of the courts and the law. Hill appealed to that side of Quincy's nature. But, the next day, Quincy heard a different account.

> But as is common on the next day. Breakfasted with Col. Dry, the Collector of the Customs and one of the Council.—A friend to the Regulators and seemingly warm against the measures of British and Continental administrations he gave me an entire different account of things. I am now left to form my own opinion[322]

Quincy's ambivalence was symbolic of the danger that separatist movements would present to the new Republic. As Richard Beeman's excellent account of the Regulator Movement has pointed out, an independence movement predicated on resisting authority, like the American Revolution, could not, at the same time, tolerate divisions that could be exploited by the British or other enemies.[323] The Regulator Movement, eventually, was so exploited by the British, and a similar uprising, Shays' Rebellion (1786–1787), was to occur in Quincy's own state after the Revolution.[324] As Beeman noted, all such movements "were testimony to the existence of at least an underlying threat to political integration within the new nation."[325]

In any event, Quincy found the aftermath of the uprising "problematical."[326] Sympathy for resistance to royal authority was one thing, but here "[n]one can recover their debts . . ." a point of importance to a wealthy man like Quincy.[327] "The people are in great consternation about the matter."[328]

---

321. *Id.*, pp. 96–97.

322. *Id.*, p. 97.

323. See Beeman, *supra*, pp. 169–177.

324. "The profound alienation that typified these outbursts of violence in the Regulator movement had its payoff during the Revolution, when the eastern rulers of North and South Carolina society asked the back country settlers for their support during the Revolution." *Id.*, p. 176. The result was more violence, the "Uncivil War." *Id.*, pp. 176–177.

325. *Id.*, p. 177.

326. *Southern Journal*, p. 116.

327. *Id.*, p. 116. See Wood, *Radicalism*, pp. 68–69, on the reliance of gentry like Quincy on income from loans.

328. *Southern Journal*, p. 116.

Nor did any of this bode well for colonial unity. Even North and South Carolina had little in common. "There is very little, if any kind, of commerce or intercourse between the No[rth] and So[uth] prov of Carolina, and there is very little, if any more, of regard in the Inh[abitan]ts of the one Colony for those of the other."[329]

No wonder Quincy took a pragmatic view of the struggle for colonial autonomy!

C. Proprietorial Politics: Virginia, Maryland and Pennsylvania

At the conclusion of the *Southern Journal,* Quincy "hazard[ed] an eccentric Conjecture."[330] It was "that the Penn, Baltimore or Fairfax familys will hereafter contend for the dominion—and one of them perhaps attain the sovereignty—of North America."[331] This extraordinary idea, from a man whose views of the future were often prescient,[332] was based on his experiences in the three colonies dominated by actual proprietorship parties, in the case of Pennsylvania and Maryland, or the *de facto* proprietorship of the Fairfax family in Virginia.[333]

Although Quincy visited Williamsburg and "Spent the Evening with two of the Councils of the Province, and our conversation was wholly political (and inquisitive),"[334] there is very little about Virginian politics that has survived in the *Southern Journal.* (The two excised pages, cut from the *Southern Journal,* were in the section on Virginia.)[335] Quincy had to turn down an offer to meet the Governor, the Earl of Dunmore, and most of his attention was directed to defects in the court systems[336] and the sorry state of religion.[337]

It is particularly frustrating that pages 125 and 126 were cut out, as the next words are directed to Quincy's view of the Virginian constitution.

---

329. *Id.,* p. 116.

330. *Southern Journal,* p. 184.

331. *Id.,* p. 184.

332. On the threat of slavery to the unity of the colonies, Quincy was a brilliant prophet. See the discussion at Section V, "Race and Slavery," pp. 28–40, *supra.*

333. See *Id.,* pp. 184–185 and accompanying notes.

334. *Id.,* pp. 123–124.

335. These would be *Southern Journal,* pp. 125–126. See *Editor's Foreword, supra,* and *Transcriber's Foreword,* pp. 3–9, *supra.*

336. *Southern Journal,* pp. 121–122.

337. *Id.,* p. 124.

[PAGES 125 AND 126 ARE CUT OUT]

_____

safe-guard from future invasions and oppressions. I am mistaken in my conjecture, if in some approaching day Virginia does not more fully see the capital defects of her constitution of gov:t and rue the bitter consequences of
them.[338]

It is possible that Quincy was continuing to refer to the General Court, with
its "amazingly defective, inconvenient and dangerous, not say absurd and mischievous" mixture of common law jurisdiction with discretionary equitable
relief, discussed above.[339] But Quincy may also have addressed the serious
political problems of Virginia's pre-revolutionary elite, so well described by
Beeman as the "pursuit of the deferential ideal."[340] Certainly the power of the
Fairfax and Carter families in the House of Burgesses would have been dis-
quieting to a Whig. And Quincy had a poor view of the Virginia gentry. "They
have several wise men and patriots; but even these are much belied, if they
have not been guilty of practices inconsistent with common honesty."[341] The
yeomanry was little better. The average man was a good farmer, but not well
educated or politically sophisticated. "The Commonality and farmers thro'
this province were vastly more ignorant and illiterate kind of people than with
us . . ."[342]

The "commonality" of Maryland appeared to be an improvement.

> The commonality seem in general thro' this province to be well dispositioned
> and friendly towards strangers, and pretty industrious: But I saw nothing to
> lead me to suppose they in any measure surpassed the New Englanders in
> either of these respects.[343]

But that colony was also locked in internal divisions. There was "the very bitter, important contest" about the clergy tax, already discussed.[344] In addition,
two of the colony's most prominent men, "men of prodigious fortunes," were

338. _Id.,_ p. 127.
339. _Id.,_ pp. 121–122.
340. See Beeman, _supra,_ p. 31.
341. _Southern Journal,_ p. 130.
342. _Id.,_ p. 131.
343. _Id.,_ p. 141.
344. _Id.,_ pp. 134–135. See the discussion at Section VI, "Religion," pp. 40–49, _supra._

locked in a political battle "with amazing mutual hatred and bitterness."[345]
The two protagonists were Daniel Dulany (1722–1797), the Attorney General
of the Province, and Charles Carroll (1736–1832). "[T]heir families have been
at open enmity many years."[346]

> A most bitter and important dispute is subsisting and has long subsisted in this
> province touching the fees of this officers of the colony and the Governor's
> proclamation relative thereto.—At the conference of the two houses (which I
> have in print) the Dispute was conducted (by it is universally said) by Daniel
> Dulany of the Council and the Speaker Tillingman and [blank] of the Lower
> House. This dispute tho' managed with good sense and spirit, breaths an acri-
> mony, virulence, and unmannerly invective not honorary to the parties and
> inconsistent with the rules and dignity of parliament.[347]

The two men attacked each other regularly in the press, Dulany writing as
'Antilon' and Carroll as 'First Citizen.'[348] Carroll was a leader of the colony's

---

345. *Southern Journal*, p. 139.
346. *Id.*, p. 140.
347. *Id.*, pp. 138–139.
348. *Id.*, p. 139. Derrick Lapp, Carroll's biographer, described the struggle as follows:
"As the relationship between Great Britain and her North American colonies became
more and more strained in the early 1770's, events in Maryland would provide an opportunity for the Carrolls to re-enter the political stage. The lower house of the Maryland
legislature began an investigation of the amount of revenue earned by proprietary officials
by virtue of the office held. The high earnings revealed by this probe led the lower house
to propose a reduction in fees, which, of course was rejected by the upper house. The
ensuing 'fee controversy' pitted Daniel Dulany, the deputy secretary of Maryland (and
one of the officials found garnering huge annual sums) against Charles Carroll of Carrollton, who took up the pen and the persona of 'First Citizen' to publish a series of essays
in the *Maryland Gazette*. In their debate, 'First Citizen' and 'Antilon' (Daniel Dulany's
pseudonym) battled over the nature of government, the rights of Man, and the role of
religious affiliation. In his first letter, which appeared on February 4, 1773, 'First Citizen'
wrote: 'Government was instituted for the general good, but Officers intrusted with its
powers, have most commonly perverted them to the selfish views of avarice an ambition;
hence the Country and court interests, which ought to be the same have been too often
opposite, as must be acknowledged and lamented by every true friend of Liberty . . .'"
    See Derrick Lapp, *First Citizen Charles Carroll of Carrollton* (Maryland State Archive Online
Publication, 2004), (hereafter, "Lapp"). See also Charles Carroll, Daniel Dulany, *Maryland and
the Empire*, 1773; *The Antilon – First Citizen Letters* (Johns Hopkins, 1974); *Dictionary of American Biography*, V, p. 499.
    The origin of the pseudonyms is interesting. According to the *Dictionary of American Biog-
raphy*, Dulany

"upwards of 5000 Roman Catholicks,"[349] and Quincy observed that Carroll and his father "each of them [kept] a Priest and Private Chapel in their respective houses."[350] Carroll would become a leading patriot, and a signer of the Declaration of Independence, while Dulany would later lose his property as a loyalist.[351]

The irony in all this is Quincy was an admirer of Dulany!

> I spent about 3 hours in company with the famous Daniel Dulany, Esq. (author of the Considerations) [*Considerations on the Propriety of Imposing Taxes in the British Colonies* (1765)] the Attorney General of the province and

---

"on January 7, 1773, published a letter in defense of the government signed 'Antilon,' a pseudonym which it was generally understood concealed the identity of Daniel Dulany [*q.v.*]. This letter, in the form of a dialogue in which the arguments of 'First Citizen' against the government's position were overcome by Dulany speaking as 'Second Citizen,' gave Carroll his opportunity. Dramatically enough he stepped into the clothes of the straw man Dulany had knocked down and under the signature of 'First Citizen' reopened the argument. The controversy was carried on in the *Maryland Gazette* until July 1, 1773, and when it was over Carroll had become indeed something like the First Citizen of the province." *Id.*, vol. III, p. 532.

Thus Dulany actually invented "First Citizen" as a straw man for argument, and Carroll adopted it for his use in a counterattack! But what about "Antillon"? According to Edward C. Papenfuse, Dulany "chose 'Antilon' which combines 'anti' and an old English word for unfair taxes ["Lon"]." "Remarks by Dr. Edward C. Papenfuse on the occasion of the presentation of *First Citizen Awards* to Senator Charles Smelser & Dr. William Richardson (Feb. 17, 1995), p. 1. http://www.mdarchives.state.md.us/msa/stagser/s1259/121/7047/html/ecpremar.html (hereafter, "Papenfuse"). See *Oxford English Dictionary* (2d ed., J. A. Simpson, E. S. C. Weiner, Oxford, 1989), Vol. VIII, p. 1120. ("lon" obs. forms of "loan"). This could possibly derive from the notorious forced "loans" of Charles I that resulted in the *Five Knights' Case* of 1627 and the *Petition of Right* (1628). See Coquillette, *supra*, pp. 322–325. In any event, Dr. Papenfuse believed that Dulany "wanted to remind his readers that he had once eloquently defended them against the hated Stamp Tax." Papenfuse, *supra*, p. 1. My special thanks to Mark C. Sullivan for this research.

349. *Southern Journal*, p. 140.

350. *Id.*, p. 140.

351. See *Id.*, p. 138, note 217. When Carroll died at age 91, he was the last surviving signer. According to Lapp:

Carroll of Carrollton would demonstrate himself to be a "true friend of Liberty" for nearly three decades. He served on the first Committee of Safety in Annapolis, and while Maryland wavered on the subject of pursuing independence, Carroll joined Benjamin Franklin and Samuel Chase in the effort to recruit Canada as a "fourteenth colony" in rebellion against England. As a Maryland delegate to the Second Continental Congress, Carroll served on the Board of War. He also helped to frame the Maryland constitution and would serve in the new state government as well as the Federal Congress as a U.S. Senator for Maryland. Lapp, *supra*.

several others of the Bar, and Gentlemen of the province. Dulany is a Diamond of the first water:—a gem that may grace the cap of a patriot or the turban of a Sultan.[352]

In fact, Quincy's entire account of the Dulany-Carroll conflict seems little concerned with the merits, on which one would assume Quincy would favor Carroll's position. Rather, Quincy's real concern was focused on the simple inappropriateness, "not honorary [sic] to the parties," of the political invective.[353] This, of course, would be consistent with Quincy's sense of "gentry" and genteel conduct, which caused him to conceal his outrage during Charleston dinner parties.[354] But it also was consistent with Quincy's fear of internal dissensions within the colonies. Indeed, here was another example of internal dissension within the colonies which—as it turned out—would again play itself out during the Revolution, with Carroll the patriot, and Dulany the loyalist.

Quincy did not like Baltimore, "poor, diminutive, little city" making "a very contemptible appearance,"[355] but he saw Pennsylvania as a model of good government. "As soon as you enter Pennsylvania—government the regularity, goodness, and the strait, advantageous disposition of Public Roads are evidences of the good policy and laws of this well regulated province."[356] In Pennsylvania, Quincy met with important colonial leaders, such as "The Farmer," John Dickinson (1732–1802),[357] Joseph Reed (1732–1802),[358] and Jonathan Smith (1742–1812).[359] He also met with men who would be loyalists, such as Jared Ingersoll (1722–1781).[360] "Our Discourse altogether political, polite and entertaining."[361] It was here that Quincy encountered criticism of Benjamin Franklin from the likes of Chief Justice William Allen (1704–1780) and others.[362] This was ironic, and not just because of Quincy's later close col-

---

352. *Southern Journal*, p. 138.
353. *Id.*, p. 139.
354. See the discussion at Section III, "Gentility," pp. 18–21, *supra*.
355. *Southern Journal*, p. 142.
356. *Id.*, p. 143.
357. *Id.*, p. 148, and accompanying notes.
358. *Id.*, pp. 149–150, and accompanying notes.
359. *Id.*, p. 148, and accompanying notes.
360. *Id.*, pp. 149–150, and accompanying notes.
361. *Id.*, p. 149.
362. *Id.*, pp. 155–156.

laboration with Franklin, for Franklin was one of the chief architects of the Whig nature of Philadelphia so attractive to Quincy.[363] The people were prosperous, and even the streets were orderly:

> The streets of Philadelphia intersect each other at right angles, and it is probably the most regular and best laid out city in the world:—perhaps equal to Babylon of Old; and peradventure in other less-eligible respects may equal it, within the compass of two centuries:—I mean in numbers, wealth, splendor, luxury and vice.—[364]

But "wealth, splendor, luxury and vice" did not deflect these hardworking burghers from the solid middle-class values so central to Quincy's Whig ideology.

> The Pennsylvanians as a body of people may be justly characterized as industrious, sensible and wealthy: the Philadelphians as commercial, keen and frugal: their economy and reserve have sometimes been censured as civility and avarice, but all that we saw in this excellent city was replete with benevolence, hospitality, sociability and politeness, joined with that prudence and caution natural to an understanding people who are alternately visited by a variety of strangers differing in rank, fortune, ingenuity and character.[365]

This was combined with a liberal toleration for differences in religion, an investment in public buildings, and a legislative body acting "in names of the Governor by and with the consent and advice of the freeman of the prov:[ince]. . . ." Here was much to be admired.[366]

But all was not well. Quincy, like Franklin, saw civic virtue constantly undermined by the special interests of the proprietary party, acting under the influence of the Penn establishment: John, Thomas and Richard Penn.[367]

> There is a proprietary influence in this prov:[ince] destructive of a liberal conduct in the legislative branch and of [blank] in the executive authority here. The House of Representatives are but 36 in number, as a body held in great, remarkable and general contempt: much despised for their base acquiescence

---

363. See Morgan, *Franklin*, pp. 49–70; Wood, *The Americanization of Benjamin Franklin*, pp. 17–60; Walter Isaacson, *Benjamin Franklin: An American Life* (New York, 2004), pp. 146–174.

364. *Id.*, p. 168.

365. *Id.*, p. 161.

366. *Id.*, p. 162.

367. See Morgan, *supra*, pp. 100–103, 114–115.

with the laws and measures of the proprietary party, and singularly odious for certain provincial maneuvers too circumstantial to relate.[368]

This infected the legislative system with "influence," i.e., the special interests that Quincy detested as the antithesis of civic virtue. Even the sessions were secret.

> Their debates are not public, which is said now to be the Case of only this house of Commons throughout the Continent. Many have been the attempts to procure an alteration in this respect but all to no purpose. The influence which governs this house is equal if not superior to anything we hear of but that which governs the British parliament; and the proprieter is said to have as dead a set ["Fix"] in a Pennsylvania Assembly as Lords Bute or North in the English house of commons. This Government is in great danger from this quarter.[369]

Fortunately, the Penn aristocracy was crippled by weakness of character and ability. "But a lineal successive defeat of capacity, want of policy, glaring avarice and oppressive measures in the Penn-family is said to have prevented and guarded against much of the mischief which might otherwise have taken place."[370] But there was always a danger that a Penn of real ability might "arise from this [stalk]."[371]

> But should a subtle and genuine keen modern statesman (a Sir Robert Walpole for Instance) arise from this stoic [stalk], great and important maneuvers may be expected. This family lost much of their Prov:[incia]l influence by renouncing the Religion of their Ancestors and of the Colony in general for that of Episcopacy.[372]

The political power of the Proprietor was often offset by the Quakers, but when the two interests combined, the result was worrisome.

> Notwithstanding the Prop:[rietor]y influence before spoken of, there is a certain Quaker Int:[eres]t which operates much against the Proprietor in land causes in the Courts of Common law, where the Jury frequently give verdicts

368. *Southern Journal*, p. 164.
369. *Id.*, pp. 164–165.
370. *Id.*, p. 165.
371. *Id.*, p. 165.
372. *Id.*, p. 165.

against the opinion of the judges. In the house of Reps the Leaders of the Quaker party are often of the Proprietory likewise. All general questions and points are carried by the Quakers: that is, by their union they defeat the operations of all other sects in questions which any way relate to or may in the end affect religious concerns.—But they are very public-spirited.[373]

Like Franklin, Quincy feared what he saw of the "proprietary influence,"[374] hence his observations about a "sovereignty of North America" for the "Penn, Baltimore or Fairfax families" at the conclusion of the *Southern Journal*.[375] On the other hand, the Quakers and the Moravians opposed a militia, another potential problem for the colonial resistance.

> There is no militia in the prov:[ince] and of course no seeking after petty commissions, etc.—The advantages and disadvantages of this is a topick of doubtful disputation:—we shall never all think alike on this head.—Many of the Quakers and all of the Moravians hold defensive war lawful; offensive otherwise.[376]

But, all in all, Pennsylvania appealed deeply to Quincy's Whig faith. "There is . . . throughout the whole province among the husbandmen a spirit of industry and useful improvement."[377] It was the natural capital of the colonies—a great concession from a Bostonian! "This city & prov:[ince] are in a most flourishing state: and if numbers of buildings, men, artificers, and trade is to settle the point, Philadelphia is the Metropolis of this Northern region."[378] And, most importantly for Quincy, there was an absence of the internal civil strife that was so worrisome in the Carolinas and Maryland. "The political state of Pennsylvania is, at this time, the calmest of any on the Continent."[379] Franklin would have been proud.

---

373. *Id.*, p. 165.

374. According to Morgan, "what <u>rankled</u> most, at least to Franklin, was the interposition of the proprietary power between George II and his Pennsylvanian subjects . . . 'the Proprietaries claiming that invidious and odious Distinction, of being exempted from the Common Burdens of their Fellow subjects.'" Morgan, *Franklin*, *supra*, pp. 100–101.

375. *Southern Journal*, *supra*, pp. 184–185.

376. *Id.*, p. 166.

377. *Id.*, p. 166.

378. *Id.*, p. 168.

379. *Id.*, p. 171.

IX. CONCLUSION

There is a sea of secondary accounts about the origins of the American Revolution, but relatively few accessible original sources.[380] Among these, Quincy's *Southern Journal* is remarkable for its candor, authenticity, breadth of interest and—dare I say it—sensitivity. As an evidentiary account, it certainly cannot be seen as "typical" or "representative," because Quincy was none of these things. He was unusual, even as an example of his social class and his Whig ideology, because of his intelligence and perception. But the picture painted by the *Southern Journal*, like a remarkably original poem or sketch, remains a compelling insight to the world of the American patriots in 1773.

Quincy understood clearly the risks facing the colonial cause. The very challenge of the geography, the distances and the hardship so graphically described by the *Southern Journal*, worked against it. So did the separate evolution of the colonial governments, reinforced by these barriers. Even in the Carolinas, there was a wall between North and South. "There is very little, if any kind, of commerce or intercourse between the No[rth] and So[uth] prov of Carolina, and there is very little, if any more, of regard in the Inh[abitan]ts of the one Colony for those of the other."[381] Worse, Quincy witnessed the bitter disputes that divided the colonies internally. For example, there was the war between the Regulators and the Tryonists in the Carolinas, that pitted the coast against the back country. Then there was the "very bitter, important contest" over the clergy in Maryland[382] and the "acrimony, virulence and unmannerly invective"[383] between the Dulany and Carroll factions in the legislature. And there were the fierce family, class, and proprietorial disputes that divided Virginia and Pennsylvania. What Quincy saw of religious differences also concerned him deeply and what he saw of civic corruption or—as in North Carolina—actual lawlessness, concerned him even more. Finally, there was the horror of slavery, "the peculiar curse of this land."[384]

Today we see the path to Revolution as inevitable, and its glorious success as preordained. Our predetermined evolutionary view of history, so popular

---

380. See *Editors' Foreword to the Quincy Papers, Quincy Papers*, vol. 1, pp. xvii–xxvii.
381. *Southern Journal*, p. 116.
382. *Id.*, p. 134.
383. *Id.*, p. 139.
384. *Id.*, p. 91.

with our Whig ancestors, sees to that. But the cards did not look that way to Quincy in 1773. British mistakes, "bad policy on the other side of the water,"[385] was the strongest card in the colonial hand. The immediate danger of "a different policy,"[386] a better British strategy, designed to divide the colonies against each other, and to exploit internal rivalries within each colony, seemed obvious to Quincy.[387] The barriers were huge; the risk of failure, great.

It is popular for historians today to eschew what is called 'diachronic' history, and to prefer 'synchronic' history.[388] 'Diachronic' is simply a fancy term for the old idea, popular with Whigs and lawyers, that we should trace important ideas and political forces as they develop through time—such as the link between the Magna Carta of 1215 and the Due Process Clause as interpreted today—and to invest these developments with a presumption of inevitability. Quincy himself, as a good Whig lawyer, thought and wrote that way.[389] 'Synchronic' history, on the other hand, focuses intently on a particular point in time, and attempts to demonstrate the broad interaction of politics, ideology, social forces, law, religion, and other forces on that defined period.

The irony is that Quincy, the good Whig, produced, in the *Southern Journal*, a synchronic source beyond compare. Here is a snapshot of a crucial moment in time, the overture of the American Revolution, which incorporates geography, sociology, gender, race, religion, law, and politics, recorded by a sensitive, nuanced, and sophisticated mind. Now add the other surviving products of that mind, Quincy's *Political Commonplace Book* (1770–1774), his *Law Commonplace* (1763), his *Reports* (1761–1772), and his *London Journal* (1774–1775), all being published as part of this five-volume Quincy Project, and you have a 'synchronic' historian's dream.

385. *Id.*, p. 86.
386. *Id.*, p. 88.
387. *Id.*, p. 85.
388. For this insight into the latest academic controversies, I am grateful to my dear friend and colleague, Charles Donahue. See his masterful Washington and Lee Lecture of 2004, "Why and Whither Legal History?" pp. 2–9 [unpublished MS]. Quincy's *Southern Journal* also fits neatly into two other current trends, "micro-history" and "prosopography," both focusing on detail and the individual as tools for comprehending complex developments. "Prosopography" derives from the Greek "prosopan," or "face" and refers to "a description of a person's appearance, personality, social and family connections, career, etc." *The Concise Oxford Dictionary* (8th ed., R. E. Allen, ed., Oxford, 1990), p. 959.
389. See Introduction, *Law Commonplace, Quincy Papers*, vol. 2.

But the most striking of that rich mix is the *Southern Journal*. It vividly demonstrates three things. First, how fortunate we are, as Americans, in our national identity. This is not just a question about the outcome of the Revolution, but, ultimately, about the survival of the Union itself—faced at its very core with the menace of slavery and inherently torn by geopolitical division. Quincy clearly foresaw all this danger in 1773.

Secondly, there was the countervailing strength of American notions of civic virtue, public dignity, and classical patriotism. These defined Quincy's genteel political faith. Initially, these were the ideas, even the conceits, of a narrow elite. But their appeal grew to all classes, and, eventually, they drove the ideology of the American Revolution itself.

The most lasting impression, however, is one of cold courage, the cold courage with which patriots like Quincy faced the drama of our nation's birth. Quincy risked his life in his voyage to Charleston to help overcome "the prevalent and extended ignorance of one colony of the concerns of another."[390] He risked his life again in his complicity with the colonial cause in Boston.[391] He risked it again, and lost it, on his mission to London.[392] This was without any reassurance that he was on one of history's great winning teams. Rather, even at the moment of Quincy's death, he only knew the hand of cards he described in the *Southern Journal*, the strengths and deep weaknesses of the patriot cause throughout the colonies. It was a dangerous, gambler's hand.

390. *Southern Voyage*, p. 184.

391. See York, "The Making of a Patriot," Part I, "A Life Cut Short," *Quincy Papers*, vol. 1, pp. 32–35.

392. See *The London Journal* (1774–1775), vol. 1, pp. 267–269.

THE SOUTHERN
JOURNAL

(1773)

[inside front cover]

Mem[orial] of L[etters] wrote during my Journey.

			to			
1773	Mar:	1	AQ			
		4	AQ	from Charlestown	So Carolina
		29	AQ			
	Apl:	1	AQ	from Brunswick	No Carolina
		2	AQ	from Newbern	No Carolina
		2	JQ	from Newbern	No Carolina
		3	AQ	from Bath	No Carolina
		3	WT	from Edenton	Do
		3	SQ	Do	Do
		3	AQ	Do	Do
		13	AQ	Williamsburg	Virginia
		15	JQ	Portroyal	Do
		24	PM	Philadelphia	Pennsylvania
		26	AQ	Do	Do
		28	PM	Do	Do
	May	9	AQ	Do	Do

[Note: The initials stand for the recipients of the letters. Thus, "AQ" is for Abigail Quincy (wife), "JQ" is for Josiah Quincy (father), "SQ" is for Samuel Quincy (brother), etc. "WT" is possibly for William Tryon (1729–1788), former Governor of North Carolina (1765–1771) who became Governor of New York. "PM" is for Perez Morton (1750–1837). Harvard College 1771. He studied law with Quincy, and was admitted to the bar in 1774. Morton became Attorney General of Massachusetts 1810–1832. See Coquillette, Brink, Menand eds., *Law in Colonial Massachusetts*, p. 347. Special thanks to my co-editor Neil York.]

[1]

———

The design of the ensuing Journal is, among other things;
to gratify one who has a right to a very
large share of my thoughts and reflections, as well
as to participate, as far as possible, of
all my amusements and vicissitudes:[1]
to be a memorial of my thoughts, as they
rises, and to remain a future witness to my
self of the changes of my own sentiments and
opinions:
to record those kindnesses and little civilities,
which might otherwise imperceptibly
fleet from the memory; but which ought
nevertheless to be held in rememberance
till we shall embrace an opportunity
fully to return them.
To thou therefore into whose hand this Journal, either
before or after my death, may chance to fall, the forego-
ing considerations may serve as some Excuse for those
trifles and impertinencies I foresee it will contain,
and shall not strive to avoid.
Boston Mar: 6th 1773   J. Quincy, junr.

---

1. A reference to Quincy's wife Abigail, the daughter of William Phillips of Boston. They
married in 1769. She was referred to in Quincy's journals as "E . . ." or "Eugenia," as Howe
observed "according to the affectations of the day." Mark DeWolf Howe, *Proceedings of the
Massachusetts Historical Society*, vol. 50 (October 1916 – June 1917), p. 434, n. 3. (Hereafter,
"Howe, *Proceedings*, 1916-1917.") Howe was the editor of this journal in its first, and only, publication before this newly edited version, which is obviously indebted to his efforts. See Neil
York's tribute to Howe in the appendix to the *Political Commonplace Book*, *Quincy Papers*, vol. 1,
pp. 219–221. Howe's notes are integrated into this edition, as noted, with amendments.

[1]*

———

A Journal,
interspersed with observations and remarks, by Josiah Quincy junr.
"Eye nature's walks, shoot folly as it flies,
"And catch the manners living as they rise."
"Laugh where we must, be candid where we can."
                              Pope[2]
Mark the affections of thy <u>youth</u>, and
engrave the observations and sentiments
of thy <u>manhood</u>; the review shall
solace thy <u>old age</u> and bring a
kind of re-juvenescence to thy <u>hoary</u>
<u>head</u>.   Zoroaster. lib. IX, fol. 5.[3]

*[following page numbered "2" is blank]

2. Alexander Pope (1688–1744), poet. Quotation from Pope's *An Essay on Man* (London, 1733), Epistle 1, 1.13. Quincy owned all of the Pope's works at his death. See *Reports*, Appendix 9, item 312 ("Catalogue of Books Belonging to the Estate of Josiah Quincy, Jun:Esq Decease'd). (Hereafter, "Quincy, Estate Catalogue.")

3. Zoroaster: Prophet of ancient Iran in the latter half of the seventh century before the Christian era; the period of his activity falls between the closing years of Median rule and the rising wave of Persian power. Forerunner of Confucius, Zoroaster was a Magian, a.k.a. the famed Magi. The Persian wars brought Rome into contact with Zoroastrian. A.V. William Jackson, *Zoroaster, The Prophet of Ancient Iran* (London: MacMillan Co., 1899), pp. 140–142.

[3]

AD
1773
February 8th

——

Sailed in the Bristol Packett,[4] John Skimmer[5]
commander for So Carolina, with design of taking
the tour of the Southern provinces for my health.
The "Nos patriae fines, nos dulcia linquimus Arva"[6]
of Virgil was uppermost in my mind, and
when I came in sight of my father's cottage,[7]
"Te, Tytere, lentus in Umbra"[8] seemed
the sweetest harmony I ever caroled.
A perpetual involuntary repetition of the
five first lines of the first Eclogue employed
my first hour on shipboard. No lines I ever
read seemed to contain so much sentiment
and harmony of numbers. Every word was a
beauty, and every reflection discovered some new
charm. I begun to think no one had ever
seen how much the Poet conveyed, and was fully

4. "One of the last remaining uses for sailing ships was transoceanic mail delivery. Called packet boats after the British nickname for the mail dispatch, mail ships were built for speed. They carried mail to overseas locations, usually under the control of the home country." Such ships usually offered the fastest and cheapest oceanic fares. *Ships*, Encarta Encyclopedia. Microsoft, Inc. 2002.

5. Howe, *Proceedings*, 1915–1916 [FN 427-2]. Capt. Skimmer was killed in an engagement with a letter of marque brig in August 1778.

6. Virgil, Eclogue I: "We have left our country's borders and sweet fields."

7. Quincy's father's mansion stood in what was then Braintree, now Quincy. Completed in 1770, it would have been visible from the channel leaving Boston. See *Illustration 1*. Quincy's father lived there until his death in 1784, at which point it was inherited by his grandson, Quincy's son, Josiah "the Mayor." See Neil L. York, "A Life Cut Short," Introduction, *Quincy Papers*, vol. 1, pp. 15–46.

8. Virgil, Eclogue I: "You, Tityrus, calm in the shade."

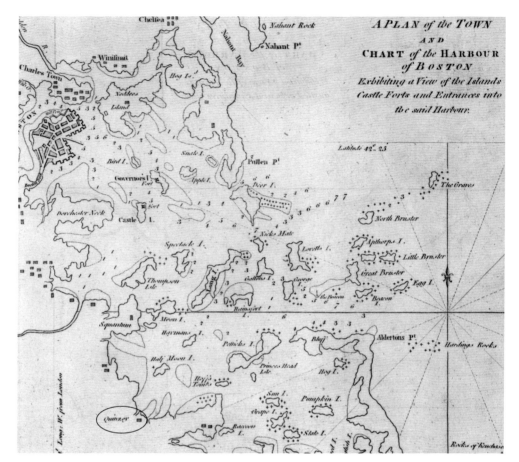

ILLUSTRATION 1. Map of Boston Harbor (London, c. 1775). Courtesy, Library of Congress, American Memory Collection. The Quincy homestead in Braintree is indicated in the lower, middle left (circled). The shipping channel would have been in sight above. See p. 89, *Southern Journal*, p. 3, "my father's cottage."

[*3 continued*]

convinced no English translation had ever
reached half the force, sense and grace of the
original. What was to be done? I had nothing to do. I immediately set about a
new translation of my favorite Roman.[9]

9. Virgil. "In his Eclogues he added a new level of meaning to the pastoral's idealization of
country life . . ." *The Oxford Companion to English Literature* (5th ed., M. Drabble ed.), 1031.
(Hereafter, "Drabble.") See Quincy, Estate Catalogue, p. 3, item 118, "Virgil."

[4]

———

Before I had got well engaged in my labours, and
before (I am sure) I had one draught of Helicon,[10] my employment was changed, and my attendants were Randall and the Cabin-boy, instead of the Muses and Graces. A bowl of thin
water-gruel was preferred to a goblet of
Nectar and Ambrosia, and Randall stood
                    "Mihi magnus Apollo."[11]
However at intervals the paroxysm of Mount
Parnassus came on, and I was soon convinced
that he who has little to do will soon have
his Hobby-horse. And why may not I up
ride as Yorick[12] says, so that I injure no
passenger in the way?
By the 3d watch of the Night I had finished my
task: it appeared the best brat I had ever seen:
But misfortunes attend the Poet. Upon a comparison with the original, my translation exceeded it
almost 2 thirds in length. It will not do, said I.

---

10. The Helicon was the largest mountain of Boeotia, a legendary mount of the muses. The
fountain supplied by the mountain's streams "were believed to inspire those who drank from
them." *The Oxford Companion to Classical Literature* (2nd ed., M. C. Howatson, ed.), p. 264.
(Hereafter, "Howatson.") "A draught from Helicon could once inspire / The bard to wing in
song his loftiest flight; But poets of these later times require / A draft from Wall Street, payable
at sight." By Anne C. Lynch: *Poems*, 1852. Epigram.

11. Translation: "To me as great Apollo." From Virgil, *Eclogue* III.

12. Yorick: Pseudonym of Laurence Sterne (1713–1768), whose nine volumes of *Tristam
Shandy*, published between 1760–1768, were the most popular literary productions of England
during the 1760s. "The book was read enthusiastically at Sterne's own university, Cambridge,
[where] a group at the university signed a mock deposition, stating that it contained the 'best
& truest & most genuine original & new Humour, ridicule, satire, good sense, good nonsense'
ever published." Alan B. Howes, *Yorick and the Critics* (New Haven: Yale University Press,
1958), pp. 2, n. 7; 5, n. 7. The pseudonym was probably inspired by the King's jester whose skull
was dug up in Shakespeare's *Hamlet* (v. 1). See Drabble, *supra*, 7.

[*4 continued*]

I must try again "and strain from hard-
bound brains nine lines a day." Thus I continued my very variegated employ, alternately
busied

[5]

——

busied with the Cabin-boys and the muse, til
I fitted my expressions and numbers to my
author. This will do, cried I. Who would
not be sea-sick a little, if it will purifie
and sublimate a Common Lawyer into a poet.
I am sure no body has given the forte of
Virgil so well: no translator has done it
I am sure. I will continue the vein, and
publish a translations of the first Eclogue
as a specimen of my improvement by
traveling. Alas how short-lived
are the pleasures of Imagination! A few minutes recollection reminded me that I
could remember only Trapp's translation,[13] which was the one I used while a
school-boy: This was a damper with
a witness, and the words of the wit, who wrote
over Trapp's door while he was in his
labour did the business. I have never made
another attempt from that time to this; and
believe I shall not to my dying day.
"Trapp mind thy bible, and translate no further,
"For it is written—"thou shalt do no murder."[14]

13. Howe, *Proceedings*, 1915–1916 [FN 428-2]. Joseph Trapp (1679–1747), poet and pamphle-
teer, *Dictionary of National Biography*, LVII, 155.

14. Howe, *Proceedings*, 1915–1916 [FN 428-3]. By Abel Evans (1679–1737). The epigram usually reads: "Keep the commandments, Trapp, and go no further, For it is written, that thou shalt
not murther."

[6]

——

These lines made a much deeper impression upon
me, than on the good Doctor to whom they were
particularly applied; and I forthwith determined to take the Poet's advice—
                    "Keep your piece nine years."
A considerable time before my taking
this wise resolution, I had taken to my
bed. A very high wind and large sea
had given a quietus before I had reached the Light house.[15] An instant applica-
tion of diluters[16] however rendered my
exercises less painful at first; and little
incidents kept turning up to divert
my attention or chear my spirits.
I observed Randall to be
over assiduous in holding my head and calling for liquid, while his sides and body
shook as if he would die. I pretty soon
discovered my situation had excited
his immediate laughter and all his over-officious

15. Almost certainly the Boston Light on Little Brewster Island at the harbor's entrance. The first light was built in 1716, and greatly improved after a fire in 1751. See *Illustration 2*, showing the Light as Quincy would have known it. It was damaged by both American and British troops during the Revolution and was replaced in 1783. See S. R. Snowman and J. G. Thomson, *Boston Light: An Historical Perspective* (Plymouth, Mass., 1999), pp. 7–14.

16. A solution. Apparently a sea sickness remedy. See Samuel Johnson, *A Dictionary of the English Language* (concise edition, London, 1756), n.p. "diluter." (Hereafter, "Johnson, *Dictionary*.") I have chosen this edition of Johnson's dictionary as the one more likely to be available to American colonists than the massive unabridged version. "Samuel Johnson's dictionary, as well as his theory of language . . . remains an invaluable guide to what our founders had in mind when they set the democratic experiment in motion." Jack Lynch, "Dr. Johnson's Revolution," *New York Times* (July 3, 2005), p. A-27.

To the Merchants of Boston this View of the LIGHTHOUSE is most humbly presented, By their Humble Servt Wm Burgis

ILLUSTRATION 2. Boston Light was "the first modern-style lighthouse in the New World." As Quincy saw it, it would have been rebuilt as of 1751. See *Mapping Boston* (eds. A. Krieger, D. Cobb, A. Turner, Cambridge, Mass., 1999), p. 104. This view was based on a rendition of William Burgis in 1729, pictured on the front of *Massachusetts Magazine*, February 1789, just after the light was rebuilt in 1783. (Courtesy, Library of Congress.) See S. R. Snowman, J. G. Thomson, *Boston Light: A Historical Perspective* (Plymouth, Mass., 1999), p. 9. Many thanks to my Editorial Assistant, Patricia Tarabelsi. See p. 95, *Southern Journal*, p. 6, "reached the Light house."

[7]

———

over-officiousness intended to conceal his mirth. He would perhaps have
received some indications of my discovery
had not my memory reminded me
of a time when I was a like over-
taken and had recourse to a very similar artifice—

[1.5 lines crossed-out with ink]

Exhausted nature soon called for some
repose; a return of my illness
however soon disturbed it. But when
in calling for my servant I was told
he had taken to his bed, my revenge
was satisfied, tho' if I would have moved
he should have seen my sides shake in
his turn. Thus I was relieved with
trifles and mirth at every interval of
my labours. For the noises which came
almost every instant thro' the bulkhead
convinced me that the Corners of Randall's
mouth no longer made enchroachments
on the domain of his ears: no position in

[8]

———

Euclid was clearer than that R[andall]'s Jaws
now oscillated with quickness between the Zenith and Nadir[17], and that their
motion was no longer horizontal,
but vertical.
Thus—"Trifles please the idle mind."
The Cabin-boy who has now become my
assistant afforded new matter for entertainment, and consolation. Tho' he had
been three years accustomed to the sea,
yes the swell and motion of the water was
so great as to work him as much as
my self. And while the poor little fellow extended his arms to my assistance, he lay with his breast on the floor
and was exercised with strains and throws
more violent than my own. My
own situation made me compassionate.
Good Heaven! Thôt I, how various, how

17. From Euclid's *Elements* (c. 300 B.C.). See Howatson, *supra*, 223–224.

[9]

———

unsearchable are thy allotments, "Every
reflection of my mind now served to
reconcile me to my own afflictions:
their number decreased on comparison, and
in proportion as calamities humanized my heart: towards the poor
prostrate boy, their severity dissi-
pated apace. Gay's fable[18] of the Cook-maid, turnspit and the ox, which I had
learned when very young lulled
me to repose (for the first time on Ship-
board) about 3 in the morning.
A more disagreeable time can hardly be conceived,
than the season of my first days and nights. Exhausted to the last degree, I was too weak to rise, and in
too exquisite pain to lie in bed. Unable to take
any manner of food, I remained wholy confined to my state-room, till the pains of
my body and limbs forced me to make one
effort to get fresh air. Assisted by two people
I reached the foot of the Companion-stairs, but

18. John Gay (1685–1732), poet and dramatist. Gay's first series of 'Fables' was issued in 1727; the second series, his principal posthumous work, was issued in 1736. It is in this posthumous edition that the fable of "The Cook-maid, the Turnspit and the Ox" first appears. See Gay, *Fables*, pp. 228–232. The gist of the fable is the cook-maid envys her masters, the dog kept to turn the roasting-spit by running on a treadmill, i.e. "the turnspit," envys the cook-maid, but neither is as badly off as the ox on the spit. "Let envy then no man torment: think on the ox, and learn content." *Id.* Gay was among the main representatives of burlesque comedy in the 18th century, "[w]ith his famous *Beggar's Opera* (1728) he produced one of the funniest and most orig-inal stage works of the age." Michel-Michot, Paulette, Marc Delrez, and Christine Pagnoulle, *History of English Literature, 2d part, 1660–1840* (University of Liege, Belgium, *unpublished*). See Drabble, *supra*, pp. 384–385. Gay composed his own epitaph for his memorial in Westmin-ster Abbey. "Life is a jest, and all things show it. I thought so once and now I know it." *Id.*, p. 383. Special thanks to Mark Sullivan.

[10]

___

was not able to proceed further. The fresh air
instead of refreshing, as first, overcame me.
My sickness came on with redoubled violence,
and after several fainting turns, I was carried
back to bed. At the end of fifty eight hours,
I took the sustenance of one rusk, and soon after
of a little broth. The night passed very heavily away, and at about 4 in the morning, my pains
came on so violent, and my cabin was so sultry and hot, [that] to rise or perish seemed the
only alternative. I knocked for the watch
upon deck, and with the assistance of two of them,
got seated on a hen-coop by side of the
Binikle.[19]
Scenes altogether new and surprising presented themselves to my view. I had never
before been on deck since passing the Light house,[20]
and had never before been out sight of land.
The heavens were overcast with black and heavy
clouds, with here and there a light flying wild cloud
interspersed. With a hard North East wind, the
weather was extremely close and muggy, and distant flash-

19. [Binnacle]: a housing for a ship's compass and a lamp. *Merriam Webster's Collegiate Dictionary*, Tenth Edition.
20. The Boston Light. See *Illustrations 1* and *2, supra.*

[11]*

————

es of lightening gleamed all round the horizon,
the waves seemed to curl with flames just
sufficient to make the darkness visible and
successive peals of distant thunder all con-
spired to make deep impressions and fit the
mind for meditation. To know how
all this affected me, a person must consid
er my weakness, my situation and cast of
mind.
What a transition have I made and am still
making!—was the exclamation of my heart.
Instead of stable earth, the fleeting waters: the little hall of ~~Justice~~ right and
wrong is changed for the wide-expanding
immeasurable ocean: instead of petty jarrs[21]
and waspish disputations; waves contend
with waves, and billows war with billows:
seas rise in wrath and mountains
combat heaven; clouds engage with clouds
and lightenings dart their vengeful
corruscations; thunders roll and oceans

21. "Justice" is crossed out in the manuscript. Quincy is referring to his law practice before the Massachusetts Superior Court. Johnson defines "jar" as "[c]lash; discord; debate." Johnson, *Dictionary, supra,* n.p. "jar."

[12]

———

roar: All other flames and distant
shores, sea, air and heaven reverbe-
rate the mighty war and eccho awfull
sounds:
"The Sky it seems would pour down livid flames,
"But that the Sea, mounting to th' welkin's cheek,
"Dashes the fire out."22
Vast field for contemplation! Riches for
mind and fancy!
Astonishing monuments of wisdom; magni-
ficient productions of power!
The ingenuity, the adventurous spirit, the
vast enterprises of man next succeed to employ reflection. A little skiff, scarce a speck
in this wide expanse, flew threw the waves
and plyed this angry flood;—braved the
threatening dangers—this world of night
and chaos.

Shakespear's
Tempest
[left margin, ll. 6–7]

22. Howe, *Proceedings*, 1915–1916 [FN 430-1]. From William Shakespeare, *The Tempest*.
"[P]robably written in 1611, when it was performed before the King in Whitehall." Drabble, p.
968. The first line reads, "The sky, it seems, would pour down stinking pitch." Act 1, scene 2.
See p. 179, *infra*.

[13]

——

While thus surprised and gratified, I rejoiced to think of my undertaking, and
was pleased with the <u>hopes</u> being wiser and
better for my excentric motion.
Suddenly the weather changed, became
redoubly inclement, and cold rain and sleet
threatened my health if I tarried longer.
But to go in my enfebled state to a
hot confined cabin

[half of l. 9, all of l. 10, half of l. 11 scratched out]

was intol-
lerable. Rain and cold appeared less
dreadfull than heat and foul air. I sent
for my hussar, which with my sourtout,[23]
was to fit me for a companion to the
sailor at helm till sun rise.
The weather increased in badness—
I became fretfull—'twas death
almost to retire to my hole—
an exclamation escaped me—
I repined—I murmured—I
exclaimed again.—When—(I

23. [Hussar:] a member of any of various European units originally modeled on the Hun-
garian light cavalry of the 15th century. Also used to describe "jacket" or "waistcoat" as in "hussar jacket." See *The Compact Edition of the Oxford English Dictionary* (Oxford, 1971), vol. 1, p.
1353. (Hereafter, "*Oxford English Dictionary*.") [Surtout:] a man's long close-fitting overcoat.
Merriam Webster's Collegiate Dictionary, Tenth Edition.

[14]

———

shall never forget the sensation)—
the seaman at helm carrolled
with his marine pipe—
"How little do these landmen know,
"what we <u>poor</u> <u>sailors</u> undergo."
The best divine, moralist or philosopher
could not have devised a better care for
my spleen and vexation. I was all sympathy in a moment. Upon comparison how little reason had I for complaint? How much ground of gratitude
to heaven? Each thôt now tended to
reform me, every new reflection became more and more sentimental.
I was humanized—
            "Hence pity found place in my breast."—
The honest tar continued his carolls, and his
notes were truly musick to my ear.
            "A concord of sweet sounds."
I was perswaded the fellow chaunted his
naval tune to divert me, but when
then he expected to do it by the harmony
of sounds and numbers or by the sentiment
of his song to alleviate my afflictions

[15]

_____

in calling me to consider those of others,
I doubted. but it was wholly imma-
terial to me; either way I was e-
qually obliged to him.—(Some
passages of Yorick at this instant
came across my mind—and it
would have been infamous, if they
had no influence upon my heart.)[24]
My hand mechanically went to
my pockett, but searched in vain
for my purse: this was deposited in my sea-chest the day before I sailed. Luckily a small
remnant of my Cash fee was in the
Lining of my desert-pockett—I
threw it to the helmsman who in
endeavouring to catch it struck it
half thorough one of the scupper-
holes. It was now out of his
reach, he could not leave his helm
to get it, I could not rise from any seat without
help,

24. See note 12, *supra*.

[16]

———

help, and no one was on deck but,
us two.—The witty, careless,
good humoured fellow looked
a little shagreened at first,
(for every roll of the sea threatened it's loss) but with great ease
and indifference turning upon
his heel warbled with ineffable
harmony
"Hah! why should we quarrel for riches,
"Or any such glittering toys,
"Since a light heart and a thin pair of breeches,
"Goes thoro' the world brave boys."
To know how this turn of the
sailor was relished, to realize the
pleasures it gave, one must
know every circumstance of
my situation and every feeling
of my heart.
If there is any merit in the motive—any in the
action—all is thine Oh Yorick, Prince of
sentiment!

[17]

———

Days of heat, cold, wind and rain now
rolled on. Confined to my cabin
almost wholly I became pale, wan
and spiritless; and as I have since learned from my servant every person
on ship-board gave me over and
concluded I should never reach land.
I was perfectly sensible of my danger,
but by being carried upon deck,
night and day, when it did not
storm violently, my spirits re-
vived, but my appetite never.
My second week at sea was now
passing, with only little incidents,
perhaps, nor more worthy of record-
ing than those which for want of
better materials has engaged my idle
time, and found a place in the preceeding
pages.

[18]

_____

With us came passenger one Mr. John
Alexander Hunter late a purser on
board his majesty's 20 gun ship war lying
in Boston: a gentleman lately oblidged
to ask leave to quit the service, for his
following the practices and examples of
his superiors: which in them escaped with
impunity. "See Little villains hung by great."[25]
  Mr. Hunter was one day uttering
his complaints, when among other things
an expression escaped him, remarkable
as coming from he who had been
15 years in the Crown-service, and retained much
of the peculiar sentiments and manners
of such an employ. He was speaking
of the partiality of a Court of Enquiry which

25. For an account of John Alexander Hunter, see "Introduction," *Southern Journal, supra,* at Section VIII, A., "Hunter, the Dishonest Purser," pp. 64–66.
  The quotation comes from a satirical poem by Sir Samuel Garth (1661–1719), a distinguished physician and friend of Alexander Pope, written to ridicule the opposition of the London apothecaries to a charitable dispensary established by the College of Physicians that gave free drugs to the poor. See Drabble, *supra,* pp. 381–382. The poem, in its final corrected version, was published by John Nutt as *The Dispensary: A Poem in Six Cantos* (2nd ed., London, 1699). The relevant verses read as follows:

> Not far from that most celebrated place [the Old Bailey],
> Where angry Justice shows her awful face;
> Where little villains must submit to fate,
> That great ones may enjoy the world in state;
> There stands a dome [the Dispensary], majestic to the sight,
> And sumptuous arches bear its oval height;
> A golden globe, placed high with artful skill,
> Seems, to the distant sight, a gilded pill:
> This pile was, by the pious patron's aim,
> Raised for a use as noble as its frame.

Id., pp. 1–2. As always, my gratitude to Mark Sullivan, superb reference librarian.

[*18 continued*]

had sat upon him and the little reason to hope
for justice in a Court martial with which he
was threatened, unless he would ask leave
to quit his birth [berth?].—"Good GOD!, cried he,
why do I complain? What reason had

[19]

——

I to expect any thing better. <u>A</u>
<u>government that is arbitrary is</u>
<u>always unjust: a tyranny in one</u>
<u>or more is always cruel and unrighteous</u>."
Such sentiments from him surprised
me. I was impatient to know whether these reflections were founded in
his heart, or only the over-flowings
of spleen, disappointment and revenge.
For great is the sense of wrong, when oppression touches ourselves, weak, weak
indeed, when we are exempted from
all apparent danger of a like misfortune.

      Hunter was a man of good na-
tural powers; considerably acquainted
with essays and the Belles Lettres, tho' not
learned or conversant with the severer
studies.[26] I took this opportunity
to start the controversy between G[reat] B[ritain]
and the Colonies. I spoke of the conduct
of both; of present measures and

26. ["Belles Lettres"] "Writings on studies of a literary nature . . ." *The Concise Oxford Dictionary* (Ed. R. E. Allen, 8th ed., Oxford, 1990), p. 101. (Hereafter, *Concise Oxford Dictionary*.) "Severer studies" are advanced studies, such as law.

[20]

————

of the probable consequences. I hoped
hence to draw the general opinions of
his Core and also what must have
frequently transpired in his company for the last 7 years.

"Very true, said he, Mr. Q[uincy] we all
know this. Great Britain has no right
to tax you. The ministry know it as
well as you, but money must be had
some where. Every thing is strained to
the utmost at home. The people of England
see, as well as you, that N[orth] America
must one day be independent, and tis
her interest and most certainly of the present
administration to prevent this as
much as possible: And they will prevent it for a much longer time than
you imagine. For you can't contend with
the powers of Britain, whose navy conquers
the World; and your first men are all
bought off and will be more and more so

[21]

——

in proportion as the ministry are
wise and well informed. And who
can blame them for it, they are
in the right of it to do it, and you are
in the right of it to make opposition, but
all will not do. You must
submit for a great while yet to
come. Why all the world are slaves,
and N[orth] America can't hope to be free."
     A train of conversation of
this kind pleased and exasperated.
I reasoned, spoke of facts, of history, of human nature, of glorious
sacrifices—till from inveighing
I almost stormed. The agitation did my
health good, if nothing more; for
I wanted my blood to circulate.
     Upon my telling him, that
the present steps of the British government were to the last degree iniquitous, re-
pugnant to the first notions of right

[22]*

———

and wrong:—"Oh (Mr. Q[uincy] (he replied)
what do you tell of that for, there
can be no government without fraud
and injustice!—All government is
founded in corruption. The British
government is so. There is no doing without
it in State-affairs." This was a
clencher. Well I hope Mr. H[unter] you
will never more complain of arbi-
trary proceedings and wrong and cruelty
seeing such is the government you have served
and are now raging to be employed
by. ""Yes, yes, when it touches
one's-self, we have right to complain.
Damn it, was ever any one served
as I have been? Admiral M.[27] has
himself to my knowledge done
ten times as bad, and yet the rascal,
the scoundrel persecuted me with
unrelenting, brutal cruelty."

27. Admiral John Montagu (1719–1795), commander-in-chief on the North American station, 1771–1774. See *Dictionary of National Biography*, XXXVIII, 258. See also Howe, *Proceedings*,
1915–1916 [FN 434-1].

[23]

———

Here I let matters drop, making
only a few natural reflections
on the character of man.
How little variant is this Gentleman from those
Zealots for Liberty, who are the Enslavers
of Negroes?
      In the course of this time I had
a good opportunity of discovering the great
corruption of Administration and the gross
fraud of the Servants of the Crown.
Mr. H[unter] frequently owned to me that
his salary and birth was only worth
45£ sterling a year: but that the
year before last he made 300£
and the last 6 months at the rate of
400£ sterling a year.[28] And this
will not seem at all incredible
to those who are informed of the
ways and means of doing it and the
sharers and connivers of it.

28. Approximate Currency Equivalencies: £45 Sterling = $45,000 (2004); £300 Sterling = $300,000 (2004); £400 = $400,000 (2004). In a freewheeling way, I have arrived at these values by comparing costs of contemporary commodities, including books and hogsheads of wine. See pages 77 and 119, *infra*. Other comparative costs are to be found at pp. 44, 53, 61, 67, 71, 76–78, 82, and 119, *infra*. For example, Longfellow House on Brattle Street in Cambridge sold in 1781 for $4,264. Modern houses of comparable size and desirability sell for about $4 to $5 million. The same ratio is true of most commodities mentioned by Quincy. While the ratios are higher than those usually employed, I believe they are more realistic. See John J. McCusker, "How Much is that in Real Money? A Historical Price Index for use as a Deflation of Money Value in the Economy of the United States," *Proceedings of the American Antiquarian Society*, vol. 101, pl. 2 (Worcester, 1992), 297–373. See also John J. McCusker, *Money and Exchange in Europe and America 1600–1775: A Handbook* (Chapel Hill, 1978); Leslie V. Brock, "Colonial Currency, Prices and Exchange Rates," *34 Essays in History* (1992), 70–132, set out at http://etext.lib .virginia.edu/users/brock. Most importantly, these values make intuitive sense in comparing our world with Quincy's. Many thanks for the assistance of Patricia Tarabelsi with this note.

[24]

21st Feby. 1773.

——

This morning we were within 30 leagues
of our port, which should have probably
have reached the preceeding day had
we not been becalmed 24 hours.
At about 7 o'Clock AM a black cloud
hung over the North eastern
part of the Hemisphere, and at 8 the
wind rose extremely high at NNE.
Before night the wind blew a hurricane:
Every thing threatened a terrible tempest.
We were in the latitude of Bermudas,[29]
a latitude remarkable for storms
and whirlwinds. The hurry, noise and
confusion of preparing for the storm
was astonishing to one, never in a like
situation. Rain, hail, snow and
sleet descended with great violence and
the wind and waves raged all night.
About 4 in the next morning Capt.
Skimmer called to me, Saying "Mr. Q[uincy]
"come and see here: you may now say

29. Bermuda is located at 32.20 N and 64.45 W. This was particularly significant to Quincy, whose brother Edmund (1733–1768) was lost by shipwreck in these latitudes. See note 35, *infra*.

[25]

———

you have seen a storm at sea. I
never saw so dismal a time in my
life."
      The scene beggars all description.
As the day advanced, at times light-open-
ings in the clouds gave a view of the horrors
all around us: such apertures were
ever attended by a tenfold gust of wind.
The seas rose in mountains on each side,
and we were alternately elevated to the
clouds and sunk in the deep. I frequently
saw the yards plunged in the waves, and
was often sent by force of the motion
across my cabin. I used to keep myself in bed by throwing my left
arm over my right shoulder
and then twisting a cord (fastened to the side) round my
wrist prevented being pitched out of
bed. It was so dark by reason
of immense thick fogs that at
mid-day you could not see the end

[26]

———

of the Bowsprit,[30] and often scarce discern the
yards. The exhalations from the water
resembled in density and much <u>in</u>
<u>smell</u> the vapour from a burning
lime-kiln. In short horror was
all round Us. Our Capt. had been
31 years a seaman, Mr. Hunter had
been on all the Coasts of Europe and
America, and the Mariners had one
or other of them visited most parts
of the ocean, but none had seen so
terrible a time. Seas struck us
repeatedly with terrible concussions,
and all seemed to expect instant
deaths. In this manner day succeeded day, and night closed upon night;
here a gleam of hope, and then anon a
bitter disappointment. In vain did we
look for change, tempest and whirlwinds
seemed to have attained stability.
   "In every place
"Flamed amazement.—Not a Soul
"But felt a fever of the mind."[31]

30. [Bowsprit:] a large spar projecting forward from the stem of a ship. *Merriam Webster's Collegiate Dictionary*, Tenth Edition.

31. Shakespeare, *Tempest* (Act I, Scene 2, ll. 201–203). The line reads: "Not a soul but felt a fever of the mad and play'd some tricks of desperation."

[27]

25 Feby.

_____

On Wednesday (24th Feby) night, the rain
much abated, but the clouds did not dis-
perse, nor the wind lull. I put my head out
of the Companion door in order to take a
view, I could not help repeating those
beautiful lines of our Poet
          Unmuffle ye faint starrs, and thou fair moon,
That wont'st to love the traveler's benizon [blessing],
Stoop thy pale visage thro' an amber cloud,
And disinherit Chaos, that reigns here
In double night of darkness and of shades;
Or if your influence be quite damm'd up
With black usurping mist, some gentle taper,
Though a rush-candle from the wicker hole
Of some clay habitation, visit us
With they long levell'd rule of streaming light,
And thou shalt be our Star of Arcady,
Or Tyrian Cynosure.[32]
On Thursday things remained much as they
were; towards night the clouds dispelled, starrs
were here and there to be seen, and every thing seemed
to promise better times: but our hope was as

32. John Milton's 1634 play, *Comus* (l. 343). "Cynosure," "[t]he star near the north pole, by
which sailors steer." Johnson, *Dictionary*, *supra*, n.p. "cynosure."

[28]*

———

the morning cloud and evening dew. Before
day light seas, winds, snow and rain raged more
than ever. All matters had previous to
this been disposed to encounter the worst.
Everything was either lashed upon deck or removed off it: Axes were delivered out and all
stood prepared for cutting away the masts,
which we expected to be obliged to do every
minute. We had long laid under bare-poles,
except what is called a balanced mainsail to
keep her head to the wind and seas as far as
possible. All now retired to steerage
or cabin: none remained upon deck: we
drew towards the Shore with incredible swift-
ness, considering we carried no sail: Seas
broke over us often; now and then one would
strike with enormous force. I had no
way to keep myself in bed, but by throwing
my left arm over the right shoulder and then
twisting a cord (fixed to the side of my state-
room) round my wrists. The whole of
this night, (after eight o'Clock) I believe
every soul on board expected to perish. Δ
          We were now in that latitude

Δ [Added, Left Margin, at "Δ"]
"Who knows but _he_,
whose hands the light'ning forms,
"Who heaves Old Ocean,
and who wings the storms,"
"Pours fierce ambition

[*28 continued*]

in a Caesar's mind,
"Or turns young Ammon
loose <u>to</u> <u>scourge</u> mankind."[33]

[left margin, ll. 17–22]

33. Alexander Pope, *Essay on Man*, 1733 (ep. I, l. 157). Ammon was an Egyptian god with the head of a ram. Howatson, *supra*, pp. 31–32.

[29]

———

in which the remains of my Elder Brother[34] lay deposited in the Ocean; and probably very
near the spot were Mr. John Apthorp[35] and lady were foundred. It was
impossible at this season to exclude
this from rememberance the mind
dwelt upon it. Especially as in case
of our loss, there would have been a like
ignorance of our fate and length of expectation of friend, as in the unhappy
case of Mr. A[pthorp] and his lady. To consider
to ruminate, to waver, to despond,
to cheer and ponder anew was
natural to the scene—⊗
—   "A thousand fantasises
—   "throng into the memory;
"Of calling shapes, and beckoning shadows dire,
"And airy tongues, that syllable mens names
"On sands, and shores, and desert wildernesses.
"These thoughts may startle well, but not astound
"The virtuous mind.—
"Peace—be not over-exquisite

⊗ [Added, Left Margin]
"He who thro' immunity can peirce,
"See worlds on worlds compose one universe,
"Observe how system in system runs,

34. Howe, *Proceedings*, 1915–1916 [FN 436-1]. Edmund Quincy (1733–1768). See note 29, *supra*.
35. Howe, *Proceedings*, 1915–1916 [FN 436-2]. John Apthorp married, December 12, 1765, Hannah, daughter of Stephen Greenleaf.

[*29 continued*]

"What other planets circle other suns,
"What vary'd Being peoples ev'ry star,
"May tell why Heav'n has made us as we are."[36]

[left margin, ll. 13–20]

36. Alexander Pope, *Essay on Man*, 1733, (ep. I, ll. 17–28).

[30]

———

"To cast the fashion of uncertain evils;
"For grant they be so, while they rest unknown,
"What need a man forestall his date of grief,
"And run to meet what he would most avoid?
"Or if they be but false alarms of fear,
"How bitter is such self-delusion?"37
      Providence now gratified a
frequent desire of my heart:—that I might
be in a situation so circumstanced as to be fully convinced of a
speedy departure—
—   "To that bourn
"From which no traveller returns:"—
that I might have the exercise of my
understanding—time to examine the
heart—to reflect upon the past—
look forward to the future—weigh
and consider—Whether I leaned
—"Upon the pillared firmament,
Or rotteness."38
      To notice the operations of the mind
and observe the emotions of the spirits at such

37. John Milton's 1634 play, *Comus* (l. 362).
38. William Shakespeare's 1602 play, *Hamlet* (Act III, sc. 1, line 87ff.) reads "But that the dread of something after death, The undiscover'd country from whose bourn, No traveler returns . . .". John Milton's 1634 play, *Comus* (l. 597), reads: "The pillar'd firmament is rottenness, And earth's base built on stubble." Quincy was a very literate young man!

[31]

——

seasons is certainly a duty and very profitable employ. The justness of our sentiments
opinions and judgments concerning all
subjects is here brôt to the test; and
the propriety, right and equity of our
past lives must stand an audit.
We hence are powerfully taught
what is folly, what wisdom, what
right and what wrong:—the duties
we have omitted and those we have
performed: a reflection upon the one is
pungent, a review of the other exquisitely joyous. That <u>procrastination</u>
<u>is the theif of time</u> we had heard
in doctrine: It's truth now shines
not in theory, but in fact: experience
gives weight and energy to what before
was fluctuating and feeble.
"<u>Tomorrow, tomorrow and tomorrow</u>
"Creeps in this petty space
"To the last syllable of recorded time;
"<u>And All our Yesterdays have *lighted* fools</u>

[32]

____

"The way to study wisdom."[39]
  I had often in past life expressed
my creed that every man died a hater
of tyrants, an abhorrer of oppression,
a lover of his country, and a friend to
mankind. I shall never forget how
my conviction upon this head now
received confirmation. No period of my
life now gave such solid solid satis-
faction, such heart-felt joy, as those
few in which I had contributed a
mite towards exhibiting certain men and
measures in what now appeared a true light and in annoy-
ing those who at this test still
appeared the enemies of country.
Perhaps I was now more an en-
thusiast than ever, for the review
was delightfull.—I regretted nothing
more than that in past-times I had not
been more of the true citizen of my
country and the world;—more assiduous,
more persevering, more bitter more

39. Shakespeare, *Macbeth* (soliloquy) Act 5, Scene 5, ll. 19–28. The last line has been altered by Quincy from "The way to dusty death" to a more optimistic "The way to study wisdom"! He also omitted "from day to day" in the second line, but, if from memory, it was quite an accurate recollection.

[33]

———

implacable, more relentless
against the scourges of my country,
and the plagues of mankind. I shall
never, I hope I shall never, forget
the resolutions I now formed, the
sentiments I now entertained; my
determination to remember them
in future and make this minute
I am now writing of, as a memorial of the past and a memento
for the future; And to aid me in
engraving them on the tablet
of my heart.
  At the making of this minute I
have not reached the land; the day is more
cheerful but Danger not at an end.
I pray GOD to seal instruction at this
instant;—that every thought and
sentiment which is just and true; that
every resolution which is good and noble
may not be shipwrecked in the future
current, whirl or tempest of base,

[34]

26 Feby.

———

ignoble appetites, tumultuous, exe-
crable passions;—Become the
fleetings of a bird of passage—"The
baseless fabrick of a vision"—but
stable as the pillared firmament and
influential as the mid-day sun.
　　　Upwards of an 100 hours had
now passed without sight of the Sun: the
Wind had set almost wholly from NNE;
the Gulph Stream (said to run along
the Carolina—shore upwards of 5 knots
an hour) directly opposite: All of a
sudden the waters changed their colour:
we threw the lead and found soundings; the terror
and confusion on Shipboard was now
great indeed: whether this land was off
the Barr of Carolina, off Roman Shoals
or the Bahama Sands was altogether
uncertain to every person on board.[40]

40. With no opportunity to make lunar or solar observations, the longitude of the ship would
be unknown. A chronometer would have been most unlikely on Quincy's ship in 1773. Although
invented by John Harrison (1693–1776) in 1759 and used by Captain Cook in his voyages between
1772 and 1776, chronometers were not widely deployed on commercial ships until much later.
See Rupert T. Gould, *The Marine Chronometer: Its History and Development* (London, 1923), pp.
40–70. Thus, the ship could be as far west as the Carolina barrier beaches, or as far east as the
Bahama shores. Latitude was an easier matter, if sightings of the polar star, or "cynosure," were
possible, and Quincy remarks that they were "in the latitude of Bermudas"; (32.20 N) and in the
latitude where his elder brother died. See pp. 24, 29. Latitude could be determined by the height
of the polar star above the horizon.

[*34 continued*]

New dangers now stared us in the face.
Necessity compelled to venturing upon
deck and hoisting a reefed foresail;

[35]*

———

for the wind set violently on the shore
at this time, about 8 in the morning;
in the afternoon the clouds seemed again
to scatter, and tho' we flattered ourselves less than before, yet the signs
of better wheather worked forcibly on
our hopes. At night however, new
clouds arose with redoubled heaviness
and blackness, and our Capt. said he believed we should have a harder time,
than ever. The winds changed almost every minute, and what is very extraordinary considering their
violence these variations were
to directly opposite points of
compass.[41] WE had the greatest reasons to fear the consequence. But
the rains falling in incredible
floods imperceptibly layd
the seas and assuaged the storm.
And after a prodigious trying

41. True hurricanes, being swirling winds circling about an "eye," would appear to have a calm, and then winds from exactly the opposite direction. But such storms tend to occur in the late summer or fall in these latitudes.

[36]

27 Feby

——

night to those sailors who kept the
Deck, the morning broke with
signs of fair weather. At XII o'Clock
(27 Feby) we had a tolerable good
observation, and found ourselves to the
Southward of Our port. Our Crew
were spent, pale and spiritless. The
pleasures of a returning sun are
not to be conceived but by those who
have been in like jeopardizes and
trials.[42]

      We had once during the storm dis-
covered a ship near us: we now again
saw her. Each made a signal to speak
together, and each bearing down upon the
other, we met just at XII o'Clock. It

42. An attached newspaper clipping reads: "From an English Print of the 3d of March, which we are favored with by one of the Passengers, we find that on the 26th and 27th of February they had in England a prodigious high Wind, or rather Hurricane, by which great Damage was done in London and other Places, by blowing down Houses, Chimnies, etc. and to the Shipping in the River, as almost every Vessell from Greenwich to London Bridge, were drove from their Moorings; and by running foul of each other several of the smaller ones were sunk, and many Lives lost; others dismasted, and some drove ashore; among the latter were the Ships Earl of Dunmore, and Dutchess of Gordon, in the New-York Trade: Great Damage was like-wise done at Cowes, Portsmouth, Downs, and other Seaport Places, the 'Elements (as the Paper says) seemed to be all over in a Ferment, and the Clouds appeared of a fiery Red for many Hours:' Capt. Hall, of this Place, in a Ship just arrived in the Downs from Dartmouth, was drove ashore off Kingsdown, and lost her Rudder and received other Damage." See Howe, *Proceedings*, 1915–1916 [FN 138-1].

[*36 continued*]

proved a ship from St. Croix: she had
scarce a rag of sail standing, most of
her running rigging gone: her hand[s]
alternately at the pump: she looked dis-
tressfully enough: Each one on board
our brigg began now to compare our

[37]

————

case with that of our fellow voy-
ager who appeared bound to the same port
with us: all were moralizing
on the scene. For we had comparatively suffered no such damage
in the Storm. Extreme precaution,
watchfulness, and steadiness in our
master, great activity and courage
in our crew; all knowing and willing
to do their duty; with extreme
fine sails, rigging etc. had saved
us from much injury which we should
otherwise certainly have suffered.
The Capt. of this Ship told us that
he had been a seaman 21 years
and never had seen "such a time
in his days!" No person on board us
had ever been to Carolina, which occasioned our Capt. to asked the master of the
Ship whether he had ever been the
like voyage before: to which he answered
"yes about 21 years ago." And our

[38]

——

replying that we had never been there;
the hearty fellow commanding the
Ship cheerfully said—"Give us this
sun and this breeze and we'll soon
be better acquainted with the way."
     I could not helped being sur-
prized with this sort of ease and jollity
immediately after such hair-breadth 'scapes
and in a shattered condition.
Our Crew were mightily tickled with
his courage—And a horse-laugh-
"hearty-cock-brave fellow" and
reechoed thro' our bark.
     This interview also was one
of those we must experience before
we can form a true idea of its plea
-sure. 'Twas far beyond what a mere landman
would suppose.
     We soon outsailed the Ship, but before
we had gone far our Capt. on a sudden seemed
very angry with himself: no one knew the
cause of his agitation; when he ordered the peak

[Added, Left Margin]
The Crew of this
ship was so weakened
with incessant pumping
and fatigue that when they
came off Charlestown

[*38 continued*]

strength of lungs
sufficient to answer
the hailing; and
it was finally made
by a signal.
[left margin, ll. 4–11]

[39]

——

of the mainsail droped and to bear down
again on the Ship:—which being done
we all waited to know the cause of
it; the countenances seemed to express wonder at what it could
mean, and the hurry of executing
the orders of the master prevented us
from asking questions. While
we were thus waiting with expectation, the speaking trum-
pet resounded "<u>Do you want</u>
<u>any thing that I have got</u>—
provisions, water, canvass,
or rigging?" Heavens! what
were the sensations of my heart at
this question? And how was my
blood and spirits moved, when the
hoarse reply was—"No! no!
<u>plenty</u>, <u>plenty</u> here <u>yet</u>—thank
GOD!—Who's the Commander
of that Brigg?" "John Sckimmer!"
"GOD send you well in!"

[40]

—

This scene made me almost beside myself.
I was weak and feeble:—misfortunes
humanize the mind. Adversity ⊗
makes us susceptible of the finer
feelings. My brain turned—my ♥
throbbed—my pulse rose and fell,—
I almost—and should have quite—fainted
had not tears bursting from my eyes
and rolling down in a torrent gave
me ease.   —Here was a most
beautiful assemblage of sympathies and
virtues: and my mind was so softened by
disease and misfortunes, that it was well
fitted to feel the energy of such a union.
Humanity and benevolence—gratitude
and thankfulness shown reciprocally in
the offer and return and vied in lustre: a
similitude of calamity inspired
friendship and charity, and sublimity of
action.—It has been said that necessity
was the mother of invention;[43] may we
not also say, that misfortune is
the parent of virtue?
—"What Sorrow is, thou bid'st us know,
"And from our own, we learn to melt at others' woe."[44]

43. "Necessity, who is the mother of invention." Plato, *The Republic*, Book I, 344 (c), Jowitt translation.

44. "What sorrow was, thou bad'st her know, And from her own she learn'd to melt at others' woe." Thomas Gray (1716–1771), *Hymn to Adversity* (1742) stanza 2, lines 15–16.

⊗ [Added, Left Margin]

"<u>Daughter of Jove</u>, relentless power, Thou tamer of the human breast,
Whose iron scourge, and tort'ring hour. The bad affright, afflict the best!
When first thy <u>Sire</u> to send on Earth VIRTUE, his darling child design'd,
<u>To thee</u> he gave ye heavenly birth, And bad to form her infant mind.
Thy form benign, Oh Goddess wear, Thy milder influence impart,
Thy philosophic train be here <u>To soften</u>, <u>not to wound the heart</u>,
The generous spark extinct revive, <u>Teach me to love</u> and <u>to forgive</u>,
<u>Exact my own defects to scan</u>, <u>What others are to feel</u>, <u>and know myself a
man</u>."[45]
[left margin, ll. 1–20]

45. *Ode to Adversity* (1753) by Thomas Gray (1716–1771), author of "Elegy Written in a Country Churchyard" (1751), is among the most celebrated, and most quoted, poems of the 18th century.

[41]

1773
28 Feby

———

We now were off Charlestown-Bar,
and the wind being right in our teeth we
were the whole day beating up. Just
before sunset we passed the fort.
Charlestown[46] appeared situated between two large spacious rivers,
(the one on the right called Cooper
River and—the other on the left,
Ashley-River) which here emp-
tie themselves into the sea. The
number of shipping far surpassed
all I had ever seen in Boston. I
was told there were then not so
many as common at this season,
tho' about 350 sail lay off the town.
The town struck me very agreeably;
but the New Exchange[47] which fronted the
place of my landing made a most
noble appearance. On landing,
Sunday Ev[enin]g just before dark, the numbers of Inhabitants and appearance
of the Buildings far exceeded my expectation. I proceeded to the Coffee house,

46. See *Illustration 3*. Charleston, situated on neck of land between Ashley and Cowper rivers; in 1787 contained about 800 houses. Lat. 42.10.N. Long. 72.15.W. *The American Gazetteer*, Containing a Distinct Account of all the Parts of the New World, printed for A. Millar and J. & R. Tonson, 1762. 1787—15,000 inhabitants, including 5400 slaves. Jedidiah Morse, D.D., *The American Gazetteer*. Printed in Boston, 1797.
47. See *Illustration 4*.

ILLUSTRATION 3. Charleston Harbor in 1742. From the collections of the South Carolina Historical Society. Courtesy, South Carolina Historical Society.

[42]

Lavinus
Clarkson
[left margin, ll. 5, 7]

1 March 1773

——

where was a great resort of company as
busy and noisy as was decent.

I hear met with Mr. Lavinus
Clarkson[48] to whom I had Letters who
much befriended me in getting
lodgings, which we were put to very
great difficulty to obtain. By X
o'Clock however we procured one
near the State-house, and this night I

---

48. Levinus Clarkson (1740–1798). Born in Jamaica, Long Island. Married Mary Ann Van Horne and had 10 children. *The Sawyer Family History*, www.sawyer-family.org, 2000. Clarkson was an active patriot and apparently had business with the Secret Committee of the Continental Congress, as evidenced by the following record:

THURSDAY, JULY 10, 1777: A petition from Joseph Belton, and a petition from Captain James [Joseph] Lees, were read: 11 The petition of Joseph Belton is in the Papers of the Continental Congress, No. 42, I, folio 137. Ordered, That the petition of J. Belton be referred to the Board of War, and the petition of Captain Lees to the Marine Committee. The Secret Committee laid before Congress a letter of the 8 June last, from John Dorsius, for self and Levinus Clarkson, and a bill of exchange, drawn by Alexander Ross on John Dorsius, in favour of Willing, Morris & Co. Ordered, That the same be referred to the Board of Treasury, in order to bring in a report for paying the before mentioned bill here, and directing Mr. Dersius to apply the amount of the said bill in discharge of the debts incurred in consequence of orders from the Secret Committee, and also to enable the agents of the Secret Committee 0170 543 in South Carolina, to receive all the money arising from the sale of the State lottery tickets in that State, towards discharging the debts aforesaid. Library of Congress: Journals of the Continental Congress 1774–1789. Edited from the original records in the Library of Congress by Worthington Chauncy Ford, Chief, Division of Manuscripts, Volume VIII. 1777: http://memory.loc.gov/ll/lljc/008/lljc008.sgm_old

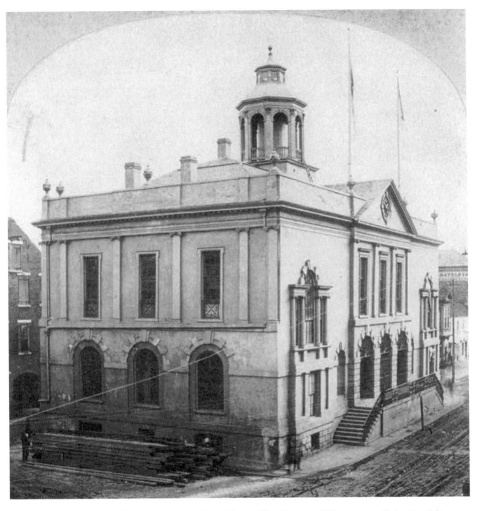

ILLUSTRATION 4. The Exchange Building, Charleston. The core of the building, built in 1767–1771, would be identical to the one Quincy saw. Courtesy, Library of Congress. Date, circa 1865. See p. 138, *Southern Journal*, p. 41, "the New Exchange."

[*42 continued*]

had the most sound and refreshing slum-
ber I ever enjoyed.

In the morning the same
gentleman politely attended me
to introduce me to those to whom I had
Letters of recommendation.

This and the next day I spent in
traversing the town from one end
to the other, viewing the publick
buildings and most elegant mansion
houses.

[43]

1773
March 2d.

David
Deis
[left margin, ll. 4, 6]

This day I was waited upon by several gentlemen to whom yesterday I had
delivered Letters—those who came in
my absence left Cards with their names.
Received a ticket from David Deis
Esq.[49] for the St. Cecilia Concert,[50] and now
quit my journal to go.

March 3.
[left margin, l. 8]

——

The Concert-house is a large inelegant
building situated down a yard at
the enterance of which I was met

49. Howe, *Proceedings*, 1915–1916 [FN 441-1]. David Deas (d. 1775), treasurer of the Chamber of Commerce of Charleston, December 1773.

50. Howe, *Proceedings*, 1915–1916 [FN 441-2]. Mention of this Society is found in the *South Carolina Gazette*, November 30, 1767. From 1766–1771, concerts were held in Charleston's most prominent public-house, or tavern, located on the north-east corner of Broad and Church Streets; sometimes referred to as "the Corner." *Votaries of Apollo: The St. Cecilia Society and Concert Music in Charleston, South Carolina, 1766–1820* (Indiana University Dissertation [2003] by Nicholas Michael Butler, unpublished, pp. 186–190).

[43 continued]

by <u>a Constable with his staff</u>. I
offered him my ticket, which was <u>sub-
scribed by the name of the person giving
it</u>, and directing admission of me <u>by</u> <u>name</u>,
the officer told me to proceed, I did and
was next met by a white-waiter,
who directs one to a 3d to whom I
delivered my ticket and was conducted in. The Hall is preposterously
and out of all proportion large, no Orchestra for the performers,

[44]

———

tho' a kind of loft for fiddlers at the Assembly.[51]
The performers were all at one end of
the hall and the Company in front and on
each side. The musick was good.
The two Base-viols and French horns
were grand. One Abbercrombie,[52]
a Frenchman just arrived played
a first fiddle and solo incomparably,
better than any I ever had heard:
I have several times heard John
Turner and Morgan[53] play a solo.
Abbercrombie can't speak a word
of English and has a salary of 500
Guineas[54] a year from the St. Cecilia
Society.—Hartley[55] was here, and
played as I thôt badly on the harpsi-

51. The room lacked a raised platform for musicians to perform, having only an elevated gallery or loft on one of the walls where musicians would stand during dancing assemblies. Ergo, Quincy's observation, "no orchestra for the performers, tho' a kind of loft for fiddlers at the Assembly." *Votaries of Apollo: The St. Cecelia Society and Concert Music in Charleston, South Carolina, 1766–1820,* pp. 186–190.

52. John Joseph Abercrombie (c. 1745–1808), descendant of an old Scottish family, was raised by his mother in her native town of Arras, France, and was then educated at the Jesuit College of Douai, French Flanders. *Votaries of Apollo: The St. Cecelia Society and Concert Music in Charleston, South Carolina, 1766–1820,* pp. 186–190.

53. Boston musicians, later turned rivals. See *Music in Colonial Massachusetts, 1630–1820: A Conference held by the Colonial Society of Massachusetts, May 17 and 18, 1973* (Boston [1980], pp. 1094–95).

54. Approximate Currency Equivalencies: 500 Guineas = £525 (Guinea being an English coin issued from 1663 to 1813 worth 1£ 1 shilling) = $525,000 (2004).

55. George Harland Hartley. Organist, arrived in Charleston in 1773, but returned to England four years later because of his loyalist views. Barnwell, Robert Woodward, Jr., ed., "George Harland Hartley's Claim for Losses as a Loyalist." *South Carolina Historical Magazine* 51 (1950), p. 50.

[*44 continued*]

chord. The capital defect of this
concert was want of an organ.

    Here was upwards of 250
ladies, and it was called no great show.
I took a view of them, but I saw

[45]

———

no E—.[56] However I saw
"Beauty in a Brow of Egypt:"
To be sure not a Helen's.[57]
  In loftiness of head-dress these
ladies stoop to the daughters of the
North: in richness of dress surpass
them: in health and floridity of countenance veil to them: in taciturni-
ty during the performances greatly
before our ladies; in noise and flirtations after
the musick is ever pretty much on
a par. If Our Women have any
advantage it is in White and red,
vivacity and fire.
  The Gentlemen many of them
dressed with a richness and elegance uncommon with us—many with swords
on. WE had two Macaronis[58]

56. "E" for "Eugenia," his nickname for his wife, Abigail.
57. "The lunatic, the lover, and the poet
 Are of imagination all compact:
 One sees more devils than vast hell can
 hold,
 That is, the madman: the lover, all as
 frantic,
 See Helen's beauty in a brow of Egypt."
William Shakespeare, *A Midsummer Night's Dream*, Act V, Sc. 1, l. 7. Was Quincy referring to a black, mulatto, or quadroon mistress? Later, he remarked that "[t]he enjoyment of a negro or molatto woman is spoken of as quite a common thing: no reluctance, delicacy or shame is made about the matter." *Southern Journal, infra*, page 113.
58. See *Illustration 5*. ["Macaroni"]: a "British dandy affecting Continental fashions." *Concise Oxford Dictionary*, p. 710. The term came from an "overblown hairstyle" that resembled a popular Italian pasta, "as well as to the dandy wearing it," and later achieved fame in the patriot anthem, "Yankee Doodle." See Corby Kummer, "Pasta 101: Where it Came From and How It got Here," *Atlantic Monthly* (July 1986). "Macaronis were constantly castigated as effeminate."

ILLUSTRATION 5. *Welladay! Is this my Son Tom!* from an original drawing by Grimm, printed for Carington Bowles, London, Pub. 1773 (litho), English School, (18th century) / Private Collection, The Stapleton Collection; Courtesy, the Bridgeman Art Library.

[*45 continued*]

present—just arrived from London.
This character I found real, and not
fictitious. "See the Macaroni" was a

See Kate Haulman, "A Short History of the High Roll," *Common – Place*, vol. 2 (October 2001), p. 3. Contemporary English explorers named the Macaroni Penguin for its resemblance to a "macaroni." See *Illustration 6*. My thanks to my extraordinary former editorial assistant, Patricia Tarabelsi.

[46]*

David
Deis
[left margin, ll. 4, 6]

March 3.

——

common phrase in the hall. One may
well be stiled the Bag and the Other
the Cue-Macaroni.[59]
     Mr. Deis was very polite:—
he introduced me to most of the
first character. Among the
Rest to Ld. Charles Gr:[eville] Montagu,[60]
the Governor (who was to sail next day for London),
and to the Ch:[ief] Justice[61] two of the
assistant Judges, and several of the
Council.
     Nothing that I now saw raised my
conceptions of the mental abilities of this
people: but my wrath enkindled
when I considered a King's Gov[ernment].

59. A reference to the "bag," or body, and "cue," or pigtail, of the wig? "Carlyle, Fredk, Gt. II, vi. vii., 213 'He cannot . . . change the graceful French bag into the strict Prussian queue in a moment.'" *Oxford English Dictionary* (compact vol., 1971), vol. 1, p. 621, defining "bag." See note 58, *supra*, and *Illustration 5, supra*.

60. Howe, *Proceedings*, 1915–1916 [FN 442-1]. Governor, 1765–1773. His successor, Lord William Campbell, was commissioned July 8, 1773.

61. Howe, *Proceedings*, 1915–1916 [FN 442-2]. Thomas Knox Gordon.

ILLUSTRATION 6. A Macaroni Penguin, named by eighteenth-century English sailors for its resemblance to the popular hairstyle. Photo by Cliff Wasserman. Courtesy, photo-escapes.com. See pp. 147–149, *Southern Journal*, p. 45.

[*46 continued*]

Spent in viewing horses, riding
over the town and into the vicinity,
and receiving formal complements.

[47]

1773
4 March
Thursday

David
Deis
Esq:
[left margin, ll. 4, 6, 7]

———

Dined (with four other Gentlemen) with David Deis, Esq.
Table decent and not inelegant: Provisions
indifferent, but well dressed: no apology:
good wines and festivity. Salt fish brôt in
small bits in a dish made a corner. The
first toast the king: the 2d a lady: The
3d Our friends at Boston and your
(meaning my) fire-side. The master of
the feast then called to the <u>Gentlemen</u> on his right
hand <u>for a</u> <u>Lady</u>:—this was done to every
one, except to the Ladies at table (Mr.
D's daughters about 16 and 10) who were
called upon <u>for a Gentleman</u> and gave one
with ease. The ladies withdrew after
the first round—the father seemed displeased at it. Glasses were changed
every time different wine was filled.
A sentiment was given by each Gentleman
and then we were called to Coffee and tea.

[*47 continued*]

No compulsion in drinking, except that
a Bumper was called for at the 3d toast.[62]
Politicks an uninteresting topick.

---

62. Bumper: "a cup filled." Johnson, *Dictionary, supra*, n.p. "bumper."

[48]

1773
5 March: Friday

John
Matthews, Esq.
[left margin, ll. 4–5]

———

Dined at a very elegantly disposed and
plentiful table at the house of John
Matthews, Esq.[63] (son-in-law of Col. Scott)[64]
in company with the Ch[ief] Justice of St.
Augustine,[65] and several other Gentlemen.
        Puddings and pies brôt in hot
after meats taken away. The flour
of the place in general is indifferent.
First toast The King and his friends. The
master of the feast calls upon <u>his lady</u> for
<u>a Gentleman</u> as a 2d toast: given with
ease. Ladies go round as toasts. The
females withdraw, and sentiments succeed.
No compulsion in drinking: no interesting conversation. Good wines.

63. N.B. Not to be confused with John Mathews (1744–1802), Governor of South Carolina,
1782–83; admitted to South Carolina bar on September 22, 1766. *Dictionary of American Biography*, XII, 404. Howe, *Proceedings*, 1915–1916 [FN 443-1]. In the Hayne Records (*S.C. Hist. and
Gen. Mag.*, XI, 92) is found the entry: "John Mathews, Goosecreek, Sally Scott S[pinster],
Boston, Jan. [1770]."
    64. Despite much effort, not identified.
    65. William Drayton (b. 1732). Born at Magnolia, served as Justice for Carolina, Chief Jus-
tice for the Province of Florida, Aide to General Lyttleman in the Cherokee War of 1759, and
Member of the South Carolina Supreme Court. Appointed by President Washington as a First
Judge of the United States District Court. *Magnolia Plantation's Historical Notes of Interest*, Carolina Internet, Inc. 2000. The family home, Drayton Hall, built between 1738 and 1742, still
stands outside of Charleston. See *Illustration 7*.

ILLUSTRATION 7. Drayton Hall, built 1738–1742. The hall survived the Civil War, and Gen. Sherman's troops, because it was in use as a smallpox asylum. Today it remains the only complete plantation home on the west bank of the Ashley River. It still hints at the elegant lives of Quincy's hosts, and the background of slavery. Courtesy, Library of Congress.

[49]*

1773
6 March.

Thomas
Loughton
Smith
Esq.
[left margin, ll. 3, 4, 6, 8]

———

This day was to have been spent with Thomas Loughton
Smith, Esq.[66] at his country seat. Bad
weather prevents, and I take what is
called a family dinner with him. A
prodigious fine pudding made of what
they call Rice flour. Nick-nacks
brôt on table after removal of meats.
Ladies ask the Gentlemen to drink a glass of
wine with them: Upon a Gentleman's asking
a Lady to do the like, she replies :G—
bless you, I thôt you never would ask
I have been waiting for you this
½ hour."

66. Howe, *Proceedings*, 1915–1916 [FN 443-2]. Thomas Loughton Smith (1741–1773) married, 1763, Elizabeth, daughter of George Inglis, merchant. Died in April 1773, from injuries received after falling off his horse. *S.C. Hist. and Gen. Mag.*, IV, 252.

[*49 continued*]

1st Toast, Our Boston—friends and their Good health
Sir:—the Unmarried Lady (of 19) at my right
"your good health and best affections Sir!"
Miss ____ your toast madam. "Love and
friendship and they who <u>feel them</u>!"
Toasts called for from the Guests, etc. till Coffee etc.
Mr. Smith's house furniture, pictures, plate
etc. very elegant—wines very fine.

[50]

————

Mrs. Smith shewed me a most beautiful
White Sattin and very richly embroidered
Lady's work bag, designed as a
present for a lady in London. Miss
Catherine Ingliss, her Sister, a still more
finely embroidered festoon (as they called it) of flowers.
Both their own work; and surpassing
anything of the kind I ever saw.
Before dinner a short account of the
late disputes with the Governor Lord Charles G.
Montague, and the state of matters at
present.
No Politicks after dinner.
In walking with ____ occurred a
singular event, of which Balch[67] could
make a humorous story.

67. Howe, *Proceedings*, 1915–1916 [FN 444-1]. Howe described Balch as "a hatter, of 72 Corn-hill, Boston, opposite the head of Water Street, a wit of the day." Sidney Willard described him as "a very worthy and respectable man . . . a frequent guest of Governor Hancock, and enter-tainer of his other guests, adding zest to the viands and the *vina* at the dinner-board by anec-dotes and stories, mimectic art, humor, witticism, and song, drawn from his inexhaustible storehouse." Sydney Willard, *Memoirs of Youth and Manhood* (Cambridge, Mass., 1855), vol. 1, pp. 209–210. Samuel Breck observed that Balch's hat shop "was the principal lounge even of the first people in the town." *Recollections of Samuel Breck* (ed. H. E. Scudder, Philadelphia, 1877), p. 108. Breck added, "Such, as late as 1788, was the unsophisticated state of society." *Id.*, pp. 108–109. Balch was a member of the Sons of Liberty. *Id.* p. 107. See also note 186 *infra* and accompanying text. Quincy never indicated what the "humorous" story was, nor did he identify his companion.

[51]

1773
7 March
Sabbath

——

Went to St. Phillips Church:[68] Very
few (comparatively speaking) present,
tho' this former part of the day is the most
full: A young scarcely-bearded boy
read prayers, with the most gay, indifferent and gallant air imaginable: very
few men and no women stand in
singing time: a very elegant peice
of modern declamatory composition
was decently delivered by another
clergyman, by way of sermon from
these words in Job "Acquaint now
thyself with GOD, thus good will or may come
of it."[69]   Having heard a young
church-parson very coxcomically[70]
advance a few days before, that no sermon
ought to exceed 25 minutes, I had the

68. Howe, *Proceedings*, 1915–1916 [FN 444-2]. Built in 1723 and destroyed in the fire of February 15, 1835. An account of it is in the Year Book of Charleston, 1880, 265; 1896, 319. The rector
at this time, Rev. Robert Smith, was in England. His assistant was Robert Purcell. Both were
born in England. The rebuilt St. Phillips Church survived the Civil War and is, today, one of
Charleston's principal churches.
69. Howe, *Proceedings*, 1915–1916 [FN 444-3]. "Acquaint now thyself with him, and be at
peace: thereby good shall come unto thee." Job XXII. 21.
70. "Coxcomical:" "[from coxcomb.] Foppish, conceited," Johnson, *Dictionary*, *supra*, n.p.
"coxcomical."

[*51 continued*]

curiosity to see by my watch whether
our clerical instructor was of the same
sentiments, and found he shortened the
space above 7 ½ minutes. It was
very common in prayer as well as

[52]

———

sermon-time to see gentlemen conversing
together. In short, taking a view
of all things, I could not help remarking the time of it, that here was not,
certainly, "<u>solemn</u> mockery."
This Church is the most decorated within,
tho' not the most splendid without, of
any in the place.
I find that in the several places of public
worship, which I have visited, that a
much greater taste for marble monuments prevail here, than with Us to the
northward.
I had noticed before, and could not help renewing
a remark, that a majority of both Sexes
at public assemblies appear in mourning.
I have seen and have been told, that mourning apparel at funerals is greatly in
fashion.

This divine after shewing that avocations, business etc.
precluded a certain species of acquaintance with GOD,
very sagely said "I come now to show that <u>there</u>
<u>is</u> a certain <u>allowable</u> acquaintance with GOD."
Qu. What kind of <u>acquaintance</u> can the Creature
have with the Creator which is <u>not allowable</u>?
[left margin, ll. 5–16]

[53]

1773
7 March
[left margin, l. 1]

Miles
Brewton
Esq.

[left margin, ll. 4, 6, 7]

———

Dined with considerable company at
Miles Brewton Esq.'s[71], a gentleman of very
large fortune: a most superb house[72]
said to have cost him 8000£ sterling.[73]
The Grandest hall I ever beheld, Azure Bleu
Satten-window Curtains, rich bleu paper with gilt, Mashee
Borders,[74] most elegant picture, excessive
grand and costly looking glasses etc.
Politicks started before dinner: a hot
sensible flaming tory, one Mr. Thomas
Shirley[75] (a native of Britain) present: he had advanced that
G[reat] B[ritain] had better be without any of the
Colonies; that she committed a most

71. Howe, *Proceedings*, 1915–1916 [FN 444-5] (1732–1775). See *S.C. Hist. and Gen. Mag.*, II, 142. He was lost at sea, with his family, in going to Philadelphia.

72. One of Charleston's finest homes. The house still stands today. See *Color Plate 1*. See also George C. Rogers, Jr., *Charleston in the Age of the Pinckneys* (2nd ed., Columbia, S.C., 1980), pp. 69–70. The house was built at 27 King Street in 1765. Brewton was "the leading slave merchant of his day." *Id.*, p. 69. See the illustrations in J. Thomas Savage, *The Charleston Interior* (Greensboro, N.C., 1995), pp. 15–18.

73. Approximate Currency Equivalencies: £8000 = $8 million (2004).

74. Paste borders. See *Oxford Dictionary*, *supra*, vol. I, p. 1735.

75. Howe, *Proceedings*, 1915–1916 [FN 445-1]. One of the name was president of the St. Cecilia Society.

COLOR PLATE 1. The Hall at Miles Brewton House (1765) 27 King Street, Charleston. "The Grandest hall I ever beheld, Azure Bleu Satten-window Curtains, rich bleu paper with gilt . . ." See p. 163, *Southern Journal*, p. 53. Courtesy, J. Thomas Savage, *The Charleston Interior* (Greensboro, N.C., 1995) and Jane Iseley, the photographer, and the generous Manigault family. With special thanks for the assistance of Mrs. Grant Whipple. See note 72, *supra*.

[53 continued]

capital political blunder in not ceed-
ing Canada to France: that all the Northern Colonies
to the Colony of New York and even
NY also were now working the Bane of
G[reat] B[ritain]: that GB would do wisely to renounce
the Colonies to the North and leave them a
prey to their continental neighbors or foreign
powers: that none of the political

[54]

———

writings or Conducts of the Colonies would
bear any examination but Virginia
and none could lay any claim to incomium[76]
but that province etc.
—Strongly urged that the Massachusetts
were aiming at sovereignty over the
other provinces; that they now took
the lead, were assuming, dictatorial
etc. "You may depend upon it (added
he) that if G[reat]B[ritain] should renounce the
Sovereignty of this Continent or if the
Colonies shake themselves clear of her
authority that you all (meaning the
Carolinas and the other provinces) will
have Governors sent you from Boston;
Boston aims at Nothing less than
the sovereignty of the whole continent;
I know it."
It was easy to see the drift of this discourse:
I remarked that all this was new to me;
that if it was true, it was a great and good ground
of distrust and disunion between the

76. [Encomium:] "Panegyrick; praise, elogy," Johnson, *Dictionary*, *supra*, n.p. "encomium."

[55]

———

colonies; that I could not say what
the other provinces had in view or
thôt but I was sure that the
Inhabitants of the Massachusetts paid a
very great respect to all the
Sister provinces, that she revered,
almost, the leaders in Virginia and
much respected those of Carolina.
Mr. Shirley replied, when it comes
to the test Boston will give the
other provinces the shell and the
shadow and keep the substance. Take
away the power and superintenden-
cy of Britain, and the Colonies must
submit to the next power. Boston
would soon have that—power rules
all things—they might allow the
other a paltry representation, but
that would be all.
The Company seemed attentive—and incredulous—were taking sides—

[56]

——

when the call of dinner turned the
subject of attention.
Shirley seemed well bred and learned in the
course of the Afternoon, but very warm and
irascible.
From his singular looks, and behavior I suspected he knew my political path.
A most elegant table—3 courses.
(Nick nacks), jellies, preserves, sweet
meats etc.
After dinner, two sorts of nuts, almonds
raisins, 3 sorts of Olives, apples, oranges
etc.
By Odds the richest wine I ever tasted:
Exceeds Mr. Hancock's, Vassall's, Phillips's
and others much in flavour, softness
and strength.
I toast all your friends, Sir. Each gentleman
gave his toast round in succession.
A young lawyer Mr. Pinckney,[77] a gentleman
educated at the temple[78] and of eminence

77. Likely Charles Cotesworth Pinckney (1746–1825), born in Charleston, S.C.; later a prominent delegate to the Constitutional Convention, 1787. *Dictionary of American Biography*, XIV, 614. His second cousin, Charles Pinckney (1757–1824), also a lawyer of Charleston, S.C., would only have been 16 years old. His brother Thomas, who also read law in the Temple, returned from England to South Carolina in 1774. See notes 80 and 83, *infra*, and *Illustration 9*.

78. See *Illustration 8*. "[T]he two Honourable Societies of the 'Inner' and 'Middle' Temple" form part of the Inns of Court, "survivals of a great legal university which flourished in medieval times . . ." See J. H. Baker, *An Introduction to English Legal History* (4th ed., London, 2002), pp. 159–162. (Hereafter, "J. H. Baker.") Notwithstanding the old proverb, "the Inner Temple for the rich, the Middle for the poor," the two societies produced such greats as Coke, Littleton, and Plowden. Bellot, H.H.L., *The Inner and Middle Temple*. Methuen and Co. (London, 1902). Despite the deterioration of standards of legal education in the Inns of Court by the eighteenth century, a significant number of Americans were members, mostly wealthy and mostly from the South. See E. Alfred Jones, *American Members of the Inns of Court* (London, 1914), ix–xxx. See also W. C. Richardson, *A History of the Inns of Court* (1978).

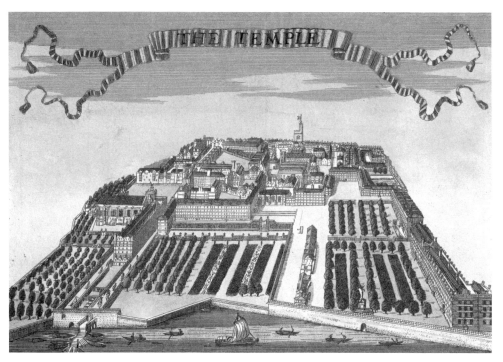

ILLUSTRATION 8. The "Temple," London in 1671. "Middle Temple" is to the left, "Inner Temple" to the right. From *'A Book of the Prospects of the Remarkable Places in and about the City of London,'* c. 1700 (engraving), Morden, Robert (fl. 1682–1703). O'Shea Gallery, London, UK. Courtesy, the Bridgeman Art Library. See p. 168, *Southern Journal*, p. 56.

[*56 continued*]

dined with us. From him and the rest of the
Company I was assured, that by the provincial laws of the place any two

[57]

———

justices and 3 freeholders might and very
often did <u>instanter</u>[79] upon view or complaint try a negro for any crime, and
might and did often award execution
of death—issue their warrant and it
was done forthwith. Two Gentlemen
present said they had issued each
warrants several times. This law
too was for <u>free</u> as well as <u>slave</u>-
Negroes and molattoes. They further
informed me, that neither Negroes
or molattoes could have a Jury;—
that for killing a negro, ever so wan-
tonly, as without any provocation;
they gave a late instance of this; that
(further) to <u>steal</u> a negro was death,
but to <u>kill him</u> was only fineable.
Curious laws and policy! I exclaimed.
Very true cried the Company but this is the
case.

79. "Instanter:" "Immediately; at once." Earl Jowitt, *The Dictionary of English Law* (ed., C. Walsh, London, 1959), p. 981. (Hereafter, "Earl Jowitt.")

[58]

[blank]

———

[59]

[blank]

———

[60]

———

At Mr. Brewton's side board was very
magnificent plate: a very large
exquisitely wrought Goblet much
excellent workmanship and singularly beautiful.
A very fine bird kept familiarly
playing over the room, under our
chairs and the table, picking up the Crumbs
etc. and perching on the window, side
board and chairs: vastly pretty!

[61]

1773
March 8th

――――

Received complimentary visits, from Charles
Cotesworth Pinckney, Esq.,[80] Messrs.
Bee,[81] Parsons, Simpson, and Scott,
all Gentlemen of the Bar, and others.
Was much entertained with Mr. Pinckney's conversation, who appeared
a man of bright natural powers,
and improved by a British education at the Temple.[82]
This Gentleman presented me with the only
digest of the laws of the province,[83] made

80. Charles Cotesworth Pinckney (1746–1825). Studied at the Middle Temple and attended the lectures of Blackstone at Oxford. Was offered and declined the command of the army, a seat on the U.S. Supreme Court, and the secretaryships of war and state. A lifelong Federalist, nominated for Vice President in 1800 and for President in 1804 and 1808. *Dictionary of American Biography*, XIV, 614. See note 77, *supra*, and note 87, *infra*. See also *Illustration 9*.

81. Likely Thomas Bee (1725–1812) of Charleston admitted to the South Carolina bar, 1761, and delegate to the First and Second Provincial Congresses, 1775–1776. See note 96, *infra*. Howe, *Proceedings*, 1915–1916 [FN 448-2] (1729–?). Married his first wife, Susannah Holme, in 1761, and married Sarah McKenzie, March 16, 1773.

82. Most Americans of the period, like Quincy himself, learned law by apprenticeship. A few were sent to study at the Inns of Court in London. Middle Temple was particularly favored by those from South Carolina. See *Illustration 8*. "South Carolina is more strongly represented at this Inn in the eighteenth century than any other colony. This is not surprising in view of the double fact that few of the prosperous inhabitants of . . . Charleston had not crossed the Atlantic before the American Revolution and that sons of successful planters, merchants and professional men were sent to England for their education and general culture." E. Alfred Jones, *American Members of the Inns of Court* (London, 1924), ix. Charles Pinckney matriculated at Christ Church College, Oxford, on January 19, 1764, was admitted to Middle Temple and called to the English bar on January 27, 1769. *Id.*, 171–172.

83. Howe, *Proceedings*, 1915–1916 [FN 446-2]. *The Practical Justice of the Peace, and parish-officer of . . . South Carolina*, 1761, by William Simpson. The full title was *The Practical Justice of the Peace*

[*61 continued*]

some years since by Mr. Simp-
son, late Atty. General in the Absence of
Sir Eagerton Leigh.[84] This present

---

and Parish-Officer, of his Majesty's Province of South Carolina (Charleston, Robert Welk publisher, 1761). See Morris L. Cohen, *Bibliography of Early American Law* (Buffalo, 1998), vol. III,
p. 25, No. 8001. There were no up-to-date collections of statutes, but in 1736, Chief Justice
Nicholas Trott had published *The Laws of the Province of South Carolina* (Charleston, 1736), an
ambitious attempt to reproduce all of the colony's statutes, plus the text of the two charters and
the relevant Act of Parliament. Thus, Quincy may have been a bit unfair. The first South Carolina reports covered 1783–1804 (*Bay's Reports*), and the *Public Laws* (1694–1790) were published
by Grimke in 1790. See *Catalogue of the Library of the Law School of Harvard University* (Cam-
bridge, Mass., 1905), vol. II, pp. 626, 628; Charles G. Soule, *The Lawyer's Reference Manuel of
Law Books and Citations* (Boston, 1884), pp. 53–54. Many thanks, as always, to Mark Sullivan.
Quincy was right that the *Practical Justice* was "the only digest of the laws of the province,"
Southern Journal, p. 61, but Peter Timothy had published the Chief Justice's *Charge to a Grand
Jury* (Charleston, 1741), well before, and there were several "extracts" for the proceedings of the
High Court of Vice-Admiralty, published shortly afterwards. *Id.*, vol. I, p. 151 (see No. 1521), vol.
IV, p. 32 (No. 11215), p. 33 (Nos. 11218, 11219, 11220). In 1704, there was an anonymous *Abridg-
ment of Laws in Force and Use in her Majesty's Plantations* (London, 1704), including "Carolina,"
and in 1721 Nicholas Trott published his *Laws of the British Plantations in America, relating to the
Church and Clergy, Religion and Learning* (London, 1721). In 1736 he published *The Laws of the
Province of South Carolina, in 2 Parts. The first containing all the perpetual Acts in force and Use,
with the Titles of all such Acts as are Repealed, Expired, or Obsolete, placed in their Order of Time.
The second Part, containing all the temporary Acts in force and Use; to which is added, the Titles of all
the Private Acts, and the two Charters granted by King Charles the II., to the Lords Proprietors of
Carolina, &c.* (2 vols., folio. Charleston, 1736). See John G. Marvin, *Legal Bibliography*
(Philadelphia, 1847), p. 697.

84. Egerton Leigh, son of Peter Leigh, who succeeded Charles Pinckney in the 1750s as chief
justice, replaced John Rutledge as attorney general and subsequently held many royal offices.
George Rogers, Jr., *Charleston in the Age of the Pinckneys* (Norman, Okla., 1969). "The highest
court in the province was soon called upon to decide on the council's right to sit as an upper
house. Printer Powell attempted to bring an action against Sir Egerton Leigh, president of the
council, for false imprisonment. Mr. Edward Rutledge represented Powell's interests, and Mr.
Simpson, clerk of the council, appeared in behalf of Sir Egerton. After a full argument on both
sides in the court of common pleas, Chief Justice Gordon and the four assistant judges quashed
the suit, declaring in express terms that the council was an upper house of assembly and hence
had the right to commit for contempt." W. Roy Smith, Ph.D., *South Carolina as a Royal
Province, 1719–1776* (New York, 1903), pp. 393, 413.

Attorneys General of South Carolina:

John Rutledge 1764–65;	Sir Egerton Leigh 1765–1774;	James Simpson 1774–1775
	Surveyor-General of Lands 1772–75	

ILLUSTRATION 9. Charles Cotesworth Pinckney (1746–1825). "Friend and confidant of George Washington, and one of the founders of the American Republic." E. Alfred Jones, *American Members of the Inns of Court* (London, 1924), p. 172. From the collections of the South Carolina Historical Society. Courtesy, South Carolina Historical Society. See p. 173, *Southern Journal*, p. 61.

[*61 continued*]

was the more acceptable as there is no
collection of the Laws of this Province in
a book to be had.—No wonder
their lawyers make from £2000
to £3000 sterling a year![85]—The rule
of Action altogether unknown to the people![86]

85. Approximate Currency Equivalencies: £2000–£3000 Sterling = $2 million to $3 million (2004). Quincy's observations were not entirely fair. *The Laws of the Province of South Carolina* had been published in 2 volumes in Charleston in 1736. See note 83, *supra*. But they were now 37 years out of date! Massachusetts, on the other hand, had regularly published its statutes and digests of the laws, as early as *The Lawes and Libertyes* (Cambridge, Mass., 1648). See Morris L. Cohen, "Legal Literature in Colonial Massachusetts," in *Law in Colonial Massachusetts* (Coquillette, Brink, Menand eds., Boston, 1984). See also Daniel R. Coquillette, "Radical Lawmakers in Colonial Massachusetts: The 'Countenance of Authorities' and the *Lawes and Liberteyes*," 67 *New England Quarterly* (1994), 179–211.

86. Does Quincy mean "Rules of Actions," i.e., pleading by causes of actions? See "Introduction," *The Southern Journal, supra*, Section VII A., "Law and Lawyers: South Carolina," pp. 52–56.

[62]

1773
March 9th

———

Spent all the morning in viewing the
Public library, State-house, public
offices etc. being waited upon by
Messrs. Pinckney and Rutledge,[87] two
of the Gentlemen lately from the temple,
where they took the degree of Barrister at law. The public library is
a handsome, square, spacious room,
containing a large collection of very
valuable books, cuts, globes etc.
I received much entertainment and information from the above gentlemen and Mr.
Charles Cotesworth Pinckney informed
me of an anecdote to which he was per-
sonally knowing, which I desired him
several times to repeat that I might
be the better able to relate it.
He said, that two Gentlemen being at a tavern
one of them gave <u>the Pretender's health</u>,
the other refused to drink it, upon which
he who gave the toast threw his glass of wine
in

87. These were Charles Cotesworth Pinckney (1746–1825) and Edward Rutledge (1749–
1800). See *Illustration 9* and discussion at notes 77 and 80, *supra*, and 113, *infra*. See also James
Haw, *John and Edward Rutledge of South Carolina* (Athens, GA, 1990, pp. 18–21). For the Pinckney mansion (c. 1747), see *Illustration 10*.

ILLUSTRATION 10. The Pinckney mansion in Charleston (c. 1747) on Colleton Square. Pinckney designed it himself. Courtesy, National Archives, Brady Collection.

[63]

———

in the refuser's face. For this an
action of trespass was brôt, and
Sir Fletcher Norton[88] closed the
cause on behalf of the plaintiff, before
Lord Mansfield[89] at Nisi Prius.[90]
His Lordship in summing up the
case told the Jury it was a most
trifling affair, that the action ought
never to have been brôt, and they ought
to find the defendant Not Guilty. Sir
Fletcher after his Lordship had sat
down rose immediately in some

88. Sir Fletcher Norton (1716–1789), barrister; solicitor-general, 1762; knighted, 1762; attorney-general, 1763; elected speaker of the House of Commons, 1770. He was usually nicknamed 'Sir Bull-face Double Fee' in satires and caricatures; attacked by Junius in Letter 39. *Dictionary of National Biography*, XLI, 209. The "Pretender" was probably James Edward Stuart (1688–1766), the exiled heir to James II, or his son, "the young Pretender," Charles Edward Stuart (1720–1788), "Bonnie Prince Charlie."

89. William Murray (1705–1793), 1st Earl of Mansfield, Lord Chief Justice, 1756–1788. Mansfield "was one of the greatest judges that ever lived, and perhaps the most important Anglo-American jurist to date to convey his or her ideas primarily through decided cases." Coquillette, *Anglo-American Legal Heritage* (Durham, N.C., 2nd edition, 2004), p. 444. These included several cases that transformed the law merchant. *Id.*, pp. 444–453. But his most famous case was Sommersett's Case (1772), 20 St. Tr. 1, in which Mansfield granted a writ of habeas corpus and freed a negro slave, James Sommersett, who had been brought to England. This case established that slavery was not part of the English law. See also C.H.S. Fifoot, *Lord Mansfield* (Oxford, 1936); Edmund Heward, *Lord Mansfield* (London, 1979). There is now an excellent new account of Sommersett's Case, 20 St. Tr. 1 (1772). See Steven H. Wise, *Though the Heavens May Fall: The Landmark Trial That Led to the End of Human Slavery* (Cambridge, Mass., 2005).

90. "Before a jury and one presiding judge." *Black's Law Dictionary*, 1197 (Revised 4th ed. 1968). "*Nisi prius*" ("unless before") refers to the fact the case would be tried in Westminster "unless before" the assize judge visited the county town. See Earl Jowitt, *supra*, 1227–1228.

[*63 continued*]

heat and asked his Lordship if he did
not intend to say anything more
to the Jury?
Lord M[ansfield]   No, Sir Fletcher I did not.
Sir F[letcher]   I pray to be heard, then; and I do
here public[ly] aver it to be law, that
if one man throws wine out of a Glass
at another in anger, this is an
assault and battery; this I declare for

[64]

―――

law, and I do here pawn my reputation as a lawyer upon it.
Lord M[ansfield]   Poo, poo, poo! Sir F[letcher] it is a
most trifling affair.
Sir F[letcher]   Poo, poo, poo! my Lord, I don't
intend to be poo, poo, poo'd
out of it neither!—I renew my
declaration, and affirm it for law—
and <u>if the Jury don't hear</u>
<u>law from the Court</u>, <u>they</u>
<u>shall from the Bar</u>. I affirm
again that it is an assault and battery.
Here Sir Fletcher sat down, and
spoke so loud as that the whole
Court, bar and Jury heard him,—
"He had as good's retract his opinion now, as do it at another time."
Meaning on a motion for a new trial
for misdirection of the Judge on a point
of Law.

[65]

March 10th
Same day

Thomas
Smith
[left margin, ll. 13, 14]

———

Lord Mansfield did not think fit to
take any notice of all this.
Compare this with some
maneuvres of the <u>little</u> GODS
of the North.[91]
Mr. C C Pinkney who was a member
of the General Assembly told me that the
members of the house, like those of the
Commons of England always sat with
their hats on.
Dined with Mr. Thomas Smith;[92]
several Gentlemen and ladies: decent and
plenteous table of meats: the upper cloth removed, a compleat
table of puddings, pies, tarts, custards
sweet-meats, oranges, Macarones
etc. etc.—profuse
Excellent wines—no politicks.

91. According to my co-editor Neil York, the reference almost certainly refers to John Stuart, 3rd Earl of Bute (1713–1799), who was notorious for legal manipulation. See *Dictionary of
National Biography* (concise edition), *supra*, vol. 2, p. 2024. This was not a reference to the justices of the Superior Court of Judicature of Massachusetts! While some of the justices, particularly Chief Justice Hutchinson, could be sensitive and a bit pompous, Quincy rarely criticized
them. See, for example, Hutchinson's Charge to the Grand Jury, March term, 1768, *Reports,
Quincy Papers*, vol. 4, pp. 258–270.
    92. Residing on Broad Street. *Charleston in the Age of the Pinckneys.*

[66]*

Evening
March 11th

——

Spent the Evening at the Assembly. Bad musick,
good dancing, elegantly disposed
supper, bad provisions, worse
dressed.

Roger
Smith
[left margin, ll. 7, 10]

March 11th
[left margin, l. 5]

Dined with Mr. Roger Smith,[93] son
to Mr. Thomas Smith: good deal of
company, elegant table, and the best provisions I have seen in their town.
One Cloth removed, a handsome
desert of most kinds of Nicknakes.[94]

93. Roger Smith (1745–1805), cousin of Thomas Loughton Smith. Supporter of Whigs and
early advocate and committee member of Non-importation Association, 1769. Married to Mary
Rutledge, daughter of John Rutledge. Walter Edgar and N. Louise Bailey, *Biographical Directory of the South Carolina House of Representatives, Vol. II, 1692–1775* (Columbia, S.C., 1977), p.
635.
94. From "knick-knack," "trifle," here a dessert consisting of different kinds of "light, dainty"
sweets. See *Oxford English Dictionary, supra,* vol. 1, p. 1546.

[*66 continued*]

Good wines and much festivity.
Two ladies being called on for toasts,
the one gave—"Delicate pleasures
to susceptible minds." The other,
"When passions rise may reason
be the guide."
In company were two of the
late appointed assistant Justices
from G[reat]B[ritain]. Their behavior by
no means abated my zeal against
British

NB. This Gentleman tho' he appeared not above 29, or 30, had been
4 years of the General Assembly, for St. Phillips—Parish, Charlestown
[left margin, ll. 11–16]

[67]

Bee
[left margin, l. 7]

_____

British appointments: one of
them appeared, in aspect, phiz,
conversation etc. very near an
_____[95]

In company dined on Mr. Thomas
Bee, a planter of considerable opulence.
A gentleman of sense, improvement, and
politeness; and one of the members of the
house;—just upon the point of marrying
Mrs. McKenzie, a young widow of about 20
with 8000 or 9000 guineas independant
fortune in specie, and daughter to
Mr. Thomas Smith.[96]
From Mr. Bee, I received an assurance of the
truth of what I had before heard:
that a few years ago,[97] the assistant
Judges of the Superior Court of the province,
being natives, men of abilities,
fortune and good fame, an act of
assembly passed to settle 300 Sterling[98] a

95. Expletive deleted? An "ass"?
96. Thomas Bee (1725–1812) was an active Revolutionary from South Carolina. He served as Lieutenant Governor of South Carolina from 1779–1780, was a member of the Continental Congress from 1780–1782, and was appointed a Judge of the United States Court for the District of South Carolina in 1790. See *Biographical Directory of the United States Congress*, United States Government Printing Office (2005), p. 632. See note 81, *supra*. Approximate Currency Equivalencies: 8000–9000 Guineas = £8,400–9,450 = $8,400,000–9,450,000 (2004).
97. Howe, *Proceedings*, 1915–1916 [FN 448-3]. April 1768.
98. Approximate Currency Equivalencies: £300 Sterling = $300,000 (2004).

[68]

———

Sterling a year upon them, when the
king should grant them Commissions
quam diu se bene gesserint.[99] The
act being sent home for concurrence
was disallowed, and the reasons assigned was the above clause.
I am promised by Mr. Bee a trans-
script of the Reasons of disallowance
with the Attorney and Solicitor—general's
opinion relative to the act.[100]
Upon this, the assembly passed an
act to establish the like salary payable out of any monies that shall
be in the treasury, not restricting it
to any alteration in the tenure of
their commission.—
Mark the sequel. No Assistant Judges
had ever before been nominated in
England. Immediately upon the
king's approving this last act, Lord
Hillsborough[101] in his zeal for American

99. "As long as they shall behave themselves." *Black's Law Dictionary*, 1406 (Revised 4th ed. 1968).

100. Howe, *Proceedings*, 1915–1916 [FN 448-4]. *Acts of the Privy Council* (Colonial), 1766–1783, 166.

101. Wills Hill, Second Viscount Hillsborough (1718–1793). Secretary of State for Colonies, 1768–1772. *Dictionary of National Biography*, XXVI, 427.

[69]

———

good forthwith sends over, one Chief Justice, and two assistant Justices,
Irishmen, the other two, was the
one a Scotchman, and the other
a Welshman.[102]
How long will the simple love their
simplicity? And ye, who assume
the guileful name, the venerable
pretext of friends to Government, how
long will ye deceive and be deceived.
Surely in a political sense, the
Americans—"are lighted the
"way—to study wisdom."[103]
I have conversed with upwards
of one half the members of the
General Assembly and many other ranks of men on this matter.
They see their error, and confess it:
they own it a rash, imprudent, hasty
step, and bitterly repent it. A
Committee of the house has ranked

102. Howe, *Proceedings*, 1915–1916 [FN 449-1]. From Ramsay (*History of South Carolina*, II. 154) it may be assumed that these appointments were made in 1771. The chief justice was Thomas Knox Gordon, and the three assistants, Edward Savage, John Murray and John Fewtrell. But Quincy's characterization nevertheless assumes five appointments!
103. See FN 33, *supra*. Shakespeare, *Macbeth* (soliloquy) Act 5, Scene 5, Lines 19–28.

[70]

——

it in their list of grievances.
The only solamen[104] is—"it is done:
we will take care, never to do the
like again." The only apology
is, that the assistant Judges of the
provinces were unwilling to
have Circuit Courts without a fixed salary: the remote parts of the province
complained of being obliged to attend
all causes at Charlestown: they
had great reason of complaint:
the regulaters of this province were
up as well as those of N[orth] Carolina:
Such was the influence of some,
that upon the disallowance of the first
act, that no act for creating Circuit
Courts could be got thro' till salaries
were fixed.—May heaven for-
give, but the people never forget
them! Think you, that they who

104. Latin: *solamen*, "a means of consolation, comfort." *Cassell's Latin Dictionary* (rev. ed. J.R.V. Marchant, J. F. Charles), London, 1949, 529. (Hereafter, "*Cassell's.*") See Johnson's *Dictionary, supra*, n.p. "solace."

[71]

_____

eyed the fleece, have got it? NO!
As in like cases—American
fools—thirsting for honour and riches—
beat the Bush:—British harpies[105]
seize—<u>the poor bird</u>.[106]—Right-
eous is the measure of GOD.
Spent a most agreeable evening with
Mr. R[oger] S[mith] and was entertained with much
genteel supper.
I also have learned from several
Gentlemen that it was common in this
province for an executor of a will
to make several hundred guineas[107]
by his office;—and that with reputation.
Mr. R[oger] S[mith] told he made the last year,
by 3 ex[ecut]orships upwards of Seven
hundred guineas[108]; and Mr. Bee told me,
that Thomas L Smith's father
made 10,000 Sterling[109] and more the
same way.
Who would not be <u>his own</u> Executor?

105. "[A] kind of birds which had the faces of women, and foul long claws, very filthy crea-
tures." Johnson's *Dictionary*, *supra*, n.p. "harpy."
106. "And while I at length debate and beate the bush,
There shall steppe in other men and catch the burdes." John Heywood (1497–1580)
Proverbes, Part I, Chap. II. See also Plutarch (46–120) *Of Garruity*.
107. Approximate Currency Equivalencies: 300 Guineas = £315 = $315,000 (2004).
108. Approximate Currency Equivalencies: 700 Guineas = £375 = $375,000 (2004).
109. Approximate Currency Equivalencies: £10,000 Sterling = $10 million (2004).

[72]

1773
March 12th

Thos Lynch
[left margin, l. 3]

——

Dined with Thomas Lynch Esq.,[110]
a plain, sensible, honest man,
upon a solid, plentiful, good
table; with very good wines.

NB I was
Introduced by
Thomas
Smith Esq.
[left margin, ll. 8–11]

Spent the Evening with the Friday-night
Club, consisting of the more elder
substantial gentlemen: About
20 or 30 in Company. Conversation
on negroes, Rice, and the necessity of
British Regular troops to be quartered in
Charlestown: there were not want-
ing men of fortune, sense & attach-
ment to their country, who were
zealous for the establishing such troops
here.

110. Thomas Lynch (1727–1776). South Carolina legislator; with Christopher Gadsden and John Rutledge, represented South Carolina in Stamp Act Congress, 1765. Served as a member of the First and Second Continental Congresses, 1774–76. *Dictionary of American Biography*, XI, 523. See *Illustration 11*.

ILLUSTRATION 11. Portrait of Thomas Lynch Jnr. (1749–1779). Thomas Lynch Snr. was Quincy's dinner host on March 12th. He was known for his "plain, sensible" appearance. "He wears his hair strait, his clothes in the plainest order." E. C. Burnett, *Letters of Members of the Continental Congress* (1921) vol. 1, p. 8. He was a wealthy planter, his grandfather having settled in South Carolina shortly after its settlement. He was a member of the First and Second Continental Congresses (1774–1775). His son, Thomas Lynch Jnr., was sent to England; to Eton, Cambridge and then to Middle Temple (1764–1772), from whence he had just returned. He signed the Declaration of Independence, but had feeble health. He died in 1779 when he and his wife took passage to the West Indies and the South of France for his health and his ship was lost. See generally *Dictionary of American Biography*, XI, 523–524. From the collections of the South Carolina Historical Society. Courtesy, South Carolina Historical Society.

[*72 continued*]

I took some share in this conversation;
and can't but hope I spoke conviction to many sensible minds. At
the Close of the Evening, plans were agitated
for the making a certain part of the

[73]

with Mr. Brewton

———

militia of the province (to take
in rotation) answer instead
of foreign aid.[111]
I here learned in a side conversation,
that two of the late Assistant-Judges ⊗
of the Supreme Court (men too of
great opulence!) who were in the
General Assembly at the time of the Act
mentioned 2 pages back, were
the very means of getting it passed:
Quid non mortalia pectora cogis
Auri sacra fames?[112] That they
hoping to enjoy the Emoluments of
the grant were hot, zealous and perpe-
tually persevering till they got it
thro': He informed me also of the
specious arguments they used, and the
advantages that they took of the popular
commotions. Good heavens, how much
more noble a part might they have taken: They are
now knawing their tongues in rage.

⊗ Gentlemen now in
high and popular repute.
[left margin, ll. 7–9]

---

111. Was the plan to substitute militia, in rotation, for British regulars?
112. Virgil, *Aeneid* 3.56: "Oh cursed hunger for gold, to what do you not drive the hearts of men."

[74]

1773
March 13th

T L
Smith
[left margin, ll. 4, 5]

———

Spent all the morning transcribing
Mr. Edward Rutledge MS law
Reports.[113] At XI set off <u>in State</u> for
the Retreat of T L Smith Esq.
Dined there and spent the remainder of
the Day.
This Day spent the most agreably of
any since my arrival in Charles-
town.
A most delightful place indeed!

March 14.

Bad weather: spent the day at my lodgings.

---

113. Quincy's copy of Rutledge's Reports is still in the Massachusetts Historical Society, Quincy Family Papers, No. 60 (Micro. Reel 4). Edward Rutledge (1749–1800) was admitted to Middle Temple on January 12, 1767 and called to the English bar on July 3, 1772. He was one of five Middle Templers to sign the Declaration of Independence. Like Quincy, he initially sought a conciliation with Britain, supporting Joseph Galloway's "Plan of a Proposed Union between Great Britain and the Colonies" in 1774. Following the Revolution in which he fought bravely, he was elected Governor of South Carolina. "He was stiffly conservative and rarely conceded anything to the democratic elements of the state." *Dictionary of American Biography*, XVI, 258. John Adams strongly disliked him. See E. Alfred Jones, *American Members of the Inns of Court* (London, 1924), 189–190. See also note 87, *supra*. Quincy, of course, had begun his own *Reports* in 1762. See "Introduction," *Reports, Quincy Papers*, vols. 4 and 5.

[74 continued]

Visited by Mr. Lynch, Deis, and others.
Mr. Lynch gave me a long account of
the conduct of the Regulators[114]; with the cause
of their ill-success; the Ease with which Tryon[115]
might have been defeated.
He said he had the best information of
the facts he related, and good grounds for
his opinions on the matter.

114. "The name 'Regulator' was adopted at a meeting held at Sandy Creek . . . on the 22d of March, 1767, at which a written agreement was drawn up and an association was formed 'for regulating public grievances.' This agreement contemplated no violence, and only bound the signers to pay no more taxes until satisfied they were agreeable to law and were properly applied . . . But their leader, Herman Husbands, though uneducated, was a mischievous and turbulent demagogue and a canting hypocrite . . . He set himself diligently to work to inflame the passions of the people, to exaggerate the evils of which they justly complained, and to incite them to violence." Alfred Moore Waddell, *A Colonial Officer and His Times, 1754–1773* (Raleigh, N.C., 1890), p. 134. "At Hillsboro, in September [1770], when the Court met, with Judge Henderson presiding, the greatest outrage or series of outrages yet perpetrated by the Regulators took place. [Threatened,] the Judge adjourned the Court and that night fled the town. They then held a mock court, and made scandalous entries on the docket. On the 12th of November they burned Judge Henderson's barn, and on the 14th his house." *Id.* at 138–39. On May 16, 1771, the conflict came to a boil with 1100 of Governor Tryon's army facing 2000 Regulators at the Battle of Alamance, a river. Governor's army: 9 killed, 60 wounded; Regulators: 20 killed, unknown wounded. *Id.* at 140–41. The rebellion was ended and "Tryon left North Carolina about a month after the battle of Alamance, to become Governor of New York." *Id.* at 158.

115. Howe, *Proceedings*, 1915–1916 [FN 450-2]. William Tryon (1725–1788), governor of New York (1771) and North Carolina (1765), *Dictionary of National Biography*, LVII, 276. Upon the death of Governor Dobbs, Tryon succeeded to the Governorship and qualified on the 3d April, 1765. He still retained his rank in the British army and his place in the regular line of promotion. *Id.* at 73.

[75]

1773
March 15th

Lynch,
Rutledge
Brewton
[left margin, ll. 3, 5, 8]

———

Dined with company at Mr. Lynch's
on Turtle.[116] —
Spent the morning and afternoon in
transcribing Law reports of Edw[ar]d
Rutledge Esq. late Student in
the Temple.[117]
Spent the evening with Monday-night
Clubb; introduced by Mr. Brewton.
Cards, feasting, and indifferent wines.
NB. This was at a Tavern, and was
the first time of my meeting with
ordinary wines since my being
at Charlestown.

116. Turtle, often from Chesapeake Bay, was a delicacy of the eighteenth century.
117. Rutledge was admitted to Middle Temple on January 12, 1767. See notes 87 and 113, *supra*.

[*75 continued*]

March 16.
[left margin, l. 14]

Bee
[left margin, l. 16]

Spent this morning ever since 5 o'Clock
in perusing Public Records of the Province
which I was favored with by the worthy
Mr. Bee:—have marked many to
be Copied for me:—am now going to the famous Races.

[76]

1773
March 16.
[left margin, l. 9]

Miles
Brewton

[left margin, ll. 11, 12]

———

The races were well performed, but
Flimnap beat Little David, (who had
won the 16 Last Races) out and out: The
last heat the former distant the latter.
The first 4 mile heat was performed in
8 m[inutes] and 17 seconds, being 4 miles.—
2000£ sterling[118] was one [sic] and lost at the
Race, and Flimnap sold at Public
Vendue[119] the same Day for £300 sterling.[120]
Took a family-dinner with Mr.
Brewton—had a fine dish of
Politicks—had further light from
one of the Company (a prerogative—
man) into the Arts used to disunite
the Colonies. Sounded Mr. Brewton
and Mr. Erving[121], when alone, with
regard to a general and permanent
Continental literary correspondence:

118. Approximate Currency Equivalencies: £2,000 Sterling = $2 million (2004).
119. ["Vendue"]: "a public auction." *Concise Oxford Dictionary*, p. 1361.
120. Approximate Currency Equivalencies: £300 Sterling = $300,000 (2004).
121. For Miles Brewton (1732–1775) see note 72, *supra* and *Color Plate 1, supra*. "Mr. Erving" was possibly James Irving, merchant; who dealt dry goods in 1740s–1750s. He was associated with Robert Pringle. *South Carolina Historical Magazine*, vol. 86, pp. 200, 202.

[*76 continued*]

the matter taken mightily.
At the Races I saw a prodigious fine collection of excellent, tho' very high-prized
horses—and was let a little into the
singular art and mystery of the Turff.

[77]

1773
March 17th

Spent all the morning in copying Mr.
Rutledge's Reports. Feasted with
the Sons of St. Patrick. While at
Dinner 6 violins, 2 hautboys and basoon with a Hand-tabor beat excellently well.
After Dinner 6 French horns
in concert—most surpassing
musick!—Two solos on the
French horn by one who is said to blow
the finest horn in the world: he has
50 Guinea[122] for the Season from the St.
Cecilia—Society.

March 18th

Brewton
[left margin, l. 18]

————

Spent in Reading further reports
of Mr. R[utledge]—paying complementary
visits of Departure, and in prepe-
ration for my Journey
Northward.
NB This day advanced to Miles Brewton Esq.

122. Approximate Currency Equivalencies: 50 Guineas = £5, 6 shillings = $52,500 (2004).

[*77 continued*]

thirty one pounds sterling[123] for one pipe[124] of Best London
Particular Madeira Wine to be sent for to the house of
Puntalium Fernandez and Co. in Madeira—and
Took Mr. Brewton's Receipt of this date.

123. Approximate Currency Equivalencies: £31 Sterling = $31,000 (2004).
124. ["Pipe"]: "A liquid measure containing two hogsheads." Johnson's *Dictionary*, *supra*,
n.p. "pipe." A hogshead contained sixty gallons. *Id.*, "hogshead." Quincy had ordered 480 quarts
of Madeira, or over 738 bottles at 1.3 pints a bottle!

[78]

March 19th

——

By reason of an order of the house of
Assembly enjoining attendance of all
the members, Mr. Lynch cannot set
out:—I am therefore to be detained this day.
Spent all the morning in hearing the debates of the
House—had an opportunity of hearing the best
speakers in the province.
The first thing done at the meeting of the house
is to bring the mace **X** and lay it on the table before the speaker. This I am told is the way
in the Commons of G[reat]B[ritain].
The next thing is for the Clerk to read over in
a very audible voice, the doings of the
preceeding day.
The speaker is robed in black and has a
very large Wigg of State, when he goes
to attend the Chair (with the Mace borne before
him) on Delivery of speeches etc.
T Lynch Esq. spoke like a man of sense
and a patriot—with dignity, free, and laconism.
Gadsen Esq.[125] was plain, blunt, hot and

125. Thomas Lynch (1727–1776) was a wealthy patron of distinguished lineage. He was a member of the First and Second Continental Congresses (1774, 1776). Illness prevented further public service. See *Dictionary of American Biography*, XI, 523. Christopher Gadsden (1724–1805), with Thomas Lynch and John Rutledge, represented South Carolina in Stamp Act Congress, 1765. He served as a member of the First and Second Continental Congresses, 1774, 1776. *Dictionary of American Biography*, VII, 81.

[*78 continued*]

incorrect tho' very sensible. In many
respects he resembles Bowers.[126] In the
course of the debate, he used these very

[Added, Left Margin, next to "mace **X**"]
X A very superb and elegant one
which cost 90 Guineas.[127]
[left margin, ll. 9–11]

126. Howe, *Proceedings*, 1915–1916 [FN 452-2]. Jerathmeel Bowers.
127. Approximate Currency Equivalencies: 90 Guineas = £94, 10 shillings = $94,500 (2004).

[79]

———

singular expressions for a member of
parliament—"And, Mr. Speaker, if
"the government and Council don't see fit to fall
"in with Us, I say, let the General duty
"law, go to the Devil, Sir."—And
"we go about our business!"
Parsons, Jno. Rutledge, and Old Charles Pinckney, (the three first-lawyers in the
Province) spoke on the occasion:—the
two last very good speakers indeed.[128]
The members of the house all set with
their hats on, and uncover when they
rise to speak: they are not confined (at least they did not confine
themselves) to any one place to
speak in.
The members conversed, lolled, and
chatted much like a friendly jovial
society, when nothing of importance
was before the house:—nay once or twice
while the Speaker and clerk were busy in
writing the members spoke quite loud
across the room to one another.—A
very unparliamentary appearance.

128. Howe, *Proceedings*, 1915–1916 [FN 452-3]. James Parsons (d. 1779), of the Council of Safety. For Pinckney, see notes 77, 80, 87 and *Illustrations 9* and *10*, *supra*. For Rutledge, see note 123.

[80]

1773
March 17th

——

The speaker put the Q[uestio]ns sitting, and conversed with the House sitting: the
members gave their votes by
rising from their seats—the
dissentients did not rise.

March 20th
[left margin, l. 6]

Set out with Mr. Lynch for his plantation
on Santee river on any way to the
Northward. In crossing Hobcaw—
ferry we were awed by 6 Negroes
4 of whom had nothing on but
their kind of breeches, scarce sufficient for covering.
Had a most agreeable ride, and received much
information from Mr. Lynch of the
maneuvers at the Congress
in 1765: his relation was by no
means favorable to a certain celebrated Northern Patriot;[129] and the con-

129. For Thomas Lynch (1727–1776), see note 110, *supra*, and *Illustration 11*, with accompanying note, at p 191, *supra*. The "celebrated Northern Patriot" has not been identified. Possibly
James Otis Jr. or Timothy Ruggles of the Massachusetts delegation.

[*80 continued*]

duct of Livingston[130] (as L[ynch] exhibit-
ed it) ought to be remember-
ed with unrelenting indignation
[line crossed out]
Caesar Rodney of Pennsylvania[131]
Lynch and Gadsen of So[uth] Carolina
were heroes and patriots.

NB. From what I learned from Mr. Lynch it is worth trying the experiment
of planting Rice in our low, marshy lands, for the pur-pose of feeding cows
and making the most excellent flavored and yellow butter.—He said he did
not doubt it would answer well. [left margin, written with the page turned
90° counter-clockwise, ll. 9–24]

130. Probably Phillip Livingston, delegate to both Continental Congresses. Robert R. Livingston entered only the second. The Stamp Act Congress met at New York. Delegates from nine colonies attended from October 7 to October 19, 1765. Howe, *Proceedings*, 1915–1916 [FN 452-4]. Howe was incorrect, since Robert R. Livingston did indeed attend the Stamp Act Congress. While there he proposed a plan of intercolonial union to assign quotas to each colony for imperial taxes, a very controverted idea. Thus, it may well have been Robert Livingston to which Quincy referred.

131. Caesar Rodney (1728–1784), delegate to Continental Congress, 1775, 1778. *Dictionary of American Biography*, XVI, 81. Caeser Rodney did not sit for Pennsylvania, but for Delaware. Quincy was probably confused. My thanks to co-editor Neil York.

[81]

1773
March 21.

————

Mr. Lynch's plantation is very pleasantly situated and is very valuable.
[5 lines heavily crossed out]
Had a three hours tedious passage
Santee-river: Crossed Georgetown
river or Sam-pit River just at dark.
Lodged in the town and am now held
in duress by a very high equinoxial
gale from Crossing Wineyaw-bay,[132]
formed by the union of Waccamaw [Winyaw],
Pedee [Pee Dee] and Black rivers. 'Tis prodigious fine traveling weather and
requires no small share of philosophy to be contented with my
situation.
NB. I had a very fine view of a white
Squirrel this day, in traveling thro'
the woods.

132. Winyaw Bay.

[82]

1773
22nd March

Joseph
Allston
[left margin, ll. 5, 9]

———

Spent this night with Mr. Joseph Allston[133]
a gentleman of immense income all of
his own acquisition: He is a person
between 39 and 40, and a very few years
ago begun the world with only 5
negroes—has now 5 plantations,
with an 100 slaves on each. He told
me his neat income was but about
5 or 6000 £ sterling[134] a year, he is
reputed much richer. His plantation, negroes, gardens etc. are
in the best order of any I have
seen: He has propag[at]ed the Lisbon
and Wine Island grapes with great
success. I was entertained with
more true hospitality and benevolence by this family than any I
had met with. His good lady

133. Self-made fortune as planter; began with five slaves and, by 1773, had expanded to 100 slaves and an income of £5000–£6000 Sterling [$5 million–$6 million (2004)] per year. Walter Edgar and N. Louise Bailey, *Biographical Directory of the South Carolina House of Representatives, Vol. II, 1692–1775*, p. 35.

134. Approximate Currency Equivalencies: £5000–£6000 Sterling = $5 million–$6 million (2004).

[82 continued]

filled a wallet, with bread, biscuit,
wine, fowle and tongue, and presented
it next morning. The wine I declined, but gladly received the rest. At
about 12 o'Clock in a sandy pine

[83]

———

desert I enjoyed a fine regalement;
and having met with a refreshing
spring, I remembered the worthy
Mr. Allston and Lady with more warmth
of affection and hearty benisons,
than ever I toasted King or
Queen, Saint or Hero.
This Gentleman sent his servant as
our guide between 30 and 40 miles
much to our preservation
from very vexatious difficulties.

1773
24th March

Mr. Withers
[left margin, l. 14]

———

Lodged the last night at the Plantation of Mr.
Johnston,[135] (who is now at Charlestown)
Mr. Withers, Brother in law to Mr. Joseph
Allston came as our guide about 10
miles.
A most barren, deary rode: 9 cows and oxen
had perish within a week for want
of sustenance: great difficulty to get
food for man or beast.

135. Brother-in-Law to Joseph Allston; married Esther Allston. Walter Edgar and N. Louise Bailey, *Biographical Directory of the South Carolina House of Representatives, Vol. II, 1692–1775*, pp. 371–372.

[84]

1773
25th March
———

This day left the province of South Carolina
and entered that of the North

Gen[era]l remarks
            and   } on So[uth] Carolina
Observ[ati]ons

The constitution of So[uth] C[arolina] is in very many
respects defective and in an equal num-
ber extremely bad.
The inhabitants may well be divided into
opulent and lordly planters, poor and spiritless peasants and vile slaves.
Having blended with every order of men
as much as was possible and convenient, I
had considerable opportunity to learn their
manners, genius, taste etc.
The whole body almost of this people
seem averse to the claims and assump-
tions of the British Legislature over the
Colonies; but you will seldom hear
even in political conversations any
warm or animated expressions against the
measures of administration. Their fiercer
passions seem to be employed upon

[85]

——

their slaves and here to expend themselves. A general doubt of the firm-
ness and integrity of the Northern colonies
is prevalent: they say the M[assachusetts] Bay
can talk, vote and resolve—but their
doings are not correspondent:[136] sentiments and expressions of this kind
are common and fasionable; they
arise from various causes: I imagine from envy and jealously in some, and
from artifice in others: the very remarkable difference in their manners
and religious tenets and notions con-
tribute to the same effect.
It may well be questioned whether
in reality there is any 3d branch in
the Cons[titu]tion of this government.[137] 'Tis true
they have a house of assembly: but
who do they represent? The laborer,
the mechanic, the tradesman, the
farmer, husbandman or yeoman?
No. The representatives are almost
if not wholly rich planters:—the

136. "Suitable," "agreeable," "answerable." Johnson, *Dictionary, supra,* n.p. "correspondent."
137. A reference to John Locke (1632–1704), *Two Treatises on Civil Government* (London, 1690), Chap. XIX. See Quincy, Estate Catalogue, item 43.

[86]

———

Planting interest is therefore represented but I conceive nothing else (as <u>it</u>
<u>ought to be</u>.)
At present, the house of Assembly ^X are
staunch Colonists. But what is it
owing to? Bad policy on the other
side the water. The members of this
house are all very wealthy, and such
kind of men have in general but little
solicitude about the interests or concerns
of <u>the many</u>: and frequently the fittest
instruments to inslave and oppress
the commonality. Such extravagant
disproportion in property is to the
last degree impolite and dangerous.
The Council, Judges and other great offi-
cers are all appointed by mandamus from G[reat]B[ritain]
nay the Clerk of the Board and Assembly.
Who are and have been thus appointed? Indigent and ____ persons,
disconnected and obnoxious to the people.
I heard several of the planters say, "we
"none of Us, when we grow old can
"expect the honour of the State—they

[Added, Left Margin, next to "house of Assembly ^X"]
X Non-residents may be chosen to represent any town, if
they have lands in the county; and hence a great majority of
the house are dwellers in Charlestown, where the body of
Planters reside during the sickly months. A fatal kind of policy!
[left margin, ll. 4–18]

[87]

———

"are all given away to worthless
"poor rascals."
The planter (like the fox) prides
himself in saying the grapes are
sower:[138] his fortune inclines and
makes him look with contempt on
the official grandee.—Thus the
rights and liberties of the State are in
some measure safe—but from
a very unstable cause.
This government is composed of two aristocratic parts and one monarchical body:
the aristocratic parts mutually
dislike each other.—Let us suppose
a change in British policy.
Compose the Council of the first planters,
fill all the Public offices with them—
give them the honour of the State, and
tho' they don't want them, give
them it and emoluments also:—
introduce Baronies and Lordships—their
enormous estates will bear it

138. "Sour." A reference to the fable of the fox and the grapes in Aesop. See Howatson, *supra*,
p. 231.

[88]

———

What will become of Carolinian freedom?
The luxury, disipation, life, sentiments
and manners, of the leading people naturally tend to make them neglect, dispise, and be careless of the true interests
of mankind in general.—
Hence we may suppose, that when a
different policy is gone into with regard
to this people, there will be a very
calamitous alteration in the views and conduct of the Planters and therefore
also with regard to
the true interests of the province.
State, magnificence and ostentation, the
natural attendants of riches, are con-
spicuous among this people: the number and subjection of their slaves tend
this way. Cards, dice, the bottle and
horses engross prodigious portions of
time and attention: The Gentlemen (planters and merchants) are mostly men
of the turff and gamesters. Political en-
quiries and philosophie disquisitions are
too laborious for them: they have no great
passion for to shine and blaze in the
forum or Senate.[139]

———

139. Another indication of Quincy's dedication to the Republican ideals of Cicero. See
Quincy, Estate Catalogue, Item 256, *Quincy Papers*, vol. 5, *Reports*, Appendix 9.

[89]

——

The yeomanry and husbandmen make
a very different figure from those of
New England: the middling order in
the Capital are odious characters.
The state of Religion here is repug-
nant not only to the ordinances and institutions of Jesus Christ, but to every
law of sound policy.
The Sabbath is a day of visiting & mirth
with the Rich, and of license, pastime and frolic for the negroes. The blacks I saw
in great numbers playing pawpaw, huzzle-cap, push
penny,[140] and quarrelling round the doors
of the Churches in service time—
and as to their priests—Voltaire
says—"always speak well of the

---

140. "Huzzlecap" was a game of pitching pennies. "Shove-half penny" or "Shove ha'penny" was "an English pub game that involves sliding an object (usually a coin) along a polished surface towards a marked scoring area." See Adah Parker Strobell, *"Like It Was": Colonial Games 'n Fun Handbook* (Acropolis Books, 1975). "While shuffle-board was a game enjoyed primarily by the wealthy, its miniaturized form, shove-halfpenny, has always been a tavern sport. As such, it was outlawed throughout much of history. During the reign of Henry VIII, a landlord who allowed the game in his pub could be fined the sum 40s. Shove-halfpenny goes by several names: slide-thrift, shove-groat, push penny, and an 18th-century variation known as Justice Jarvis." *Id.* Special thanks to Mark Sullivan. The editor of this volume is still seeking a description of "pawpaw," perhaps a reference to the fruit? ("Picking up pawspaws, put them in a basket.") "Pawpaw" is another term for the Caribbean papaya fruit, "an elongated melon-shaped fruit with an edible orange flesh and small black seeds." *The Concise Oxford Dictionary* (ed. R. E. Allen, 8th edition, Oxford, 1990), p. 874. Games were originally discouraged by the Puritans, and the freedom to play games had symbolic importance. "So notions of 'liberty' would seem to have grown beyond the purely political definition, and games were one little expression of Americans' new freedom to enjoy life." "Gaming in the Early 19th Century," http://www .goreplace.org/newsletter/articleGaming.htm. How even more symbolic for African-Americans!

[*89 continued*]

prior."[141]—The slaves who don't
frolic on the Sabbath, do all kinds
of work for themselves on hire.
The ladies of Charlestown want
much of the fire and vivacity of the North,
or I want taste and discernment.

141. This was almost certainly an ironic comment. See page 215 [122], *infra*. Voltaire's *Letters* were in Quincy's library. See Quincy, Estate Catalogue, *infra*, Items 213, 290.

[90]

————

There being but one chief place of
trade it's increase is amazingly
rapid:—the stories you are every
where told of rise in the value of
lands seem Romantic, but I was
assured they were fact.
There is a large Colossal statue of Mr. Pitt[142]
in Charlestown much praised by
many. The drapery was exquisitely
well done: but to me, the attitude,
air and expression of the piece was bad.
The staple commodities are Rice,
Indigo, hemp, tobacco, peas, skins and naval
stores: the two first are the capital: the
general topics of conv[ersati]on, when cards,
the bottle and occurrences of the day
don't intervene are of negroes, and
the price of Indigo and Rice: I was sur-
prized to find this so general.
Compared with the Inhabitants of N[ew]E[ngland]
I think it no injustice to say there
are here few men of Letters and
science

142. William Pitt, Earl of Chatham (1708–1778), "the Great Commoner," was the most powerful Whig of his day. His consistent opposition to taxing the American colonies made him a
natural hero there. Howe, *Proceedings*, 1915–1916 [FN 456-1]. See Huger Smith, in *S.C. Hist. and
Gen. Mag.*, XV. 18; and C. H. Hart, in *Proceedings*, XLVIII, 291. Quincy also noted a statue of
Pitt in New York. See note 321, *supra*.

[91]

——

Slavery may truely be said to be the
peculiar curse of this land:
Strange infatuation! It is generally
thought and called by the people it's
blessing. Applicable indeed to this
people and their slaves are the words
of Our Milton—
—   "So perfect in their misery,
Not one perceive their foul disfigurement."[143]
A few years ago; it is allowed, that the Blacks
exceeded the Whites as 17 to 1. There are
those who now tell you, that the
Slave are not more that 3 to 1,
some pretend not so many. But
they who talk thus are afraid that
the Slaves should by some means
discover their superiority: many
people express great fears of an
insurrection, others treat the idea
as chimerical. I took great pains
(finding much contrariety of opinion) to find out the true proportion:

143. John Milton's 1634 play, *Comus* (l. 64) reads "And they, so perfect in their misery, Not once perceive their foul disfigurement." Quincy had an excellent collection of Milton's works at his death two years later. See Quincy, Estate Catalogue, items 28, 178, 182, 323.

[92]

———

the best information I could obtain
fixes it at about 7 to 1, my own
observation leads me to think
it much greater.[144]
The brutality used towards the slaves
has a very bad tendency with reference
to the manners of the people, but a
much worse with regard to the youth.
They will plead in their excuse—
"this severity is necessary." But whence did or does this
necessity arise? From the necessity
of having vast multitudes sunk
in barbarism, ignorance and the
basest and most servile employ!
By reason of this Slavery; the
children are early impressed with
infamous and destructive ideas, and
become extremely vitiated in their
manners—they contract a negroish
kind of accent, pronunciation, and
dialect,[145] as well as ridiculous kind

144. Recent scholarship agrees with Quincy. "[L]ow-country South Carolina planters [were] . . . surrounded and outnumbered by slaves—in some regions by as much as seven or eight to one . . ." Richard R. Beeman, *The Varieties of Political Experience in Eighteenth-Century America* (Philadelphia, 2004), p. 135.

145. Quincy was one of the first to observe candidly that cultural influence went both ways between blacks and whites, with important linguistic, cultural, and artistic consequences. Yet he was not advanced enough to see this could be culturally enriching.

[93]

——

of behavior:—even many of the
grown people, and especially the
women, are vastly infected with the
same disorder. Parents instead
of talking to their very young
children in the
unmeaning way with us, converse
to them as tho' they were speak[ing]
to a new imported African.
From the same cause have their
Legislators enacted laws touching negroes, mulattoes and masters which
savor
more of the policy of Pandemonium[146]
than the English constitution:—
laws which will stand eternal records of
the depravity and contradiction of the
human character: laws which would
disgrace the tribunal of Scythian,
Aral, Hottentot and Barbarian[147] are
appealed to in decisions upon life
limb and liberty by those who assume
the name of Englishmen, freemen
and Christians:—the place of trial

146. A scene of "uproar, utter confusion." The "place of all demons in Milton's *Paradise Lost*." *Concise Oxford Dictionary*, 859.

147. The Scythians were the scourge of the Greeks and the Persians, sweeping out of Southern Russia. The Arals, natives of today's Kazakhstan and Uzbekistan, had an equally unsavory reputation. The Hottentots are the native peoples of Namibia and South West Africa. They were decimated by the Dutch settlers. To the ethnocentric Quincy, they would all be "barbarians," i.e. "savages." See Johnson's *Dictionary*, n.p. "barbarian."

[94]

———

no doubt is called a Court of Justice and
equity—but the Judges have forgot a maxim of English law—
<u>Jura naturalia sunt immutabilia</u>[148]
and they would do well to remember
that no laws of the (little)
creature supercede the laws
of the (great) creator. Can the
institutions of man
make void the decree of GOD!
These are but a small part of the
mischief of Slavery—new ones
are every day arising—futurity
will produce more and greater.
Mr. Lynch told me, that he knew
several Negroes who had refused
to implore a forgiveness when
under sentence of death, tho' a

148. "The laws of nature are unchangeable." *Black's Law Dictionary*, 989 (Revised 4th ed. 1968). The marginal notation for this quotation is Sir Henry Hobart's *Reports in the Reign of James I* (London, 1641), covering the King's Bench in the years 1603–1625. It was republished several times, including a 1724 5th edition, and eventually had an American edition in 1829. See Sweet and Maxwell, *Legal Bibliography* (2nd ed., W. H. Maxwell, L. F. Maxwell), vol. 1, p. 301. See also William Wallace, *The Reporter* (Boston, 1882), pp. 220–229. The quotation is from *Day v. Savadge, Hobart's Reports* 85, at 87, where Hobart is reported to have said "even an Act of Parliament made against natural equity, as to make a man a judge in his own case, is void in itself, for *jura naturae sunt immutabilia* . . ." In this, Hobart is alluding to a similar passage in Edward Coke's famous report of *Dr. Bonham's Case*, 8 *Coke's Reports* 1136 (1610). See also Herbert Broom, *Legal Maxims* (10th ed., 1939, London, R. H. Kensley ed.), p. 72. Quincy included this maxim on page 71 of his maxims collection, citing to 7 *Coke's Reports, Hobart's Reports*, and St. Germain's *Doctor and Student*. See Appendix I, *Quincy Papers*, vol. 2, "The Latin Legal Maxims of Josiah Quincy, Jr.," p. [171]. My thanks to Elizabeth Papp Kamali for her invaluable work with Quincy's Latin Maxims.

[*94 continued*]

pardon was insured on this easy
term. Preferring death to their
deplorable state, they died with

See Lord Hobart's
Reports
[left margin, l. 4]

[95]

———

a temper deserving a better fate.
There is much among this people
of what the world call hospitality
and politeness, it may be questioned
what proportion there is of
true humanity, Christian charity
and love.

[96]

<table>
<tr><td>1773
March 26th</td><td>Wm Hill
Esq.
[left margin, ll. 3, 4]</td></tr>
</table>

———

Lodged the last night in North Carol[ina]:
at the house of William Hill Esq.[149]: a most
sensible, polite gentleman: tho' a Crown
officer,[150] a man replete with sentiments of
general liberty and warmly attached to the
cause of American freedom.—
Spent much of this day in public and
private conversation with Col. Robert
Howe,[151] a leading and active member
of the General Assembly. Fine natural parts,
great feeling, pure and elegant diction,
with much persuasive eloquence.
Tho' likewise a Crown Officer with a
lucrative post[152] a staunch whig and
colonist. I received much information
in provincial politicks and great
pleasure from his relation.
Hot and zealous in the Cause of America
he relished the proposed Continental

---

149. Possibly William Hill (1741–1816), who came to South Carolina from Ireland in 1761. Hill, a politician, served with distinction as a soldier under General Sumter. See *Dictionary of American Biography*, IX, 48.

150. Howe, *Proceedings*, 1915–1916 [FN 457-2]. Receiver of duties at Brunswick.

151. (1732–1786) Revolutionary major general, planter. Employed by General Washington until 1783. See *Dictionary of American Biography*, IX, 294.

152. Howe, *Proceedings*, 1915–1916 [FN 457-4]. Associate justice, and captain of Fort Johnston. See *Col. Rec. North Carolina*, IX, 798.

[*96 continued*]

correspondence, promised to promote it and write me by the first opportunity.
This Gentleman gave me at night a 3 hours
minute relation of the motives, views
and proceedings of the Regulators,

[97]

with a particular account of the battle of Alla-
manze,[153] and the proceedings of both
parties before and after the action.[154]
Being on the field he was able to give
me a good account.
I begun to change my opinion of the
Regulators and Governor Tryon—But
as is common on the next day.

27 March

Breakfasted with Col. Dry,[155] the Collec-
tor of the Customs and one of the Council.—A friend to the Regulators
and seemingly warm against the measures
of British and Continental administrations
he gave me an entire different
account of things. I am now left

---

153. Howe, *Proceedings*, 1915–1916 [FN 458-1]. J. S. Bassett, in *American Hist. Assn. Report*, 1894, 141.

154. The "Regulator Movement" in North Carolina (1764–1771) was an insurgency ostensibly to establish order and fight corruption. It pitted the frontier counties of North Carolina against the colonial government in the east. The former called themselves "the regulators," and doubtless had legitimate complaints against the corrupt official government. They also were seeking to avoid tax. The regulators were crushed by Governor William Tryon (1720–1788) at the Battle of Alamance on May 16, 1771. Quincy doubtless heard both sides of the story during his trip. See *Illustration 12, infra*, and note 114, *supra*. Later, many former regulators led the fighting against the British. See the excellent accounts in Richard R. Beeman, *The Varieties of Political Experience in Eighteenth-Century America* (Philadelphia, 2004), pp. 168–177 (hereafter, "Beeman"), and James P. Wittenberg, "Planters, Merchants, and Lawyers: Social Change and the Origin of the North Carolina Regulation," 34 *William & Mary Quarterly* (3rd series) (April 1977), pp. 215–238. Many thanks, again, to Patricia Tarabelsi.

155. Howe, *Proceedings*, 1915-1916 [FN 458-2]. William Dry.

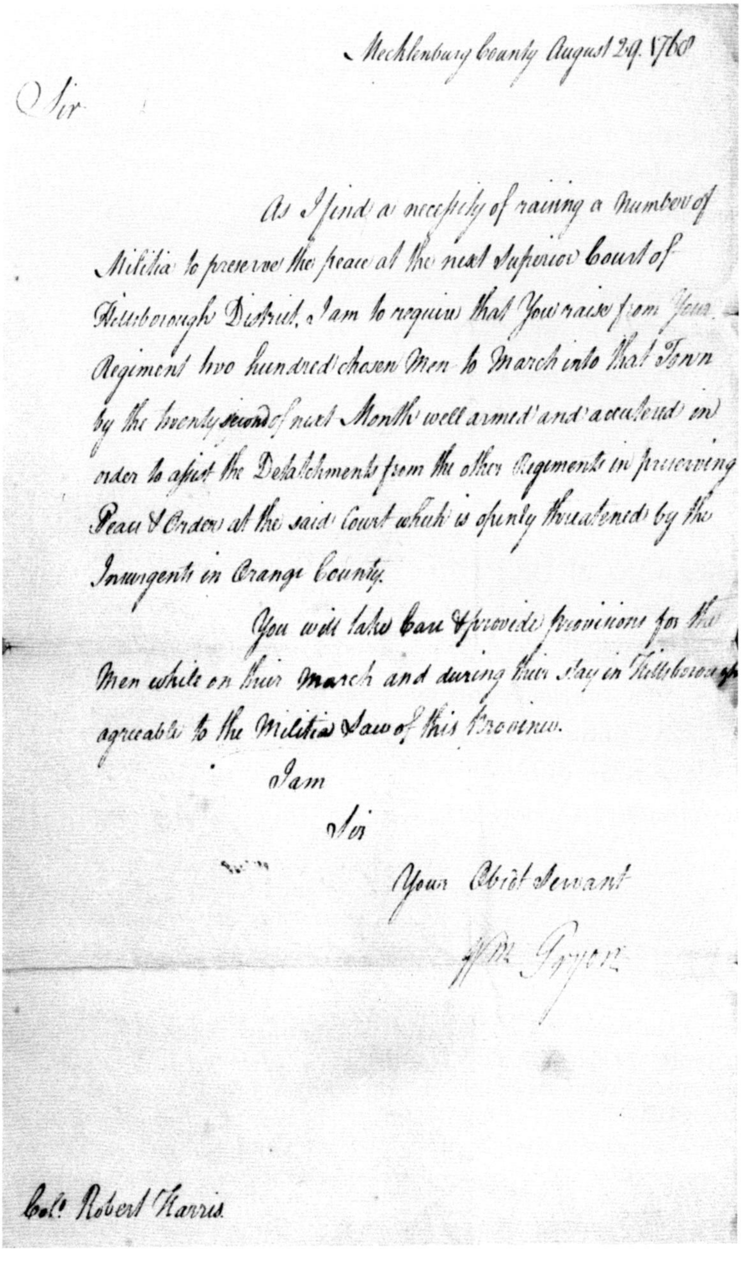

Mecklenburg County August 29. 1768

Sir

As I find a necessity of raising a number of Militia to preserve the peace at the next Superior Court of Hillsborough District, I am to require that You raise from Your Regiment two hundred chosen Men to March into that Town by the twenty second of next Month well armed and accoutred in order to assist the Detachments from the other Regiments in preserving Peace & Order at the said Court which is openly threatened by the Insurgents in Orange County.

You will take Care & provide Provisions for the Men while on their March and during their Stay in Hillsborough agreeable to the Militia Law of this Province.

I am

Sir

Your Obet Servant

Wm Tryon

Col. Robert Harris

ILLUSTRATION 12. The "War of the Regulation." Letter from Governor Tryon to Colonel Robert Harris ordering 200 of the militia to Hillsborough "which is openly threatened by Insurgents in Orange County." Courtesy, North Carolina State Archives.

[*97 continued*]

to form my own opinion—
and am preparing for a water tour
to Fort Johnston,[156] having sent
Randall forward to Wilmington.

156. At Southport near the mouth of Cape Fear River. Guarded by 10 men. Jedidiah Morse, D.D., *The American Gazetteer*. Printed in Boston, 1797.

[98]

1773
March 28th
[left margin, l. 1]

Rob
Howe, Esq.
[left margin, ll. 3, 5]

——

Yesterday was a most delightful day:
Fort Johnston is as delightful a situation:
the Commander (Rob Howe) is, if possible
a more delightful fellow. A most
happy compound of the man of sense
sentiment and dignity, with the man of the
world, the sword, the Senate and the
Bucks:[157] A truely surprizing character! The relations of his past life and adventures which he gave me in private
was moving and was ravishing:—
'Twas joyous, passing joyous! 'twas
exquisite, supremely exquisite!
NB. He has promised to transport
me some of the most finished composi-
tions in the world. I have reason to think
he will be as good as his word.
In a retired walk, Mr. Howe told me, that
in this government there was a select number
who had mutually agreed and solemnly
promised each other to keep each a regular journal not only of the Public

---

157. I.e., a sportsman. See Johnson's *Dictionary*, *supra*, n.p. "Buck."

[99]

Col
Dry
[left margin, ll. 16, 18]

––––

occurrences, but of the conduct of every
Public character! 'Tis a glorious
scheme—if executed will be fraught
with good. He told me, that having
lately had come words upon political affairs with governor Martin and one
of his council and tools, he took occasion to mention the existence
of this society and the end of their in-
situation—to record the actions (as
he expressed it) of knaves and fools—
of little villains and great and trans-
mit them in true characters to
posterity. It had the desired effect
for—Felix trembled.[158]
I go to Church this day at Brunswick[159]—
hear William Hill read prayer—dine with

158. Josiah Martin (1737–1786) was a British army officer and commissioned royal governor of North Carolina in 1771. See *Dictionary of American Biography*, XII, 343. "Felix trembled" was a reference to *New Testament*, Book of Acts, Chapter 24:25, "And as he reasoned of righteousness, temperance, and judgment to come, Felix trembled, and answered, Go thy way for this time; when I have a convenient season, I will call for thee." (King James version). Felix, Roman Governor of Israel, was questioning Paul, who had been accused by the Jewish authorities. In the end, Felix, who had hoped for a bribe, left office with Paul still in prison. See Book of Acts, Chapter 24: 26–27. All of this clearly referred to Governor Martin.

159. Nine miles north of Fort Johnston, 17 miles S.W. of Wilmington. In 1780, it was burnt down by the British, and has left only 3 or 4 houses and an elegant church in ruins. Jedidiah Morse, D.D., *The American Gazetteer*. Printed in Boston, 1797. See *Illustration 13*.

[*99 continued*]

Col. Dry—proceed to-morrow to
Willmington[160] and dine with Dr. Cobham[161]
to-morrow with a picked company.

160. Contained about 250 houses; 100 miles south of Newbern. Lat. 34.11.N. Long. 78.15.W. Jedidiah Morse, D.D., *The American Gazetteer*. Printed in Boston, 1797.

161. Dr. Thomas Cobham; maintained joint medical practice with Dr. Robert Tucker, until the partnership dissolved in 1773. "During the Regulator campaign of 1771, he participated as surgeon to the governor's forces. Dr. Cobham married Catherine Musgrove, widow of John Paine. Cobham, who owned a residence known as The Lodge in Wilmington and a plantation with two sawmills, reflected strong Loyalist sympathies as the Revolutionary era approached. Although he contributed to the New Hanover Committee of Safety, he hesitated to sign the Association supporting the Revolutionary cause and he later declared that during the war 'he was actively zealous in the Behalf of his Majesty's government.' Dr. Cobham left with the British army in 1781 and his property was confiscated." Donald R. Lennon, and Ida Brooks Kellam, eds., *The Wilmington Town Book, 1743–1778* (Raleigh, N.C., 1973).

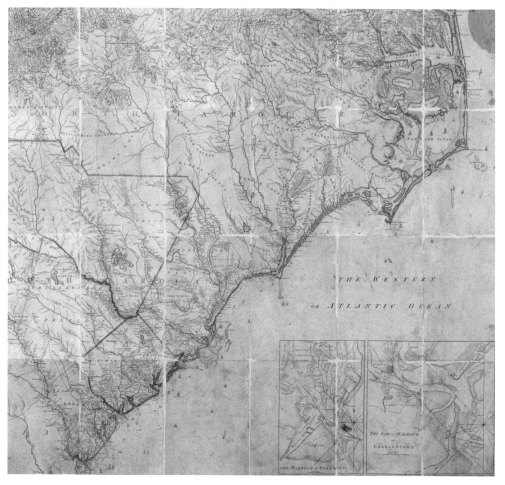

ILLUSTRATION 13. North Carolina in 1775 (Mouzon). Quincy went up the coast from Brunswick, to Wilmington, and from there to Newbern and Edenton. Courtesy, Library of Congress, American Memory Collection. See page 110, *infra*.

[100]

———

Col. Dry, a member of the Council
in this province furnished me with the
following Instruction,[162] given Governor
Martin, and as Col. Dry told me.
Governor M[artin] said to all the Colony—
Governors likewise.

Copy
George R.
[left margin, ll. 6, 7]

Additional Instruction to Our trusty
and well beloved Josiah Martin Esquire
Our Captain General and Governor in Chief
in and over our Province of North Carolina in America. Given at our
Court at St. James's the 4th day of
February 1772: In the twelfth year
of Our reign.
Whereas Laws <u>have been</u> passed in
some of Our Colonies and Plantations in A-
merica by which the Lands, tenements,
goods, chattels, rights and credits of persons, who have never resided within

162. Howe, *Proceedings*, 1915–1916 [FN 459-2]. Printed in *Col. Rec. South Carolina*, IX, 235.
The emphasis and capitals are Quincy's.

[101]

———

the Colonies where such laws <u>have been</u>
passed <u>have been</u> <u>made liable</u> to be
attached for the recovery of debts in
a manner <u>different</u> from that allowed by the Laws of England in like
Cases. And whereas it hath <u>been re-</u>
<u>presented</u> unto us, that such laws *may*
have the <u>consequence to prejudice</u>
<u>and obstruct</u> the commerce between this
kingdom and our said Colonies, and to effect Public Credit. 'Tis therefore
Our will & pleasure that
you do not on any pretence whatever
give your assent to or pass any bill
or bills in our Province under your
government by which the lands, tenements, goods, chattels, <u>rights & credits</u>

———

Qu:—How
different—
w:s essentially so?
[left margin, ll. 4–6 opposite "different"]

Stat pro
ratione—
voluntas[163]
[left margin, ll. 11–13 opposite "our will & pleasure"]

163. "The will of the people stands in place of a reason." *Black's Law Dictionary*, 1578 (Revised 4th ed., 1968).

[*101 continued*]

of persons <u>who have never resided</u>
<u>within our said Province</u> shall be
made liable to be attached for the <u>recov-</u>
<u>ery of debts due from such persons</u>

[102]

———

otherwise than is allowed by law
in Cases of the like nature within
our kingdom of Great Britain
until you shall first have trans-
mitted to us, by one of our Principal Secretaries of State, the Draughts
of such bill or bills and shall have
received Our Royal Pleasure
there upon, unless you take
care in the passing of such bill or
bills that a clause or clauses be
inserted therein suspending
and defferring the Execution there
of until Our Royal Will and
Pleasure shall be known there
upon.

$$GR^{164}$$

Copy
[left margin, l. 17 opposite "GR"]

164. Thus a royal decree of George III (1738–1820). Quincy would have had a dim view of the direct interference with colonial legislation, but the legal principle of whether colonial laws could bind non-colonials other than by English common law was a very close question, and was debated in Quincy's *Reports*. See Introduction, "First Flower—The Earliest American Law Reports and the Extraordinary Josiah Quincy Jr. (1744–1775)," *Quincy Papers*, vol. 4.

[103]

———

Col. Dry is justly called the house
of universal hospitality—his table a-
bounds with plenty—his servants excel
in cookery—and his sensible lady exceeds
(at least I think equals) Sister Q[uincy]
in the pastry and Nick-nack way.[165]

1773
March 29th

Dined at Dr. Thomas Cobbam's in company
with Harnett,[166] Hooper,[167] Burgwin,[168] Dr.
Tucker[169] and others, in Willmington. Lodged
also with Dr. Cobbam, who has treated me
with great politeness, tho' an utter stranger and one to whom I had no Letters.
Spent the Evening with the Great Company of the place.

165. For "knick-knack" see Page 66, note 94, *supra*.

166. Cornelius Harnett (1723–1781), Revolutionary statesman, "the Samuel Adams of North Carolina." Member of the Assembly, 1754–1775. Served three terms in the Continental Congress. See *Dictionary of American Biography*, VIII, 279.

167. William Hooper (1742–1790), lawyer. After 1764, practiced in North Carolina. Member of Continental Congress, 1775–77, and signer of Declaration of Independence. See *Dictionary of American Biography*, IX, 204.

168. Howe, *Proceedings*, 1915–1916 [FN 460-3]. John Burgwin.

169. Dr. Robert Tucker, doctor of physics; "remained loyal to Great Britain during the American Revolution and in 1782 was declared inimical to the state." Shared joint medical practice with Dr. Thomas Cobham, n. 161, *supra*. Donald R. Lennon, and Ida Brooks Kellam, eds. *The Wilmington Town Book, 1743–1778*.

[*103 continued*]

30th March

Dined with about 20 at Mr. William Hooper's—
find him apparently in the Whig interest—
has taken that side in the house—is caressed
by the Whiggs—and is now pushing his election
thro' the influence of that party.

[104]

1773 March
   30th

——

Spent the evening and night at Mr. Harnett's,
the Samuel Adams of North Carolina
except in point of fortune.[170]
Robert Howe, Esq., Harnett and myself
made the Social triumvirate of the Evening.
The plan of Continental correspondence
highly relished, much wished for and
resolved upon, as proper to be pursued.
Mr. H[arnett] lives in taste—with philosophy
and virtue.
At about 11 o'Clock, Col Howe took his
leave of me, having scarce been
absent from each other since our first
acquaintance 5 days ago. From
perfect strangers we became inti-
mate—From some cause or other
we have formed an apparent affection
and at parting both seem to be mutually and alike affected.—"I will
not take a final leave (said he at our
parting) for I feel an impulse that

170. Samuel Adams (1722–1803), Boston patriot and signer of the Declaration of Independence, later Governor of Massachusetts (1794–1797). Samuel Adams was not a wealthy man, at
least compared to Harnett. See John K. Alexander, *Samuel Adams: America's Revolutionary
Politican* (Lanham, Md., 2004).

[105]

——

we shall—we must—meet again!!
This gentleman is a very extraordinary
character. Formed by nature and his
education to shine in the Senate and the
field—(in the Company of the phy-
losopher and libertine[171]—a favorite
of the man of sense and the female world.
He has faults and vices—but alas who is
without them? His faults are those
of a high spirit—his vices those of
a man of feeling.
His Adventures and intrigues expressed with
his fire and cloathed in his diction would
form a most engaging romance.
In short his Character seemed
an Assemblage of a Granderson
and Lovelace.[172]

171. Libertine: "One not confined; one at liberty" or "One who lives without restraint or law." See Johnson's *Dictionary, supra,* n.p. "libertine." Quincy must mean here "lover of liberty."

172. Literary characters of the English novelist, Samuel Richardson (1689–1761); the former from the novel bearing the same name, *History of Sir Charles Grandison* (1753–1754), the latter, Lovelace, from Richardson's tragic masterpiece *Clarissa* (1747–1748).

[106]

31st March 1773

Martin
Howard
[left margin, ll. 12, 14]

———

Set out from Mr. Harnett's for Newbern.[173]

1 April
[left margin, l. 3]

This evening maybe stiled that of <u>the
Knight—errant</u>[174]—not worth the
trouble of recital, tho' it certainly
had liked to have proved very
momentous.

2 April
[left margin, l. 8]

Reached Newbern about XI o'Clock
AM in company with Capt. Collett[175]

173. Contains about 400 houses. Lat. 35.20.N. Long. 77.25.W. 99 miles SW of Edenton; 103 miles NE by N of Wilmington. Jedidiah Morse, D.D., *The American Gazetteer*. Printed in Boston, 1797.

174. This is certainly one of Quincy's most mysterious observations. Reference is to Miguel de Cervantes Saavedra (1547–1616) *Don Quixote* (1605, 1615), widely available in popular English translations by 1773. See, for example, Miguel de Cervantes Saavedra, *The History and Adventures of the Renowned Don Quixote* (trans. T. S. Smollett, London, 1770, 4 vols.).

175. Howe, *Proceedings*, 1915–1916 [FN 460-4]. John Abraham Collett . . . This gentleman, I am sorry to find my Lord, has . . . involved himself in debt so deeply that he will never be able to shew his face again in this Country. *Governor Josiah Martin to Earl of Dartmouth, August 28, 1775. Col. Rec. No. Ca.*, X, 234.

[*106 continued*]

Waited upon Judge Howard[176] and spent
about an hour with him—Did not
present the rest of my Letters—because
of the finest of the weather for traveling
and no C[our]ts of any kind sitting or even in
being in the province. Judge Howard
waited upon me in the Evening with recom-
mendatory Letters to Col. Palmer[177] of
Bath and Col. Buncombe[178] of Tyrrell
county.

176. Howe, *Proceedings*, 1915–1916 [FN 461-1]. Martin Howard, Chief Justice.
177. Howe, *Proceedings*, 1915–1916 [FN 461-2]. Robert Palmer, secretary and Council member.
178. Howe, *Proceedings*, 1915–1916 [FN 461-3]. Edward Buncombe (d. 1778). Buncombe County, named in 1791, inspired the political term descriptive of speech or action lacking conviction.

The text visible within the illustration on the document reads:

We the Ladys
of Edenton do
hereby Solemnly
...ge not to Conform
... Pernicious Custom
... Drinking Tea, or that we the
... Ladys will ... promote ... wear
... any Manufactur from England
... ...uch time that all Acts
...tend to Enslave this our
... Country shall be Repealed

ILLUSTRATION 14. "The Edenton Tea Party": Satirical English mezzotint, March 1775. Courtesy, Library of Congress.

[107]

1773
April 4th

———

Reached Bath in the Evening—Did not
deliver my Letters to Col. Palmer,
but proceeded next morning to Mr.
Wingfield's[179] parish where I spent the
Sabbath.

April 5th
Col.
Buncombe
[left margin, ll. 6, 7, 8]

Breakfasted with Col. Buncombe
who waited upon me to Edenton[180]

179. Posssibly named after Edward Maria Wingfield, President of the Assembly at
Jamestown c. 1608 (until accused of slander).

180. Contained above 150 buildings; 97 miles north of Newbern; Lat. 36.6.N. Long. 77.11.W.
Jedidiah Morse, D.D., *The American Gazetteer*. Printed in Boston, 1797.

Edenton is famous for having its own tea party, albeit less famous than its Boston counter-
part. See *Illustration 14*. On October 25, 1774, 51 patriotic women gathered in the home of Mrs.
Elizabeth King and famously vowed "We the Ladys of Edenton do hereby solemnly engage not
to conform to that Pernicious Custom of Drinking Tea, or that we the aforesaid Ladys will not
promote ye wear of any manufacturers from England, until such time that all Acts which tend
to enslave this our Native Country shall be repealed."

News of the women of Edenton reached all the way back to London, where Arthur Iredell,
brother of the Edenton resident James Iredell, penned the following letter on January 31, 1775:

"Dear Brother: I see by the newspaper the Edenton ladies have signalized themselves by
their protest against tea drinking. The name of Johnston I see among others; are any of my sister's relations patriotic heroines? Is there a female congress at Edenton too? I hope not, for we
Englishmen are afraid of the male congress, but if the ladies, who have ever since the Amazo-
nian era been esteemed the most formidable enemies; if they, I say, should attack us, the most
fatal consequence is to be dreaded. So dextrous in the handling of a dart, each wound they give
is mortal; whilst we, so unhappily formed by nature, the more we strive to conquer them, the
more we are conquered. The Edenton ladies, conscious, I suppose, of this superiority on their

[*107 continued*]

Sound[181] and gave me Letters to his
friends there.

Spent this and the next day in crossing Al-
bermarle—sound and in dining and conversing in Company with the most celebrated lawyers of Edenton. They
appeared sensible Tryonists[182] and prerogative subjects. From them I learned
that Dr. Samuel Cooper[183] of Boston was
generally, (they said universally) esteemed the Author of Leonidas,[184] who

---

side, by a former experience, are willing I imagine, to crush us into atoms by their omnipotency;
the only security on our side to prevent the impending ruin, that I can perceive, is the proba-
bility that there are but few places in America which possess so much female artillery as Edenton. Pray let me know all the particulars when you favor me with a letter.

Your most affectionate friend and brother, ARTHUR IREDELL"

See Richard Dillard, *The Historic Tea-Party of Edenton*. North Carolina Historical Commission.

181. "For many, many years a stately cypress tree stood in the midst of the Edenton harbor.
No one is entirely sure just how long the tree was there, but legend suggests it was standing long
before the first English colonists set foot in the Albemarle region. Somehow, a curious custom
grew up around the tree. Whenever a ship of trade called at Edenton, it was almost obligatory
for the master to place a bottle of the best Jamaican rum in a hollow place in the trunk. Whenever a ship left for foreign parts, the vessel would stop at the tree, and all hands would drink to
a safe voyage. Thus it was that the old cypress became known as 'the Dram Tree.' Ships whose
crews failed to drink of the Dram Tree or, even worse, failed to place a bottle there when entering port were doomed to disaster. Many are the tales of ill-fated vessels that met violent storms
or were becalmed in the doldrums. The tree survived until the spring of 1918, when a tremen-
dous ice floe vanquished the landmark to the sound's waters." Claiborne S. Young, *Cruising
Guide to Coastal North Carolina: Edenton* (Elon College, N.C., 2000).

182. Followers of William Tryon (1729-1788), English Governor of North Carolina (1765–
1771), who suppressed the Regulator Movement. During the Revolution, Tryon was Governor
of New York (1771-1778). See notes 114 and 154, *supra*, on the "Regulators."

183. Dr. Samuel Cooper (1725-1783), clergyman, Revolutionary patriot, pastor of Boston's
Brattle Square Church, 1743-1783. See *Dictionary of American Biography*, IV, 410.

184. Leonidas was King of Sparta, in command of the Greeks at Thermopylae (480 B.C.).
The reference is to a revolutionary tract that uses this pseudonym. See Howatson, *supra*, p. 321.
Howe, *Proceedings*, 1915-1916 [FN 461-4]. *Col. Rec. No. Ca.*, X, 1021-1023.

[*107 continued*]

together with Mucius Scaevola[185] were
burnt in effigy under the Gallows by the Com[mon] hang-man in No[rth]
Carolina.
Here was a Char[acter] who Balch[186] could
by taking off sett a jovial company
in a perfect roar.—He was a man
of sense, but the most singular I ever saw.

185. Another pseudonym. Name of several distinguished Romans, including the legendary Gaius Mucius Scaevola who, to show his indifference to death, thrust his hand into a fire, hence "left-handed." See Howatson, p. 510.

186. A reference to Nathaniel Balch, "a wit of the day." See note 67, *supra*, and Howe, *Proceedings*, 1915–1916 (FN 444–1). He "entertained in good humor" the Sons of Liberty at Robinson's Tavern, Dorchester. See note 67, *supra*, and accompanying text, and http://www.oneapril.com/sons/page2.shtml(accessed 01/01/2006), and sources cited.

[108]

1773
April 6th

———

There being no C:[our]ts of any kind in this
province and <u>no laws in force</u> by which any
could be held, I found little inclination
or incitement to stay long in Edenton, tho' a pleasant town.[187] Accordingly a guide offering his direction,
just at evening I left the place, and proceeded just into the bounds of Virginia where
I lodged the Night.

Gen[era]l Reflections } No and So
and Remarks on   } Carolina
        <u>(as they rise.)</u>
The soils and climates of the Carolinas differ,
but not so much as their Inhabitants.
Tho' little more than imaginary line part
these people, you no sooner enter the No[rth]
prov[ince] before you seem to see a surprising change of men and things.
There is an affectation too prevalent in
So[uth] Carolina of superiority over the Northern colonies, especially over poor No[rth] C[arolina],
which was much misery presented to me, and
might therefore cause a prejudice in

187. At several points, Quincy emphasized his primary interest in law and the legal profession.

[109]

_____

their favour when I found things
so different from the accounts received
of them.—But all prejudice
apart.
The number of Negroes and slaves are vast-
ly less in No[rth] than So[uth] C[arolina]. Their staple—commodity is not so valuable,
being not in so great demand, as
the Rice, Indigo, etc. of the South.
Hence labor becomes more necessary, and he who has <u>an interest of his
own to serve</u> is a laborer in the
field. Husbandmen and agriculture increase in number and
improvement. Industry is up
in the woods, at tar, pitch, and turpentine—in the fields plowing,
planting, or clearing and fencing the
land. Herds and flocks become
more numerous, and they resemble not Pharoah's lean kine,[188]
so much as those of the Prov[ince] I
had just left. You see husbandmen

188. ["Lean Kine"]; "Lean fleshed" cattle from the Pharoah's dream, related to Joseph, pre-
dicting the years of famine. *Genesis*, 41:19.

[110]

———

men, yeomen and white laborers scattered thro' the country, instead of
herds of Negroes and tawny slaves.
Healthful countenances and numerous families become more common as you advance North.
In Charlestown and so thro' the Southern prov[ince]
I saw much apparent hospitality,
much of what is called good-breeding and
politeness, and great barbarity. In
Brunswick, Willmington, Newbern
Edenton, and so thro' the North prov[ince]
there is real hospitality, less of what
is called politeness and good-breeding
and less inhumanity.
Property is much more equally diffused in one prov[ince] than the other,
and this may account, for some, if
not all, the differences of Character
of the inhabitants.

[111]

———

Arts and sciences are certainly better
understood, more relished, more
attended to and better cultivated in the one prov
than the other. Men of genius,
learning, and true wit, humour, and
mirth are more numerous here
than the country I had just left:
a country too, when the civilities
I had received served to prejudice
my judgment in it's favour.
However, in one respect, I find
a pretty near resemblance between the two Colonies: I mean the
State of Religion. At a low
ebb indeed in both Provinces.
'Tis certainly high time to repeal the Laws relative to religion
and the observation of the Sabbath, or to
see them better executed. 'Tis
certainly to the last degree false

[112]

———

politicks to have laws in force
which the legislators, judges and executive officers not only break themselves, but practically and too
often openly and avowedly deride. Avowed impunity to all
offenders is one sign at least that
the Law wants amendment or
abrogation.[189]
Alike as the Carolinas are in this
respect, they certainly vary much
as to their gen[eral] sentiments, opin[ion]s
and judgments: they may well be
considered as very opposite in
character, and tis very apparent
that no great friendship or
esteemed is entertained by one
towards the other.

189. This principle, that laws should be enforced or repealed, was repeated later by the great jurist, Lon L. Fuller. See Lon L. Fuller, *The Morality of Law* (New Haven, rev. ed. 1969), 39 ("failure of congruence between the rules as announced and their actual administration").

[113]

———

The slaves in No[rth] C[arolina] are fewer in number, better cloathed and better fed, than
in So[uth], and are of consequence better servants.
A mischief incident to both these prov[inces]
is very observable, and very natural to be
expected:—the intercourse between the
whites and blacks. The enjoyment of a negro
or molatto woman is spoken of as quite
a common thing: no reluctance, delicacy
or shame is made about the matter. It
is far from being uncommon to see
a gentleman at dinner, and his reputed offspring a slave to the master of the table.
I myself saw two instances of this,
and the company very facetiously would trace
the lines, lineaments and features of the father and mother in the Child, and very ac-
curately point out the more charac-
teristick resemblances. The fathers neither of them blushed or seem
disconcerted. They were called men
of worth, politeness and humanity.

[114]

———

Strange perversion of terms and language!
The Africans are said to be inferior in point
of sense and understanding, sentiment and
feeling, to the Europeans and other white
nations. Hence the one infer a right to enslave the other. An African Black labors
night and day to collect a small
pittance to purchase the freedom of his
child: the American or European White
man begets his likeness, and with much
indifference and dignity of soul sees his
progeny in bondage and misery, and
makes not one effort to redeem his
own blood.—Choice food for
Satire—wide field for burlesque—
and noble game for wit!—
unless the enkindled blood inflame
resentment, wrath and rage; and
vent itself in execrations.

[115]

———

The staple commodities of No[rth] C[arolina] are
all kinds of Naval stores—Indian
Corn, pork, peas, some tobacco, which
they gen[erally] send into Virginia, hemp,
flax-seed and mustard seed: the
culture of Wheat and rice is making
quick progress, as a spirit of agri-
cultures is rising fast.
The favorite liquor of the Carolinas
are Claret and Port wines in preference to Madeira and Lisbon.[190]
The Commerce of No[rth] C[arolina] is much differed
thro' the several parts of the prov[ince]—
they in some respects may be
said to have no metropolis, tho'
Newbern is called the Capi-
tal, as there is the seat of Government. It is
made a Q[uestio]n which carries on most trade
whether Edenton, Newbern [New Bern], Willmington or Brunswick: It seems to be
one of the two first.

190. Lisbon, "a white wine produced in the province of Estremadura in Portugal and imported from Lisbon." *Oxford English Dictionary, supra*, vol. 1, p. 1636.

[116]

———

There is very little, if any kind, of
commerce or intercourse between
the No[rth] and So[uth] prov of Carolina, and there is
very little, if any more, of regard
in the Inh[abitan]ts of the one Colony for those of
the other.
The present state of No[rth] C[arolina] is really envious: there are but 5 laws in force
thro' the Colony,[191] and no Courts at all in
being. None can recover their debts
except before a single magistrate where
the sums are within his jurisdiction,
and offenders escape with impunity.
The people are in great consternation about the matter: What will be the
consequences are problematical: many
people, as Lord Bottetourt[192] says
"augur ill"[193] on the occasion.

191. "Envious" is used here as a synonym for "invidious" or "malignant." See *Johnson's Dic-*
tionary, supra, n.p. "invidious." Howe, *Proceedings,* 1915–1916 [FN 464-1]. "This is probably an
echo of the 'Six Confirmed Laws' of 1715, which were really a codification of all statutes prior to
that year." See *Col. Rec. No. Ca.,* XXIII. i.

192. Norborne Berkeley, Baron de Bettor (1718–1770), colonial governor of Virginia, 1768–
1770. See *Dictionary of American Biography,* II, 468.

193. Translation: bodes ill. Originally, "augur" meant "one who pretends to predict by the
flight of birds." *Johnson's Dictionary, supra,* n.p. "augur."

[117]

1773.   6th April

———

Lodged at Suffolk.[194]—

        7 April
[left margin, l. 2]

Dined at Smithfield[195]—two considerable towns in Virginia.
Ever since I have left So[uth] Carolina,
as I verge No[rth] the lands and culture
of them have gradually changed
for the better. Excellent farms
and charming large cleared tracts
well-fenced and tilled are all around
me.—Peach-trees seem to be of
spontaneous growth in the South
provinces, and I had them all-along in
their proudest bloom. Whole fields
of them looked beautifully. I saw
about 6 acres all in high bloom,
and very regularly planted, and Every
other row of trees was of the apple and pear kind,
not yet in blossom: An extent of
about 12 or 15 acres of peach-trees regularly set in equi-distant rows, in-
termixed all about with many

    194. Port-town on east side of Nansemond River. Contains about 40 houses. 110 miles SE
of Richmond. Jedidiah Morse, D.D., *The American Gazetteer*. Printed in Boston, 1797.
    195. Small port-town on Pagan Creek; 85 miles SE of Richmond. Jedidiah Morse, D.D., *The
American Gazetteer*. Printed in Boston, 1797.

[118]

———

small pine trees of exquisite verdure, formed a prospect to the
Eye most delightful and charming.

1773
9th April

I arrived this morning about 10 o'Clock
at Williamsburg,[196] the Capital of
Virginia. 'Tis a place of no trade,
and it's importance depends altogether on it's being the seat of
gov:t and the place of the College.[197]
I have just been taking a view
of the whole town. 'Tis inferior
much to my expectation. Nothing of the population of the North,
or of the magnificence and splendor
of the South. The College makes
a very agreeable appearance in
front, but in the rear it is scandalously out of repair. The large
garden before the College is
of ornament and use. There is but

196. Contained about 200 houses and has about 1400 inhabitants; 60 miles east of Richmond; Lat. 37.16.N. Long. 76.48.W. Jedidiah Morse, D.D., *The American Gazetteer*. Printed in
Boston, 1797. See *Illustration 15*.
197. Towards endowing of which King William and Queen Mary gave £2000 and 20,000
acres of land. *The American Gazetteer, Containing a Distinct Account of all the Parts of the New
World*, printed for A. Millar and J. & R. Tonson, 1762. [no page numbers, alphabetical by city].
The currency equivalent for the cash endowment would be more than $2 million [2004].

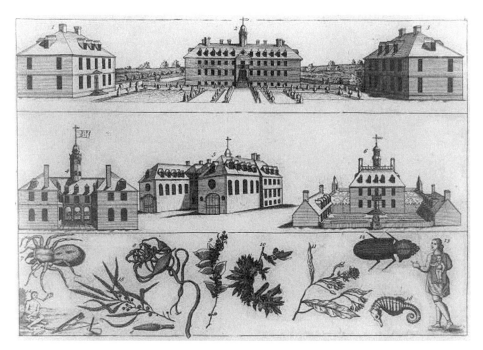

ILLUSTRATION 15. Buildings of Williamsburg, Virginia. Print from Copper Plate from Bodleian Libraray, c. 1740. Courtesy, Colonial Williamsburg Foundation. The top view shows what Quincy called "the college" (p. 118), now known as the Wren building, after Christopher Wren who "may possibly have influenced its original design." Michael Olmert, *Official Guide to Colonial Williamsburg* (Williamsburg, 1985), p. 94. It was completed in 1732. The building on the second tier, far right, was the "Govenor's House," mentioned by Quincy on p. 119. It was completed in 1722. *Id.*, p. 73. The building on the second tier, far left, is the Capitol, mentioned by Quincy on p. 120. It was completed in 1753, *Id.*, p. 54. the Attorney General's house mentioned by Quincy on p. 119 is not shown.

[119]*

———

two private buildings of Note:
the Governor's and the Atty Gen:l's.
The first is not remarkable: the
other is in the Chinese taste; and
is the handsomest of the two.
The Capitol or State-house[198] is
called a very handsome building, I have as yet seen only the
outside, I shall visit the Inward
parts of it on the morrow.
The College in this place is in a
very declined state.

This day I purchased a very handsome Edition of the Virginia Laws
of Mess. Purdie and Dixon,[199] and paid

198. As to the "Attorney General's House," Quincy may have been referring to the Peyton Randolph House, completed between 1715 and 1750. Both Peyton (1722–1775) and his brother John (1727–1787) served as Attorney General. Olmert, *supra*, pp. 26–28. See *Illustration 15*. Despite Quincy's negative remarks, George Wythe (1726–1806) had begun a law program at the college by 1779, which included John Marshall as a student in 1780. See Paul D. Carrington, "The Revolutionary Idea of University Legal Education," 31 *William and Mary* L. Rev. 527 (1990).

199. This book was in Quincy's library at his death. See Quincy, Estate Catalogue, *supra*, item 12. It was almost certainly *The Acts of Assembly, Now in Force, In the Colony of Virginia* (Rind, Purdie, Dixon, Williamsburg, 1769). See *Catalogue of Books in the Massachusetts Historical Library* (1796 Annotated edition) (Boston, 1996), p. 467.

A controversy over accusations that Joseph Royle, printer of the *Maryland Gazette*, refused to print attacks on the local government, prompted Thomas Jefferson and others to urge William Rind to move from Annapolis in 1766 to set up a rival *Virginia Gazette*. Jefferson recalled years later that "we had but one press, and that having the whole business of the government, and no competitor for public favor, nothing disagreeable to the governor could be got into it. We procured Rind to come from Maryland to publish a free paper."

Royle died shortly before Rind came to Williamsburg, and it turned out to be a fortuitous death for the new fellow. Rind was elected public printer by the House of Burgesses, giving him

[*119 continued*]

them therefore 43/ lmy[200] and they have
engaged to convey it to Boston.

---

an economic foothold in the form of printing documents and laws. As it turned out, the Assembly three years later spread the wealth to both *Gazettes* when it ordered them to print a large volume of the Acts of Assembly then in force.

Alexander Purdie succeeded Joseph Royle as publisher of the original *Virginia Gazette*. In 1767, Purdie took into the business John Dixon, who by marriage was related to Royle's widow. Purdie, dissatisfied with the partnership, withdrew to set up his own *Virginia Gazette*. The first issue appeared Feb. 3, 1775. If the reader is confused, imagine how confused Williamsburg readers were 200 years ago. By early 1775 there were three separate Virginia Gazettes, all operating in town and all under the same name: There was *Dixon's Gazette* (the original), *Rind's Gazette* and *Purdie's Gazette* (the newest). See W. C. O'Donovan, *History of The Virginia Gazette* (1986), updated 2002 and transcribed by Lew Leadbeater, http://www.vgprint.com/history.html

200. "Lmy" an abbreviation for "lawful money?" If Quincy is referring to shillings: Approximate Currency Equivalencies: 3 shillings, seven pence = $179 (2004).

[120]

1773
April. 10th
       11th
       12th

———

Hewes's crab-apple[201] is much cultivated
in Virginia. I have tasted better
cyder made it, than any I ever drank
made from Northern fruit. The
Cyder is quite pale, and clear, but of
most exquisite flavor. Tis certainly worthy taking much pains to
propogate these trees with us.

The State-house is more commodious
inside, than ornamental without.
The Council Chamber is furnished with
a large, well chosen, valuable collection of Books; chiefly of law.

201. This cider apple, also known as Hughes' Crab and Virginia Crab, was the most common fruit variety grown in eighteenth-century Virginia. In property advertisements in Williamsburg's *Virginia Gazette* (see n. 199, *supra*) from 1755–1777, the Hewes' Crab appeared more
times than all other described fruit varieties combined.
    The Hewes' is a maverick apple. Its vigorous growth habit suggests that it may be a cross
between a native American crabapple, *Malus angustifolia*, and the domesticated apple of horti-
culture. Virginian Landon Carter's "crabs" were the only apple unhurt by a late spring frost in
1772. The fruit is very small, one to two inches round, with a dull-red to bright, pinkish-red skin.
When pressing the Hewes' for cider, the juice "runs through the finest flannel like spring water,"
or, according to another writer, "the liquor flows from the pumice as water from a sponge." The
juice, described as "ambrosia" by one colleague, is both sugary and pungently tart, cinnamon-
flavored, and delicious. Hatch, Peter J. *Director, Monticello Gardens and Grounds*, January 1995.
http://www.twinleaf.org/articles/hewes.html

[*120 continued*]

The Court of Justice is very ill
contrived.
I was present at their Gen:l Court,
which is the Sup[erio]r Court of Justice and the
Court of Chancery of the prov:[ince]—But
had only an opp[ortunit]y of hearing short
motions made by their most

[121]

———

eminent counsel at the Bar: the
Chancery—business being always
the employ of the first week, and
the Crown or Civil Business that
of the second and succeeding weeks.
The Constitution of the Courts of Justice
and equity in this colony is a-
mazingly defective, inconvenient and dangerous, not to say
absurd and mischievous.
This motley kind of Court called the
Gen:l Court is composed of the Governor
and Council, who are appointed
and created by mandamus from
the Crown, and hold bene placito.[202]
I am told that it is no uncommon
thing for this Court to set one
hour and hear a cause as a Court
of Law; and the next hour, perhaps
minute, to set and audit the

202. "Mandamus" comes from the Latin "we command." This would be a prerogative order from the Crown "to compel the performance of a duty" i.e., to hold the court. *Earl Jowitt, supra*, p. 1134. Quincy would have prefered a court authorized by charter, like the Massachusetts Superior Court of Judicature, to a court appointed by royal order.

"Bene placito" comes from the Latin "well pleasing" (a phrase originally used for Crown appointments at Westminster; judges held their seats on the bench so long as it "pleased" the Crown). See J. H. Baker, *supra*, pp. 167–168.

[122]

_____

same matter as a Court of Chancery
and equity: and if my information is good, they very frequently
give directly contrary decisions.[203]
Voltaire,[204] his Huron or Pupil
of Nature might here exercise
their talent of wit and sarcasm.

203. A court of equity should, in theory, only have jurisdiction where there is no adequate remedy at law. Conceivably, the Virginia practice was to deny relief as a matter of law, then grant relief as a court of equity. To common lawyers, however, equitable relief, which was inherently discretionary, could create uncertainty as to the operation of the law, and introduce the appearance of subjectivity, both vices. See J. H. Baker, *An Introduction to English Legal History* (4th ed., London, 2002), pp. 105–115. (Hereafter, "J. H. Baker.")

204. Pseudonym of François-Marie Arouet (1694–1778), famed French writer and philosopher. Voltaire's *Letters* were in Quincy's library. See Quincy, Estate Catalogue, *supra*, Items 213, 290. Voltaire's "Huron or Pupil of Nature" first appeared in his *L'Ingenu Historie Véritable, Tirée des Manuscripts du Père Quesnal* (Utrecht, 1767), pp. 22–33, published in Geneva and in London in the same year. The book was quickly published in English translation, in London, Dublin and Glasgow, all in 1768. "The Huron" was a fictional American Indian who suddenly appeared on the coast of France, giving Voltaire full range for his usual political satire. As Donald Grinde and Bruce Johansen have observed: "North American Indians were a symbol of freedom to another French philosopher, Voltaire. Borrowing from Gabriel Sagard's work, Voltaire wrote a critique of French autocracy and hypocrisy, 'The Huron, or Pupil of Nature,' which was told through the eyes of a Huron. On the eve of the American Revolution, Voltaire's Huron proclaimed to his French companions that he 'was born free as the air.'" Donald A. Grinde Jr., Bruce E. Johansen, *Exemplar of Liberty: Native America and the Evolution of Democracy* (Los Angeles, 1991), p. 71. "As a vehicle for dreams, the Noble Savage helped reawaken Europeans to a passionate desire for liberty and happiness, which so suffused Enlightenment thought that it ignited revolution on both sides of the Atlantic. Images can do such things to reality, even when there influence is denied. For instance, although William Brandon found that Voltaire laughed at any talk of Noble Savages, his fake Huron in *L'Ingenu* (1767) sometimes echoed, and not always ironically, both Lahontan and Delisle, in spite of all Voltaire's efforts to keep him from doing so. . . . Voltaire mocked . . . himself for falling victim to such nonsense — 'My muse calls to you from America[, he complained] . . . . I needed a new world . . . . But I tremble that I'll be taken for a savage.' At the same time, on the other side of the Atlantic, Franklin, the ultimate pragmatist, often found himself called by the same muse." *Id.*, p. 13. Many thanks to Michael Hayden and Mark Sullivan.

[*122 continued*]

It was a matter of speculation with
me how such a constitution and
form of judicial administration could
be tolerable: I conversed with divers
who seemed to have experienced
no inconvenience and of course to
apprehend no danger from this
quarter; yet they readily gave
into my sentiments upon the
subject, when I endeavored
to show the political defects and
solecism[205] of this constitution.

---

205. "Solecism," "unfitness of one word to another" *Johnson's Dictionary, supra,* n.p. "solecism." Here, used to describe the unfitness of combining legal and equitable jurisdictions and
other legal inconsistencies.

[123]

_____

However I saw none who gave
me any satisfactory account of
the true reason that more
mischeivous consequences
had not flowed from this
source. Perhaps it was owing to my misfortune in
having no Letters to any of
the Bar, and but one to any
Gentlemen within many
miles of Williamsburgh,
tho' I had many to persons
of distinction expected in
town next week. I could only
regret, but many circumstances
deprived me of remedying, this
inconvenience.

1773
11th April

_____

I spent the Evening with two of
the Councils of the Province,

[124]

———

and our conversation was wholly
political (and inquisitive.)
They invited me to dine with the
Councils next day and offered
to introduce me to the Governor,
the Earl of Dunmore,[206] but I
was unfortunately obliged to
wave[207] their invitation and offer.

The State of Religion here is
a little better than to the South;
tho I hear the most shocking
accounts of the depravity and abominable wickedness of their established Clergy, several of
whom keeping public taverns
and open gaming houses: Other
crimes of which one them
(who now officiates) is charged
and

206. John Murray, fourth Earl of Dunmore (1732–1809). Governor of New York and Virginia, 1770. Returned to England, 1776; governor of the Bahamas, 1787. See *Dictionary of
National Biography*, XXXIX, 388.
    207. "Wave" for "waive."

[127]

[PAGES 125 AND 126 ARE CUT OUT][208]

———

safe-guard from future
invasions and oppressions.
I am mistaken in my conjecture, if in some approaching
day Virginia does not more
fully see the capital defects of
her constitution of gov:t and
rue the bitter consequences
of them.

The Commonality and farmers
thro' this province were
vastly more ignorant and
illiterate kind of people
than with us; yet their farms
and fields displayed great marks
of fine husbandry and much

208. Apparently, deliberately excised. By whom and for what reason are mysteries discussed by Michael H. Hayden in the Transcriber's Foreword, pp. 7–8, *supra*. See also Introduction, *Southern Journal*, pp. 43, 72–73.

[128]

———

industry and improvements: but a
spirit of inquiry and literature
is thro' this whole colony manifestly subordinate to a spirit
of gaming, horse-racing and
jockeying of all kinds:—even
cock-fighting is a very predo-
minant passion. Three or four
matches of this sort where
advertised in the Public prints
of Williamsburgh and I was
a witness to five in the course
of my Journey from that
town to Port-royal.
The Hewes's Crab Apple much cultivated
in this prov:[ince] and increase fast in repute
for making the best cyder.
An Aristocratical spirit and principle is very prevalent in the Laws
policy and manners of this Colony, and the Law ordaining that Estates-tail
shall not be barred by Common Recoveries is not the only instance
thereof.[209]

209. An "estate tail" locked land into a family by requiring that land descend through blood descendents, "heirs of the body." If issue fails, the land reverts back to the original donor or his or her heirs ("possibility of reverter"). Both because of the interest of the heirs of a tenant in tail ("remainder men") and because of the interest of the original donor's heirs ("reversioners"), the tenant in tail can, in theory, never sell more than a life estate in the land, never the complete "fee simple" title. Thus land remains in the family. But in England, the courts evolved a ficti-tious law suit, the "common recovery," which effectively permitted a tenant in tail in possession of the land to bar the entail, thus permitting free alienation of the fee simple. Thus a colony which did not permit such a "common recovery" would be favoring the tying up of land and ensuring that it descended in landed families, truly an "aristocratical spirit." See J. H. Baker, *supra*, pp. 280–297. A similar result was achieved in England between 1646–1700, called the "strict settlement," which was designed to limit the common recovery. See *Id.*, pp. 293–296. Some of the cases Quincy reported in Massachusetts presented major issues of whether the entail should be favored or disfavored, a question with major gender and social significance, as

[129]

1773
April 16th

———

Crossed Potomack river and arrived
in Maryland. Thro' Virginia you
find agriculture carried to great per-
fection, and large fields (from 10 to 30 acres extent) are planted with
Peach-trees, which being all in bloom
made my journey vastly agreable.
The purpose of raising these trees
is the making a Brandy, a very favorite
liquor. The land evidently grows
better as I verge North, and as stony
and rocky ground becomes more
frequent. The melody of the fields
and woods thro' Virginia is greatly
beyond the Carolinas. The Culture
of corn and wheat is supplanting very
fast that of tobacco in this province.
I spent yesterday chiefly with young men
of fortune: they were gamblers and
Cock-fighters, hound-breeders and
horse jockies. To hear them converse,
you would think that the grand point
of

———

any reader of Jane Austen can attest. See, for example, *Dudley* v. *Dudley*, *Quincy Reports*, 12 (Case No. 9); *Elwell* v. *Pierson*, *Quincy Reports*, 42 (Case No. 20) and *Baker* v. *Mattocks*, *Quincy Reports*, 69 (Case No. 29) *Quincy Papers*, vols. 4 and 5. See generally Marylynn Salmon, *Women and the Law of Property in Early America* (Chapel Hill, 1980). "They [Virginia lawmakers] believed that the best way of preserving valuable plantations in a slaveholding economy was to allow property owners to create entailed estates of both land and slaves." *Id.*, p. 152. See Richard B. Morris, "Primogeniture and Entailed Estates in America," *Columbia Law Review* 24 (1927).

[130]

———

all science was properly to
fix a Gaff[210] and touch with dexterity
the tails of a Cock while in combat.
He who won the last match, the Last
main, or last horse race assumed
the airs of a Hero or German po-
tentate. The ingenuity of a Locke[211]
as the discoveries of a Newton[212] were
considered as infinitely inferior
to the accomplishments of him
who knew when to Shoulder a blind
Cock or start a fleet horse.
I had heretofore heard Virginia famed
for hospitality and politeness. I made not
these discoveries. It abounds with knaves
and sharpers, and those who are adroit
at Lord Bacon's Left-handed wisdom.[213]

210. "Gaff," "a harpoon or large hook," Johnson, *Dictionary, supra,* n.p. "gaff." Commonly used in fishing, but also an implement in cock fighting, "a steel spur for a fighting cock." *Oxford English Dictionary, supra,* vol. 2, p. 1103.

211. Quincy's library contained at least some of the works of John Locke (1632–1704), whose *Two Treatises of Government* (1690) were cornerstones of American political thought. See Quincy Estate Catalogue, *supra,* item 43.

212. Sir Isaac Newton (1642–1727), the great English scientist.

213. "Sharper," "a tricking fellow; a petty thief; a rascal," Johnson, *Dictionary, supra,* n.p. "sharper." Quincy's library contained the *Works* of Francis Bacon (1561–1626), including the famous *Essays* (1st ed. 1597). See Essay 23 ("Of Cunning") and Essay 26 ("Of Seeming Wise"), *The Essays* (M. Kiernan ed., Cambridge, Mass., 1985). "Left-handed" was a "sinister" wisdom. Bacon begins his Essay 22 "We take *cunning* for a sinister or crooked wisdome." *Id.,* p. 69. In his famous *A Dissertation Upon Parties,* Henry St. John Bollingbroke (Lord Bollingbroke) writes, "But there is need of that left-handed wisdom, called cunning, and of those habits in business, called experience." Bolingbroke, *Political Writings* (ed. David Armitage, Cambridge, 1997), p. 3. (First published, 1733). Lord Chesterfield, in his letters to his son, also referred to the "cunning which Lord Bacon calls left-handed wisdom." (Letter 71, written in 1749, but not published until 1774). See Roger Coxon, *Chesterfield and his Critics* (London, 1925), p. 85. Many thanks again to Mark Sullivan, exceptional reference librarian, and to Kevin Cox, my research assistant.

[*130 continued*]

They have several wise men and
patriots; but even these are much belied, if they have not been guilty of
practices inconsistent with common

[131]

———

honesty. —'Tis, according to Shakespear, the spur of the place to be
subtle & trickish.[214]

Having now finished my tour thro'
those Southern-provinces which
boast most of their politeness,
taste and the art of true living, I
am naturally led to consider the
justness of their good opinion
of themselves.
"One affronts (says Voltaire) a whole
nation, if one doubts of this being placed
at present at the summit of taste. The
best way is to wait until time and
example shall instruct a nation where-
in it errs in it's judgment and taste."[215]
It is really affecting to consider what
a prodigious number of men have not
the least spark of taste, have no relish
for the fine arts. —

214. Quincy's library contained "The Beauties of Shakespear" (2 volumes). See Quincy, *Estate Catalogue*, item 203. See *Julius Caesar*, Act IV, Scene 2, Line 20. "There are no tricks in plain and simple faith: but hollow men, like horses hot at hand, make gallant shew and promise of their mettle, but when they should endure the bloody spur, they fall their crests, and, like deceitful jades, sink in the trial." *Id.*
215. See note 204, *supra*. [Voltaire].

[132]

_____

Taste, like phylosophy, falls to the lot
of only a small select number of privileged souls. It was in vain that
(Ovid said), GOD has created us with
countenances which look towards the
heavens (<u>erectos ad sydera tollere
vultus</u>216) for men are almost
all bent towards the Earth.

216. Ovid, *Metamorphoses*, I.86: "Countenances which look upward toward the heavens."
Quincy had copies of Ovid's *Art of Love*, *Fastorum Libes* and *Metamorphoses* in his library, see
Quincy, Estate Catalogue, Items 124, 257, 310. Ovid, Publus Ovidius Naso (43 B.C.–A.D. 17) was
a favorite of young colonial gentlemen, including Quincy and John Adams. John Adams wrote
in his *Diary*, "On a Sunday I will read the Inquiry into the Nature of the human soul, and for
Amusement I will Sometimes read Ovids Art of Love to Mrs. Savel . . ." *Diary of John Adams*,
29 Sunday, Braintree, October 5, 1758 (ed. L. H. Butterfield, L. C. Faber, W. D. Garret, 1961),
vol. 1, pp. 44–45.

[133]

1773
April 19th

———

The soils thro' Virginia and Maryland are mostly of a redish colour and sandy
substance.
Maryland is very hilly and abounds
in Oak trees.
To the South of Virginia the public roads
are thro' a level, sandy, pitch-pine
barren: when you enter Virginia,
and in proportion as you come north
you change the plain for hills,
and Pitch-pines for Oaks; and the goodness, value, and improvement of the
soil is very correspondent to
this alteration of appearances.
The Tobacco of Maryland, as I
was uniformly told both there and in
Virginia bears a preference in all
foreign markets and carries a pro-
portionable advance of price.

[134]

———

The Maryland Tobacco goes under the
denomination of colored Tobacco, and
is of a bright yellow aspect, and the
very best of it verges near to a Whitish
bright colour. This colour arises
cheifly from the nature of the soil, but
in some measure also from the
mode of curing it:—the Marylander
in this respect taking more pains
than the Virginian.

The clergy and people of this prov:[ince] are
ingaged in a very bitter, impor-
tant contest, and if we may judge
by their public papers 'tis like to
prove a very wordy war.
Til this controversy began, which is not
of very long standing, the clergy received
from all taxables, which are
all men, black and white, and all women,

[135]

_____

except white women, from sixteen to
sixty, unless exempted for age or in-
firmity by the County-Court according to positive law, forty pounds
of tobacco a year: and this tax is
payable by all Religious sects and denominations without exception.
Curious Craft!—Jesuitical
policy! Rare sport for the
genius of Voltaire!²¹⁷
The clergy tell us with immaculate
truth and still more unhypocriti-
cal solemnity, "the religion
and kingdom of CHRIST and his
followers are not of this world."
'Tis certainly happy for mankind, that
these assay-masters of religion and
the faithful are inducted into their
office by nothing more than temporary State-power, and their commissions are only durante hâc vitâ:²¹⁸ 'tis

217. See notes 204 and 215 and accompanying text, *supra.* "Jesuitical" is here used in a pejorative sense, "dissembling or equivocating." *Concise Oxford Dictionary, supra,* p. 636. The situation was serious. "Church Affairs in this Part of the World continue, in a regular Progression,
to deteriorate: and, if they go on, as they have for some Months Past, I think twelve months
from this time is the longest Period it can be possible for our Church to exist. It is terrible I do
assure you. I have not received one penny for the two years I have been Incumbent of this Parish
[Prince George's County]: and to a Man, whose daily Bread depends on his Yearly, if not daily
Income, you will guess how convenient all this must be." *Jonathan Boucher to Rev. Mr. James,*
November 16, 1773. *Maryland Hist. Mag.,* VIII. 183. *Id.* Howe, *Proceedings,* 1915–1916 [FN 468-1].
    218. "During life." *Black's Law Dictionary,* 594 (Revised 4th ed. 1968).

[136]

———

well for the Cloth, that no express
positive institution is <u>in force</u>
<u>and use</u>, limiting their authority,
revenue and office <u>quam</u> <u>diu</u>
<u>se bene</u> & <u>*christianâ*</u> fide
<u>gesserint</u>.[219]

The culture of Tobacco is declining,
and that of grain is rising fast, thro'
this province.
St. George's County and Elk-
ridge Tobacco is deemed here
to be of the best quality.

219. Translation: "As long as they shall behave themselves well and with Christian loyalty."
For "*quam diu se bene gesserint*" as words of limitation in a patent granting office for life for
judges, see J. H. Baker, *supra*, 167–168 and note 202 *supra*.

[137]

1773
April   20th
          21st
          22d

———

Maryland is the finest wheat country
in the world: the vast extended feilds[sic] of that
and other grains all thro' the country affords
great pleasure to the lover of mankind
and the useful arts; and the exquisite verdure
which at this season covers these fields
presents a prospect highly gratifying
to the sensualist and lover of nature.
The Marylanders are much attached
to that vile practice—Cock-fighting—
equally degrading sense, sentiment
and humanity. I met with two parties
of the middling rank in life who had
each spent three successive days at this
inglorious amusement, and as many
nights in riot and debauchery.

[138]*

I spent about 3 hours in company with the
famous Daniel Dulany, Esq.[220] (author
of the Considerations[221]) the Attorney General
of the province and several others of
the Bar, and Gentlemen of the province.
Dulany is a Diamond of the first
water:—a gem that may grace the
cap of a patriot or the turban of a
Sultan.

A most bitter and important dispute
is subsisting and has long subsisted in
this province touching the fees of this
officers of the colony and the Governor's proclamation
relative thereto.—At the conference
of the two houses (which I have in print[222])
the Dispute was conducted (by it is universally said) by Daniel Dulany of the Council
and the Speaker Tillingman[223] and [blank] of

220. Daniel Dulany (1722–1797). Educated at Eton, Cambridge and the Middle Temple. Opposed American revolutionary action and was, resultantly, deprived of his property as a Loyalist. See *Dictionary of American Biography*, V, 499.

221. *Considerations on the Propriety of Imposing Taxes in the British Colonies* (1765). *Id.* Howe, *Proceedings*, 1915–1916 [FN 469-2]. It is reprinted in *Maryland Hist. Mag.*, VI, 374; VII, 26.

222. Howe, *Proceedings*, 1915–1916 [FN 469-3]. *Proceedings upon the Conference, the Address to the Governor [Eden] upon the Subject of his Proclamation, the Resolves therewith sent, and the Governor's Answer thereto*, 1772.

223. Note added, not Quincy, [left margin, ll. 17, 18] Tilghman, Edward T—of [?] many year Speaker. Correction by his great-grandson. W.M.Q. of Philadelphia 1875! Possibly Edward Tilghman (1750/1–1815), lawyer, born in Wye, Maryland, practiced in Philadelphia after 1774. See *Dictionary of American Biography*, XVIII, 542.

[139]

———

of the Lower House. This dispute
tho' managed with good sense and
spirit, breaths an acrimony, virulence, and unmannerly invective
not honorary to the parties and
inconsistent with the rules and dignity of parliament.

The same dispute is now kept up
in the public papers by honorable
Daniel Dulany, Esq. on one side
and Charles Caroll [Carroll], Esq. of Carl-
ton on the other, with amazing
mutual hatred and bitterness.
The Legislature of Dulany is
Antillon, that of Caroll is
the first Citizen.[224] Caroll and

224. Charles Carroll (1736–1832). Educated in colleges of the Society of Jesus at St. Omer, Flanders, Rheims and Paris. Studied law further in London. Revolutionary leader and signer of the Declaration of Independence. Member of Continental Congress, 1776–78; U.S. Senator from Maryland, 1789–92. See *Dictionary of American Biography*, III, 522.

According to the *Dictionary of American Biography*, Dulaney "on Jan. 7, 1773, published a letter in defense of the government signed 'Antilon,' a pseudonym which it was generally understood concealed the identity of Daniel Dulany [*q.v.*]. This letter, in the form of a dialogue in which the arguments of 'First Citizen' against the government's position were overcome by Dulany speaking as 'Second Citizen,' gave Carroll his opportunity. Dramatically enough he stepped into the clothes of the straw man Dulany had knocked down and under the signature of 'First Citizen' reopened the argument. The controversy was carried on in the *Maryland Gazette* until July 1, 1773, and when it was over Carroll had become indeed something like the First Citizen of the province." *Id.*, vol. III, p. 532. Thus, Dulaney invented "First Citizen" as a straw man for argument, and Carroll adopted it for his use in a counterattack! As to "Antilon," according to Edward C. Papenfuse, Dulaney "chose 'Antilon' which combines 'anti' and an old English word for unfair taxes ["Lon"]." Remarks by Dr. Edward C. Papenfuse on the occasion of the presentation of *First Citizen Awards* to Senator Charles Sprelser & Dr. William Richardson (Feb. 17, 1945), p. 1, http://www.mdarchives.state.md.us/msa/stagger/s.1259/121/7047/htmlecpremar.htm (hereafter, "Papenfuse") access date, 2006. See *Oxford English Dictionary*

[*139 continued*]

Dulany are men of prodigious

(2nd ed., J. A. Simpson, E.S.C. Weiner, Oxford, 1989), vol. VIII, p. 1120 ("lon" obs. Forms of "loan"). This could possibly derive from the notorious forced "loans" of Charles I that resulted in the *Five Knights' Case* of 1627 and the *Petition of Right* (1628). See Coquillette, *supra*, pp. 322–325. In any event, Dr. Papenfuse believed that Dulany "wanted to remind his readers that he had once eloquently defended them against the hated Stamp Tax." Papenfuse, *supra*, p. 1. My special thanks, again, to Mark Sullivan for these insights.

[140]

———

fortunes, and their families have been
at open enmity many years.
Carol [Carroll] and his father are professed Roman Catholick, each of them
keeping a Priest and Private Chapel
in their respective houses.
There are upwards of 5000 Roman
Catholicks in this province.[225]

I attended the Supreme (called the
Provincial) Court on two Days,
but no one cause or motion
was argued, and I had therefore
no good opportunity to judge
of the talents of the Bar, but from some
little specimens and appearances I
conjecture here is not much of the
superlative.

225. Maryland was originally founded as a haven for English Catholics by George Calvert (Lord Baltimore) in 1632, but Catholics were soon in a minority. After the Glorious Revolution and the coming to the British throne of the Protestant monarchs William and Mary (1689), Anglicanism became the established religion. In 1715, the Calvert family itself, the proprietors, renounced Catholicism, but toleration of Catholics continued.

[141]

———

Daniel Dulany who heretofore
practiced with great reputation is
said to have spoke with as much
sense, elegance and spirit as he
writes: if so he must equal,
if not go beyond, all I have
yet seen or heard.

The commonality seem in general
thro' this province to be well dis-
positioned and friendly towards
strangers, and pretty industrious:
But I saw nothing to lead me to
suppose they in any measure
surpassed the New Englanders
in either of these respects.

[142]

———

Baltimore[226] is the largest, most populous and
trading town in this province.
Annapolis[227] is the metropolis or seat of
government; and the place of the Residence
of many of the most wealthy citizens;
but it is a mighty poor, diminutive,
little city, and makes a very contemptible
appearance.

226. Situated on north side of Patapsco River; 1791 population was 13,503, including 1255 slaves; Lat. 39.21.N. Long. 77.48.W. Jedidiah Morse, D.D., *The American Gazetteer*. Printed in Boston, 1797.

227. Formerly called Severn, changed by act of assembly in 1694; consists of about 40 houses; Lat. 39.25.N. Long. 78.10.W. *The American Gazetteer, Containing a Distinct Account of all the Parts of the New World*, printed for A. Millar and J. & R. Tonson, 1762. 30 miles south of Baltimore. Contains about 300 houses. Jedidiah Morse, D.D., *The American Gazetteer*. Printed in Boston, 1797.

[143]

1773
April.

―――

As soon as you enter Pennsylvania—
government the regularity, goodness, and the strait, advantageous disposition of Public Roads are evidences
of the good policy and laws of this well
regulated province.
Pennsylvania is said to be not so fine
a wheat country as Maryland, but
a better grazing country.—Cattle cover the pas-
tures in great abundance.
Very fine streams of water are
every where dispersed thro this
land, and as you approach the Capital
a prospect of the River Delaware
on which Philadelphia[228] is situated affords a delightful scene.

228. See *Illustration 16.* Consists of about 2500 houses; Lat. 40.50.N. Long. 74.00.W.
Jedidiah Morse, D.D., *The American Gazetteer* (Boston, 1797).

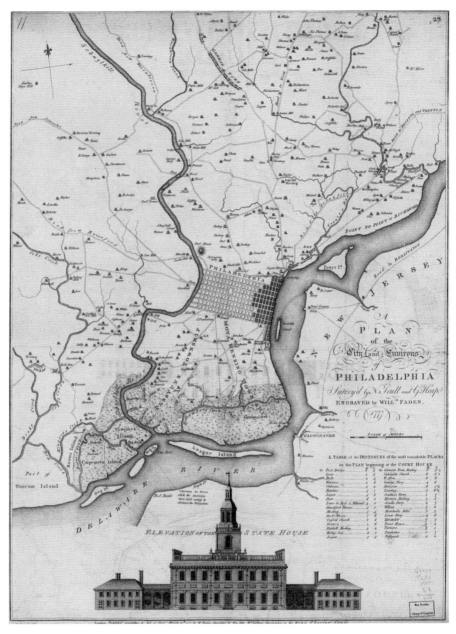

ILLUSTRATION 16. Philadelphia, plan of 1777. Courtesy, Library of Congress.

[144]

———

My journey for this several days has not
only been delightful from the gratifications
of the Eye, but the exquisite scent from
blooming orchards gave a rich perfume,
while sweetest melody of birds was
truely charming to the Ear.[229]

229. The pleasant spring weather of Quincy's overland travel north was doubtless some consolation for the rough February sea passage south to Charleston.

[145]

1773
April 24th

——

Went to public worship at St. Peter's
Church,[230] and heard the celebrated orator
Reverend Mr. [blank] Coombs,[231] an Episcopalian. He labored to
speak with propriety and was therefore not natural,
altogether; he was a little affected, but
spoke well. This may seem a paradox,
but I can't better convey my idea of him.
In prayer, he had the fault of most priests,
especially those who use established
forms, his emphasis, accent, look and
gesture was not conformable to his
subject, station and language. He made
an extempore prayer before sermon,
which in point of sentiment, propriety expression and true sublimity exceeded anything of the kind, I ever heard. This prayer he uttered with singular grace.—
His sermon was 20 minutes in length,
and was an extreme fine, moral, deis-
tical, elegant declamation—decorated
with all the beauties of polished language
and rhetorical utterance:—it closed

230. Howe, *Proceedings*, 1915–1916 [FN 470-1]. St. Peter's, founded as a chapel of ease to
Christ Church, is located on the southwest corner of Third St. and Pine St.
231. Thomas Coombe (1747–1822), Anglican clergyman, Loyalist, poet. Left America in 1779.
See *Dictionary of American Biography*, IV, 395. Howe, *Proceedings*, 1915–1916 [FN 470-1]. See
Hildeburn, Inscriptions in St. Peter's Churchyard, appendix. "John Adams described Coombe as a
'copy' of Duché."

[146]

——

most charmingly—I was in raptures.
        The Church is beautifully neat:
there is no Lord's prayer, commandments or
creed over the Communion table,[232] and
the Pulpit fronts about.
The whole congregation except the Clerk and one
other person sat all singing time, til
at the end of the Lord singing, when the whole
Church rose at the <u>Gloria Patri</u>.—The
dress and demeanor of the Audience was
quite quakerlike, decent and modest.
Reverend Mr. Blair[233] in the Evening told me that he wor-
shiped <u>this Sabbath at this church</u>. He now appears in
dress and manners quite the Layman.
In the Evening I heard that truely sensible
devout man and great Orator—Mr. Jones:[234]
Take him for all in all, and he is the best
reader and public speaker I ever heard
in the pulpit.

232. Quincy would have been familiar with churches like the King's Chapel, Boston (first church dedicated 1689), with its commandments above the altar, presented by William and Mary.

233. Howe, *Proceedings*, 1915–1916 [FN 474-1]. Samuel Blair (1741–1818), pastor of the Old South Church, Boston, 1764–1769.

234. Possibly David Jones (1736–1820), Baptist clergyman, chaplain during the Revolution and the War of 1812. Pastor in New Jersey and Pennsylvania. See *Dictionary of American Biography*, X, 165.

[147]*

1773
April 25
[left margin, ll. 1, 2]

———

This morning at sun-rise took a delightful ride of about 14 miles into the country. This country is a perfect garden.
I had almost said an Eden. However
I saw it at the highest advantage.

On my return was waited upon by young
Dr. Shippen[235] and Mr. Thomas Smith[236] a merchant
and Mr. Arodi Thayer.[237]

27th
[left margin, l. 9]

Feasted with the Superior Court Judges and all
the Bar on Turtle etc. Had much con-

235. William Shippen (1736–1808), physician, medical educator. Studied medicine in London and at the University of Edinburgh, receiving his M.D. in 1754. Appointed professor of
surgery and anatomy at the College of Philadelphia in 1765. See *Dictionary of American Biography*, XVII, 117.

236. Thomas Smith (1745–1809), born near Cruden, Aberdeenshire, Scotland. Delegate to
Pennsylvania State Constitutional Convention, 1776; member of Pennsylvania State House of
Representatives, 1776–1780; Delegate to Continental Congress from Pennsylvania, 1781–1782;
Common Pleas Court Judge, 1791; Justice of Pennsylvania State Supreme Court, 1794–1809.
Died in Philadelphia, Philadelphia County, Pa., March 31, 1809. Interment at Christ Church
Burial Ground. Joseph Illick, *Colonial Pennsylvania: A History* (New York, 1975), p. 306.

237. Arodi Thayer (1743–1831). Son of Gideon and Rachel Thayer. Born February 19, 1743.
See http://www.usigs.org/library/books/ma/Braintree1793/787.html

THE PATRIOTIC AMERICAN FARMER.
J-N D-K-NS—N Esq.ʳ BARRISTER at LAW:
Who with Attic Eloquence and Roman Spirit hath Asserted.
The Liberties of the BRITISH Colonies in America.

'Tis nobly done, to Stem Taxations Rage,
And raise, the thoughts of a degen'rate Age,
For Happiness, and Joy, from Freedom Spring ;
But Life in Bondage, is a worthless Thing.

Printed for & Sold by R. Bell. Bookseller

ILLUSTRATION 17. John Dickinson (1732–1808). Engraving by James Smither before 1797. Courtesy, the Library Company of Philadelphia. See p. 295, *Southern Journal*, p. 148.

[*147 continued*]

Joseph
Reed, Esq.
[left margin, ll. 11, 12]

versation with the <u>Farmer</u>,[238] Mr. Galloway,[239] the Speaker of the House, and [others] on
politicks:—Introduced by Mr.
Reed,[240] an eminent Lawyer,
to whom I had a Letter from the
Honorable Thomas Cushing, Esq.[241]

238. Quincy's "nickname" for John Dickinson (1732–1808), author of *Letters from a Farmer in Philadelphia* (1767–1768). See note 242, *infra*. See *Illustration 17*.

239. Joseph Galloway (1731–1803), colonial statesman, Loyalist. Rose early to eminence at Philadelphia bar. See *Dictionary of American Biography*, VII, 116.

240. Joseph Reed (1741–1785), lawyer, Revolutionary soldier and statesman. Studied law with Richard Stockton and at the Middle Temple, London. Served as president of the second Provincial Congress early in 1775. Delegate to Continental Congress, 1777–1778. See *Dictionary of American Biography*, XV, 451.

241. Thomas Cushing (1725–1788), merchant and politician. Speaker of Massachusetts General Court, 1766–1774. Member of First and Second Continental Congresses; Massachusetts lieutenant governor, 1780–1788. See *Dictionary of American Biography*, IV, 632.

[148]

1773
Ap:l 28th

John Dickinson
  Esq.
The farmer
[left margin, ll. 3, 4]

Jon:a Smith
[left margin, l. 12]

———

This forenoon John Dickinson, Esq.[242]
waited on me at my Lodgings and spent
about an hour with me, and engaged me to
dine with him 3d of May at his Country-
seat.
Compared with the honours paid the above Gentlemen
in all the other provinces, you may justly
say "A prophet is not without honour,
save in his own country."

242. John Dickinson "The Farmer" (1732–1808). Educated at home and at the Middle Temple, London. Returned to Philadelphia in 1757 and entered practice. He had an extensive
involvement in Revolutionary politics. Favored conciliation to separation and voted against the
Declaration of Independence as a matter of principle. One of only two Congressmen to volun-
teer for armed service. Member of Stamp Act Congress and Continental Congresses. See *Dictionary of American Biography*, V, 299.
    Dickinson was an accomplished essayist, his most famous writings being *Letters from a
Farmer in Philadelphia*, hence Quincy's appellation of Dickinson as "The Farmer." These *Letters* were originally written between 1767–1768, and were an attack on the Townshend Acts of
1767. See E. Alfred Jones, *American Members of the Inns of Court* (London, 1924), pp. 6–63. As
with Quincy, Dickinson was a moderate who wished to avoid bloodshed. *Id.*, p. 62. See *Illustration 17* and note 238, *supra*.

[*148 continued*]

A like complement paid me by Mr.
Stanton.[243]

Dined with Mr. Jon:a Smith[244] a very
worthy and sensible merchant with several
very worthy and sensible lawyers.

243. Mark, 6:4. Reads: "A prophet is not without honor, except in his own country, among his own relatives, and in his own house." Quincy was sensitive that he was "not admitted to the Gown" of a barrister in Massachusetts. See *Quincy Papers*, *Reports*, vol. 4, p. 317. His son believed this was because his "political course" rendered him "obnoxious to the Supreme Court of the province." Josiah Quincy, *Memoir of the Life of Josiah Quincy Jun.* (1st ed., 1825), p. 27. "Mr. Stanton" could be Daniel Stanton of Philadelphia who took a major appeal to the Privy Council concerning Rhode Island land in the late 1750s. See Mary S. Bilder, *The Transatlantic Constitution: Colonial Legal Culture in the Empire* (Cambridge, Mass., 2004), p. 171.

244. Jonathan Bayard Smith (1742–1812), merchant, Revolutionary patriot and soldier. Served on Continental Congress. See *Dictionary of American Biography*, XVII, 308.

[149]

1773 Apːl 29th
[left margin, l. 1]

———

Dined with Mr. Thomas Smith merchant
in Philadelphia and a select company:—
Was visited in the morning by the Reverend Mr. Ewing[245]
who spent 2 hours with me and with whom I
dine on 5th May. He appears quite the man
of sense, breeding and chatholicism,[246] and he gave
me much insight into the present state of
the College[247] in this place. To the South
and North of this prov:[ince] we have by
much too exalted an idea of it.

30th
[left margin, l. 11]

Waited upon this morning for about an
hour by Chief Justice Allen[248] and his sons.
Dined at the house of that very sensible

245. John Ewing (1732–1802), Presbyterian clergyman. Pastor, First Church, Philadelphia. Provost, professor of natural philosophy at University of Pennsylvania after 1779. See *Dictionary of American Biography*, VI, 236.

246. "Catholicism" in the sense of "catholic" as "universal" and "general." See Johnson, *Dictionary, supra*, n.p. "catholick."

247. First chartered as an Academy in 1751, and then, in part through Benjamin Franklin's efforts, as a College in 1765, the University of Pennsylvania established the first medical school in the Colonies in 1765. It acquired the title "University" in 1779.

248. William Allen (1704–1780), merchant and jurist. Chief Justice of Pennsylvania, 1750–1774. Founder of Allentown. See *Dictionary of American Biography*, I, 208.

[*149 continued*]

polite and facetious lawyer, Joseph Reed
Esq. in company with the Farmer,[249] Judge
Jared Ingersoll,[250] several other lawyers
and merchants. Our Discourse altogether political, polite and entertaining.
Mrs. Reed the Daughter of the late Dennis
Debert, Esq.[251] (our agent) is an ornament
of her own sex, and the Delight of Ours.

Joseph
Reed
[left margin, ll. 13, 15]

249. Again, "the Farmer" refers to John Dickinson (1732–1808). See notes 238 and 242, *supra*. For Joseph Reed (1741–1783) noted patriot and personal aid to Washington, see note 251, *infra*. *Supra*, n.p. "facetious," meaning "gay, cheerful, witty." See *Johnson's Dictionary*, n.p. "facetious."

250. Jared Ingersoll (1722–1781), lawyer and Loyalist. Judge of vice-admiralty after 1768. Officiated at Philadelphia, 1771–1775. His son, Jared (1749–1822), was counsel of many of the early leading cases before the U.S. Supreme Court. See *Dictionary of American Biography*, IX, 467.

251. Dennys De Berdt (1694–1770), merchant, colonial agent in London for Massachusetts and Delaware. See *Dictionary of American Biography*, V, 180. Howe, *Proceedings*, 1915–1916 [FN 472-4]. His daughter, Esther De Berdt (1746–1780), married Joseph Reed (1741–1785), the distinguished patriot and personal aide to George Washington, in May of 1770. Esther was certainly Quincy's "Mrs. Reed." See William B. Reed, *The Life of Esther De Berdt, afterward Esther Reed of Pennsylvania* (Philadelphia, 1853). Joseph Reed was "a member of the committee of correspondence for Philadelphia in November, 1774, and in January, 1775, was president of the 2d Provincial Congress." *Virtual American Biographies*, http://www.virtualology.com/ opjosephreed, access date October, 2006. Following his distinguished service in the Revolution, Reed became President of the Supreme Executive Council of Pennsylvania (1778–1781). He died in 1785 before being able to take a seat in Congress. Esther and Joseph had three distinguished judges among their descendents: son Joseph (1772–1846), who became Attorney General of Pennsylvania; grandson William (1806–1876), who also became Attorney General of Pennsylvania and was a distinguished diplomat; and grandson Henry (1808–1854), an academic and Vice-Provost of the University of Pennsylvania. *Id.* My thanks to my most distinguished colleague, Mary Sarah Bilder, for this information.

[150]

1773
30 April

Joseph
Reed
[left margin, ll. 7, 8]

———

Towards Evening, Judge Ingersoll and
Mr. Reed waited on me round the
town to show me its Environs and
public buildings.

May 1st
[left margin, l. 5]

Took a three hours ride with Mr. Reed round
the vicinity of Philadelphia: received much information form him relative to Mr. Dickenson (the Farmer's)[252] manners, disposition and
character: as also touching Chew[253] and
Galloway.[254]

Feasted with the Sons of St. (alias King)
Tammany.[255] (3 French horns, Bassoon,
Three fiddles, etc. before and after dinner.)

252. See notes 238, 242, and 249, *supra*.
253. Benjamin Chew (1722–1810), lawyer. Chief Justice of Pennsylvania Supreme Court,
1774–1776. See *Dictionary of American Biography*, IV, 64.
254. See note 239, *supra*.
255. Howe, *Proceedings*, 1915–1916 [FN 472-6]. On Tammany and the Philadelphia Society,
see *Penn. Mag. of Hist. and Biog.*, XXV, 433; XXVI, 7, 207, 335, 443. An account of this particular meeting is in *Id.*, XXV, 446.

[*150 continued*]

The account I have received of Bethlem[256] and it's
Inhabitants, who are all Moravians,
is truely singular and surprising.

256. 53 miles north of Philadelphia. The Renewed Church of the Brethren ("Moravian Church") was founded in Bohemia in 1467. Bethlehem, Pennsylvania, was founded by the followers of the sect in about 1740, and remains the center of the faith today.

[151]

1773
May 2

———

Went to the Public worship of
a Romish Church.[257] Such ceremony, pomp, and solemnity were
surprising, entertaining and instructive. The Devotion of priest and
people were evidences of the force
of superstition and priestcraft.
The deepest solemnity of worship
and musick: the greatest sanctity
of countenance and gesture.[258]

      While external forms and
appearances made a deep impression on my own mind, I could
easily conceive how much deeper they must impress others.
While attention held me mute,
reason lost part of her influence,
and left subsequent reflection to lead
me to a better judgment.

257. This was probably St. Mary's Church, which was completed in 1763. See *New Catholic Encyclopedia* (New York, 1967), vol. 9, pp. 972–973. Across the street and down Willing's Alley was the "Old Chapel," St. Joseph's, dating from 1733. The two churches were one Parish. Robert Molyneux (1738–1808), a Jesuit who Quincy met, would become pastor of both in 1772. Again, many thanks to Mark Sullivan, Reference Librarian extraordinaire. See also note 272, *infra*.

258. Quincy's reaction, both suitably impressed and suitably skeptical by the standards of the Massachusetts establishment, is reminiscent of similar reactions to Rome on the "Grand Tour." See Bruce Redford, *Venice and the Grand Tour* (New Haven, 1996), 30–31. Indeed, Quincy's Voyage to the South was, in a sense, his equivalent of the "Grand Tour."

[*151 continued*]

    In the words of the NEW England
psalms—"In me the fire enkindled is."

[152]

1773
May 2d

Startin
[left margin, l. 11]

———

Attended the Moravian—worship:
the softest kind of vocal and instrument-
al musick made some compensation
to the Ear for the gross affronts offered the understanding. (More incoherent, fulsome,
absurd and almost impious nonsense I
never heard.)
The prayers, addresses and worship of
this sect seem very much confined
to the 2d person in the Trinity.[259]
N.B. I dined this day with Mr.
Startin.[260]

259. In other words, the "Son," Jesus Christ.
260. Howe, *Proceedings*, 1915–1916 [FN 473-2]. Charles Startin, who married Sarah, daughter of Richard Clarke, of Boston. He presented a petition to the Continental Congress on September 24, 1776. See *Journal of the Continental Congress, 1774–1789.*

[153]

1773
May 3d

John
Dickenson
[left margin, ll. 11, 13]

———

The morning and forenoon spent between reading and amusements of the
itinerary kind.
Dined with the Celebrated Pennsylvania
Farmer John Dickenson, Esq.[261]
at his country seat about 2 ½ miles
from town. A large company
were very elegantly entertained with
Turtle and a plenteous table.
This worthy and arch-politician,
(for such he is though his views and disposition lead him to refuse the latter
appellation) here enjoys otium cum
dignitate[262] as much as any man.
Take into consideration the antique
look of his house, his gardens,
green-house, bathing house,
grotto, study, fish-pond,
fields, meadows, vista,
thro' which is a distant prospect

261. See notes 238, 242, and 249, *supra*, and *Illustration 17*. The name is correctly spelt "Dickinson."
262. Translation: "leisure with dignity."

[154]

———

of Delaware River, his paintings,
antiquities, improvements etc.
in short his whole life, and we
are apt to think him the happiest of
mortals:—I verily believe he enjoys
much true felicity: but as Whitfield[263]
said of the man in the Gospel—did
you ever see a man or his station
without a <u>but</u>. I am mistaken, if
this engaging, and stricktly speaking
charming man, has not his.
He was polite eno' to repeatedly
request my acceptance from him of
Pennsylvania laws,[264] & I was unpolite and thoughtless eno'
as often to refuse them. However I
have this excuse, I had before refused
a like offer from Mr. <u>Speaker</u> Galloway, and had engaged one of

263. George Whitefield (1714–1770), the famous Methodist preacher. He died in Newbury-
port, Massachusetts, on one of his several American trips. See *The Compact Edition of the Dictionary of National Biography* (Oxford, 1975), vol. 2, p. 2253.

264. This would most likely be either *Charters, and Acts* of *Province* [of Pennsylvania]
1682–1759 (12 mo., Peter Miller, Philadelphia, 1762), known as "Little Peter Miller" or the same
in folio, known as "Big Peter Miller." See *Catalogue of the Library of the Law School of Harvard
University*, vol. II, p. 322 (1909); *Pimsleur's Checklist of Basic American Legal Publications* (ed. M.
S. Zubrow, 2001), "Pennsylvania, p. 1." Again, my thanks to Mark Sullivan, Reference Librarian, Boston College Law School.

[155]

———

the Edition now printing:[265] —
I should have accepted this latter
offer, if I had thought better.[266]

I this day had confirmed to me, what I
ever believed—that a certain
North American Dr. [blank (Franklin)]
is a very trimmer—a very courtier.[267] Perhaps my former sentiments might make the conviction
easier—however I had (to me)
satisfactory evidence.

[Added, Bottom of page]
N.B. Jan 1775 London. I am now very well
satisfied, that the abovenamed Dr. has been
grossly calumniated:—and I have one more
reason to induce me to be cautious how I
hearken too readily to the slander of envious
or malevolent tongues. This minute I tho[ugh]t
is but justice to insert in order to take of any
impression to the disadvantage of Dr. Franklin,

---

265. This would have been *Acts of Assembly 1700–1775* (fol. Hall & Sellers, Philadelphia, 1775).
See *Catalogue of the Library of the Law School of Harvard University, supra,* vol. II, 322.

266. This was true. As of Quincy's death, there was no book of Pennsylvania laws in his
library. See Quincy, Estate Catalogue, *supra.*

267. "Trimmer," one "who changes sides to balance parties, a turn coat." Johnson, *Dictionary, supra,* n.p. "trimmer." "Courtier," one "that courts or solicits the Favor of another." *Id.,*
n.p. "courtier." These are pejorative terms.

[N.B. as continued by Quincy on left margin of page 156]

whom I am now fully convinced is one of the wisest
and best of men upon Earth:—One, of whom it may
be said that this world is not worthy. Quincy jun.

[156]

1773
May 4

———

Spent about 2 hours in private
conversation with Chief Justice Allen.
He gave me one new piece of
intelligence, which was, that Dr.
Franklin was the first proposer
of the Stamp Act. Mr. Allen
said he knew this certainly to be
fact: I might depend on it:
That George Grenville[268] told him
so, and he was certain of it from
other quarters.
I find men who are very great foes
to each other in this province,
unite in their doubts, insinuations and revilings of Franklin.

268. George Grenville (1712–1770), First Lord of the Treasury and Chancellor of the Exche-
quer, 1763–65. See *Dictionary of National Biography*, XXIII, 113.

[EXTRA PAGE INSERTED BETWEEN PAGES 156–157]

> Quincy, Massachusetts
> February 12 /1878

When the Memoir of J. Quincy Jr. was published in 1825, my father decided not to publish this passage. Some years after, the passage was read to Mr. Sparks, who regretted it was not published, and asked and obtained a copy of it. When I published a 3d Edition in 1874–5. I intended to print it, but my brother, Edmund, told me there was yet a strong dislike of Franklin in some classes in Philadelphia, who said that in some important respects, his conduct had been a great disadvantage to the young men of Philadelphia, and set them a bad example. I therefore concluded to follow my father's opinion and omit it.   Eliza Susan Quincy.

[See discussion at Editor's *Foreword*, pp. 3–4, *supra*, and Transcriber's *Foreword*, p. 8 *supra*. Everything from the May 3d entry, "If I had thought better," p. 306 [165] through "In the afternoon went with a number of gentlemen," p. 314 [159] was excised, including the visit to the Catholic chapel May 6th, most certainly by Eliza Quincy.]

[157]

1773
May 4

Wm Shippen
[left margin, l. 2]

Ewing
T. Smith.
[left margin, ll. 4, 6]

———

Dined with William Shippen, jun.
brother of Mrs. Blair.[269]

May 5th
[left margin, l. 3]

Dined with Reverend Mr. Ewing, to whom
I was recommended by Reverend Mr How.[270]
Spent the afternoon with a large
company at Mr. Thomas Smith's.

May 6th
[left margin, l. 7]

Was attended by Dr. Rush[271] to the

269. Howe, *Proceedings*, 1915–1916 [FN 474-1]. Susanna Shippen (1743–1821) married Samuel Blair (1741–1818).

270. Howe, *Proceedings*, 1915–1916 [FN 474-2]. Probably Joseph Howe, of the New South Church, 1773–1775.

271. Benjamin Rush (1745–1813), physician and Revolutionary patriot. Studied medicine with John Redman and attended first lectures of William Shippen and John Morgan at the College of Philadelphia, where he later taught chemistry. Elected to the Continental Congress, 1776, he was a signer of the Declaration of Independence. See *Dictionary of American Biography*, XVI, 227.

[*157 continued*]

mansion of one of the Super-in-
tendants of Romish Chapel. Mr.
Farmer[272] being out of town, Mr.
Molineux (an Englishman from
Lancaster in England, and joint
super intendant with Mr. F[armer]) carried
us to see the Inner Appartments
of the Dwelling house and the
Old Chapel.[273] The picture of
the Virgin Mary feeding Jesus

272. Ferdinand Farmer (1720–1786), Jesuit priest. Came from Germany to America in 1752; worked as a missionary out of St. Joseph's parish, Philadelphia. See *Dictionary of American Biography*, VI, 276. "Molineux" was Robert Molyneux (1738–1808), another Jesuit priest, who delivered the funeral sermon on Farmer's death on August 17, 1786. See *A funeral sermon on the death of the Rev. Ferdinand Farmer* (C. Talbot, Philadelphia, 1786). This was one of the first Catholic publications in what was to become the United States. Many thanks to that most extraordinary of reference librarians, Mark Sullivan of Boston College Law School. Molyneux was a close friend of John Carroll, the future American archbishop, whom he had met at the famous Jesuit school in Bruges. See *New Catholic Encyclopedia* (New York, 1967), vol. 9, p. 1016.

273. The "Old Chapel," St. Joseph's, still stands in Philadelphia. It was supplemented by St. Mary's Church, and Molyneux became pastor of both in 1772. *Id.*, vol. 9, p. 1016.

[158]

———

Christ over the Alter of the Old Chapel
was a very good peice of painting;
the Painting exhibiting his crucifix-
ion in the New Chapel is in my
opinion much better done.

    Mr. Molineux told us very
freely that he and Mr. Farmer were
both of the order of the Jesuits.[274] He and
the Sexton (a Dutchman) on enter-
ing the Chapel sprinkled themselves with holy water and crossed
themselves: on approaching
the Communion-table bowed the
knee very low, and on entering within
performed the same ceremony, and the
like at their departure.

    We were not asked to come

274. The Jesuit order was suppressed in 1773 by order of Pope Clement XIV, and finally reestablished by Pope Pius VII in 1814. This left both Farmer and Molyneux in an awkward position close to the time of Quincy's visit. For political reasons, however, the Society was not suppressed in Russia. Father Molyneux was particularly active in keeping the Society viable, associating himself to the Jesuit Society in Russia and Father Gabriel Gruber, General of the Society of Jesus there. "Molyneux rejoiced in the preliminary restoration of the Society, of which he was named American superior on June 21, 1805." *Dictionary of American Biography*, XIII, p. 82. He later became Rector of Georgetown.

    It is not surprising that the sexton was "Dutch," as Father Farmer was from a Swabian family by the name of Steinmeyer (he changed to "Farmer" on arrival). He ministered especially to the German-Catholic congregation in Philadelphia, centered in St. Joseph's parish, and engaged in the dangerous work of a traveling missionary, sometimes in the disguise of a Quaker merchant. When the British captured Philadelphia in 1777, Father Farmer extended his ministry to the Hessian regiments, but he refused to assist the British in their efforts to raise a regiment of Catholic "volunteers." In 1778, he founded the first Catholic congregation in New York City, and in 1779, he was elected a trustee of the University of Pennsylvania. See *Dictionary of American Biography*, VI, 276–277.

[*158 continued*]

within the Communion, nor presented with a sight of the Nick
nacks I had seen at a distance.[275]

The

---

275. The communion wafers? "Nick nacks" was an archaic English term for small pastry
desserts. See note 94, *supra*.

[159]

Dr. Cox
[left margin, l. 6]

———

last sabbath.
     Molineux's character is to
me problematical: Farmer
appears much of the Devotee.

May 6th
[left margin, l. 5]

Dined with Dr. [blank] Cox[276] a worthy,
sensible, polite, opulent merchant, <u>who</u>
has a most accomplished lady to his wife.
In the afternoon went with a number of Gentlemen
to see the hospital and hear a lecture from
young Dr. Shippen. The curiosities
of this hospital are far beyond anything of the kind in North America.[277]
Dr. S[hippen] gave a very learned, intelligible,
elegant and concise lecture, which did him
honor as a physician, composuist and
orator.
Returned and supped with Dr. Cox and spent
a very social night.

276. Was this the distinguished Philadelphia merchant and economist, Tench Coxe (1755–1824), or, more likely, his father, William Coxe? My thanks, again, to my most valued colleague, Mary Sarah Bilder, and that exceptional research librarian, Mark Sullivan. The Coxe papers are now available at the Historical Society of Pennsylvania.

277. The University of Pennsylvania established the first medical school in America in 1765. See note 247, *supra*.

[160]

1773
May 9th

Mr.
Whycoff
[left margin, ll. 2, 4]

Allen
[left margin, l. 8]

———

This day I was to have dined with Mr. Peter
Whycoff[278] merchant but having met with
Thomas Oliver, Esq.[279] of Cambridge, who was
returning home, I embraced the opp[ortunit]y of
so agreeable company, and set out for New
England 10 days earlier than I intended.
I was also obliged to decline the invitation of Chief Justice Allen to dine with him,
on a like account.

Our tour thro' Pennsylvania on the

278. "Whyckoff" was a distinguished New York surname, although 'Peter Whycoff' has not yet been identified. Pieter Claesen, a very important citizen of the New Netherlands, chose the name 'Wyckoff' in 1664, when the British captured New York and required the Dutch there to adopt English surnames. Claesen created for himself the name 'Wyckoff,' a combination of words meaning 'parish' and 'court,' a reflection of his duties as local magistrate. Thus, every person today bearing the name Wyckoff (in any of its countless spellings) shares this common ancestor." See http://www.nyhistory.org/nyhsqa.html. My thanks to my distinguished colleague, Mary Sarah Bilder.

279. Thomas Oliver (1734–1815), lieutenant-governor of Massachusetts, 1774. Graduated Harvard (1753); proscribed, 1778. See *Dictionary of National Biography*, XLII, 151. Oliver's house in Cambridge, Mass., "Elmwood," is now the official residence of the President of Harvard.

[*160 continued*]

borders of the River Delaware was variegated by those inchanting prospects
of sea, navigation, land, industry and plenty,
which serve to delight the senses and elevate
the mind.

[161]

———

Gen:l remarks & observons on
Pennsylvania.

The Pennsylvanians as a body of people
may be justly characterized as industrious, sensible and wealthy: the Philadelphians as commercial, keen and
frugal: their economy and reserve have
sometimes been censured as civility
and avarice, but all that we saw in
this excellent city was replete with
benevolence, hospitality, sociability
and politeness, joined with that prudence and cau-
tion natural to an understanding
people who are alternately visited
by a variety of strangers differing
in rank, fortune, ingenuity and character.

[162]

———

The legislative body of this province is composed of the Governor and the representatives
of the people, and the state of their acts are
in the name of the Governor by and with the consent and advice of the freemen of the prov:[ince]
of Pennsylvania.

I attended 3 several days the setting of the
Superior Court, (which is as contemptible a one as I ever
saw.) Without learning, dignity and order a Court
will soon loose much of it's authority and more of it's repute.
The Bar are a very Respectable body.

The Bettering-house,[280] hospital and State house[281]
are the public buildings of the City, but rather
well calculated for use than elegance or
show.

---

280. Howe, *Proceedings*, 1915–1916 [FN 476-1]. Reformatory.
281. See *Illustration 18*.

ILLUSTRATION 18. View of Philadelphia and the State House in 1778, engraving by J. Trenchard after C.W. Pleale, *Columbian Magazine*, vol. 1, no. 11 (July 1787). Courtesy, Boston Athenaeum.

[163]

————

All sects of religionists compose this
city; and the most influential, opulent
and first characters scarce ever attend
Public worship anywhere. This is amazingly general and arises
partly from policy, partly from other
causes. A man is sure to be less exceptionable to the many, more likely
to carry his point in this prov:[ince] by neglecting
all religious parties in general, than adhere-
ing to any on[e] in particular. And they who call
themselves Christians much sooner en-
courage and vote for a deist or an Infidel, than
one who appears under a religious
persuasion different from their
own. "Tantum religio potuit suadere."[282]

282. Translation: "To such (evils) could religion urge people." This is a partial quote from
Lucretius (98–c. 55 B.C.E.), *De Rerum Natura*, 1.101. See Howatson, *supra*, pp. 330–331. Quincy
may have gotten this maxim from Francis Bacon's essay "Of Unity in Religion," where Bacon
stated, "Lucretius the poet, when he beheld the act of *Agamemnon*, that could endure the
sacrificing of his own daughter, exclaimed: *Tantum Relligio potuit suadere malorum.*" See *Francis Bacon, The Essayes of Counsele Civill and Monall* (ed. M. Kiernan, Cambridge, Mass., 1985),
p. 14. Bacon was one of Quincy's favorite authors. See note 295, *infra*.

[164]

———

There is a proprietary influence in this prov:[ince]
destructive of a liberal conduct in the legislative branch and of [blank]
in the executive authority here.
The House of Representatives are but 36 in number, as a body held in great, remarkable and
general contempt: much despised for their base
acquiescence with the laws and measures of the
proprietary party, and singularly odious for
certain provincial maneuvers too
circumstantial to relate.

Their debates are not public, which is said now
to be the Case of only this house of Commons throughout the Continent. Many
have been the attempts to procure an alteration in this respect but all to no purpose.
The influence[283] which governs this house is equal
if not superior to anything we hear of
but that which governs the British parliament; and the

283. "Influence," i.e., the influence of special interests. "Ascendent power." Johnson, *Dictio-nary, supra*, n.p. "influence."

[165]

———

proprieter is said to have as <u>dead a</u>
<u>set</u>[284] in a Pennsylvania Assembly as Lords Bute[285] or North[286] in the
English house of commons.
This Government is in great danger from
this quarter.—But a lineal successive
defect of capacity, want of policy, glaring avarice and oppressive measures in the Penn-family is said to have prevented and guarded against much of the mischief which might otherwise have taken place.[287]

[Continued from preceding line down entirety of left margin]

But should a subtle and genuine keen modern statesman (a Sir Robert
Walpole[288] for Instance) arise from this stock,[289] great and important
maneuvers may be expected. This family lost much of their Prov:[incia]l
influence by renouncing the Religion of their Ancestors and of the Colony
in general for that of Episcopacy.

Notwithstanding the Prop:[rietar]y influence before spoken of, there is a cer-

284. Special influence? See "set" as in "to fix, to establish" Johnson, *Dictionary, supra*, n.p.,
"set." Today we refer to "the fix being in." Could also refer to a "packed house," using "set" as
"persons that belong together." *Concise Oxford Dictionary, supra*, 1109.

285. John Stuart, third Earl of Bute (1713–1792). Ultimately unpopular political figure; voted
against Stamp Act, 1766, and subsequently traveled abroad incognito. See *Dictionary of National
Biography*, LV, 92.

286. Frederick North, second Earl of Guilford (1732–1792). Leader of the House of Commons, 1767; first Lord of the Treasury, 1770. See *Dictionary of National Biography*, XLI, 159.

287. See note 325, *infra* on the history of the Penn family.

288. Sir Robert Walpole (1676–1745), statesman. Recognized leader of Whig party, 1703;
favored religious toleration; leader of the House of Commons, 1711; long and active political
career. See *Dictionary of National Biography*, LIX, 178.

289. See note 325, *infra* on the Penn family.

[165 continued]

tain Quaker Int:[eres]t which operates much
against the Proprietor in land causes in
the Courts of Common law, where the Jury
frequently give verdicts against the opinion of
the judges.[290] In the house of Reps
the Leaders of the Quaker party are often
of the Proprietory likewise [i.e., against?]. All
general questions and points are carried by the Quakers: that is, by
their union they defeat the operations of all other sects in questions
which any way relate to or may in the end affect religious
concerns.—But they are very

290. Quincy's *Reports* and *Law Commonplace Book* frequently focused on jury power. See *Angier* v. *Jackson*, (1763), 84; *Norwood* v. *Fairservice*, *Quincy Papers*, vols. 4 and 5, (1765), 189; and *Carpenter* v. *Fairservice* (1767), 239. See also Daniel R. Coquillette, "First Flower—The Earliest American Law Reports and the Extraordinary Josiah Quincy, Jr. (1744–1775)," *Quincy Papers*, vol. 4.

[166]

———

public spirited in all matters of public
edifices and charitable institutions.
There is also throughout the whole province
among the husbandmen a spirit of industry and useful improvement.

There is no militia in the prov:[ince] and of
course no seeking after petty commissions, etc.—The advantages and
disadvantages of this is a topick of doubtful disputation:—we shall never all
think alike on this head.—
Many of the Quakers and all of the Moravians hold defensive war lawful;
offensive otherwise.

[167]

———

There is a general disliking, not to say
antipathy among the Quakers against N[ew] Eng[lan]d:
and this aversion has it's influence in
their judgment on the men and things
of that country, and especially in
their opin:[ion] concerning the public
transaction of the Massachusetts Bay.
They are frequently calling to mind
and often relating little anecdotes of
the severities used towards their
ancestors in that province.—
No doubt the story is exaggerated,
but they give it credit, and feel
accordingly.[291]

291. In fact, there was substantial persecution of Quakers in Massachusetts during the 17th
century. See George A. Selleck, *Quakers in Boston: 1656–1964* (Cambridge, Mass., 1976), pp.
1–17. William Robinson and Marmaduke Stevenson were hanged in 1659, Mary Dyer in 1660,
and William Leddra in 1661. Later events, including intervention by Charles II, led to toleration. *Id.*, pp. 18–32.

[168]

———

The streets of Philadelphia inter-
sect each other at right angles,[292] and
it is probably the most regular and
best laid out city in the world:—
perhaps equal to Babylon of Old; and
peradventure in other less-eligible respects
may equal it, within the compass of
two centuries:—I mean in numbers, wealth,
splendor, luxury and vice.—
This city & prov:[ince] are in a most
flourishing state: and if numbers
of buildings, men, artificers, and
trade is to settle the point, Philadelphia is the Metropolis of this
Northern region.

292. See *Illustration 16.*

[169]

———

The Philadelphians boast of their
market, and most of the Southern
gentlemen justifie this vaunting:—
it is undoubtedly the best regulated
on the continent: but in point
of plenty and goodness of beaf
mutton, veal, lamb and poultry
they most certainly do not equal
Boston; I think are visibly inferior to it in these
respects.
In the Articles of Bread, Sparrow-
grass,[293] and butter, I never saw any
place equal to it.

293. Asparagus. See Johnson, *Dictionary*, *supra*, n.p., "sparrow grass." i.e., "corrupted from
asparagus."

[170]

———

The Philadelphians in respect of the
bounty and decency of table are an
example to the world; especially
to the American: with the means
of profusion, they are not luxurious,
with the bounties of earth and sea,
they are not riotous; with the
riches of commerce and industry, they
avoid even the appearance of
epicurean splendor and parade.

Very few ladies in Philadelphia
head their tables[294] on days
of entertainments of several gentlemen.
At first I was not pleased with
this custom: on reflection and further
consideration, I approve it.—
However I prophesy that it will be laid
aside here in a very few years.

294. Head, "place of honor," i.e., act as hostess at the table's head. See Johnson, *Dictionary*, *supra*, n.p. "head."

[171]

———

The political state of Pennsylvania
is, at this time, the calmest of
any on the Continent.

The attention, respect and civility paid
me during my residence in this
agreeable town is apt to byass [bias] my
judgment; as no doubt all things
receive a tincture; if not their
form, from the medium thro'
which they are received.[295]

295. A literary device of Francis Bacon. "And as veins of water acquire divers flavors . . .
according to the nature of the soil through which they flow . . . just so in these legal systems
natural equity is tinged and stained . . . according to the site of territories, the disposition of
peoples, and the nature of Commonwealth." Francis Bacon, *The Aphorism* (M. S. Neustadt ed.)
Ph.D. Thesis, University Microfilms Service, 1990, p. 273. See also Francis Bacon, *The Advancement of Learning* (1st published, London, 1605), *The Oxford Francis Bacon*, IV (ed. M. Kiernan,
Oxford, 2000), p. 102. Bacon was one of Quincy's favorite authors, and Gilbert Stuart painted
Quincy's portrait with a volume of Bacon in the background. See note 323, *infra*. Quincy owned
Bacon's *Works* at his death. See Quincy, Estate Catalogue, *supra*, item 42.

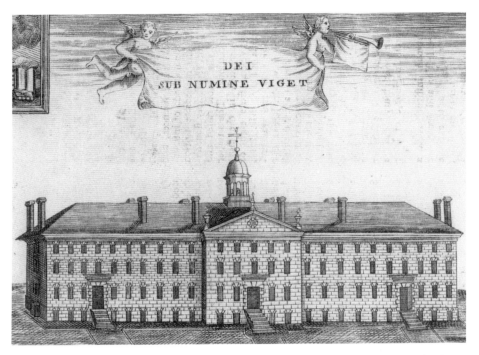

ILLUSTRATION 19. Nassau Hall, Princeton, copperplate engraving, James Parker, 1760. *New American Magazine*, No. 27 (March 1760). Courtesy, Princeton University Library, Department of Rare Books and Special Collections. See *Nassau Hall: 1756–1956* (ed. H. L. Savage) (Princeton, 1956), p. 163.

[172]

1773
May 10
[left margin, l. 1]

———

Owing to the Company with which I was now
associated I passed thro' New Jersey
with unusual, and comparatively un-
profitable speed.
Burlington[296] which I saw at a small distance, and
Trenton,[297] which I passed hastily through
are pleasantly situated and appear
flourishing.
Princetown[298] where WE tarried one night
is a delightful and healthy spot: the
College[299] is charmingly situated and is
a commodious and handsome edifice:
It is said to be in a flourishing state.
The soil and culture of the Jersies are
equal, if not superior, to any (yet settled) in
America. 'Tis indeed a fine country.

296. Situated on an island in the middle of the Delaware River, opposite to Philadelphia; Lat. 40.40.N. Long. 74.10.W. *The American Gazetteer, Containing a Distinct Account of all the Parts of the New World*, printed for A. Millar and J. & R. Tonson, 1762. 18 miles NE of Philadelphia; 160 houses; 1000 white, 140 black inhabitants. Jedidiah Morse, D.D., *The American Gazetteer*. Printed in Boston, 1797.

297. Lat. 41.29.N. Long. 72.22.W. Between 200–300 houses and 2000 inhabitants; 12 miles SW of Princeton, 30 miles NE of Philadelphia. Jedidiah Morse, D.D., *The American Gazetteer*. Printed in Boston, 1797.

298. About 80 dwelling houses. 53 miles SW of New York. Jedidiah Morse, D.D., *The American Gazetteer*. Printed in Boston, 1797.

299. Princeton was founded in 1746 as the College of New Jersey in Elizabeth, New Jersey, and was moved to Princeton in 1756. See *Illustration 19*.

[173]

———

Having passed rapidly thro' this prov:[ince]
and for that reason declined delivering
any of my Letters, I am quite an
incompetent judge of the Constitution, laws, policy, and manners of
this people.

1773
10 May
[left margin, l. 7]

In the evening we reached Powles-
Hook ferry, and next morning reached New York.[300]
In the Afternoon and Evening we traversed
the whole city: and spent the
Night at our own Lodgings in company
with Major R. Bayard[301] & Mr. Hide.

300. See *Illustration 20*.

301. In January 1773, Lord Stirling visited Mount Vernon and escorted George Washington, John Parke Custis, and a Major Robert Bayard on a trip northward. Tom J. Collins, *A Brief Summary of Some of the Pre-War Days of George Washington*, Revwar.org, 1998–2003. For Colonel William Bayard, see note 307, *infra*.

ILLUSTRATION 20. A view of New York from the North West, 1777. *The Atlantic Neptune*, 1763–1784. See Gloria G. Deák, *Picturing America, 1497–1899* (Princeton), vol. 1, pp. 85–86. I. N. Phelps Stokes Collection, Miriam and Ira D. Wallach Division of Art, Prints and Photographs, The New York Public Library, Astor, Lenox and Tilden Foundations. Courtesy, New York Public Library.

[174]

1773
May 11th

———

Breakfasted with Major Bayard.—received a
few complementary visits—and invita-
tion to dine with Col. William Bayard at his seat
in the Country.
Went to the Playhouse in the Evening—saw the
Gamester[302] and Padlock[303] performed.—the
players make but an indifferent figure
in tragedy: they make a much better in
comedy. Hallam[304] has merit in every
character he acts: Mr. Wools[305] in the Character of Don Diego, and Mrs. Morris,[306] in that
of Ursula, I thought acted with [?]
superlatively.
I was however upon the whole much
gratified, (and believe if I had stayed in town
a month should go to the Theatre every
acting night. But as a citizen and

302. Howe, *Proceedings*, 1915–1916 [FN 478-2]. By Edward Moore (1712–1757). See Drabble, *supra*, p. 665. *The Gamester* dates from 1753.

303. Howe, *Proceedings*, 1915–1916 [FN 478-3]. By Isaac Bickerstaff (1733–?1808). See Drabble, *supra*, pp. 99–100. *The Padlock* was first performed in London in 1768.

304. Lewis Hallam (1740–1808), theatrical manager. See *Dictionary of American Biography*, VIII, 148. Howe, *Proceedings*, 1915–1916 [FN 478-4]. In "The Padlock" he portrayed Mungo and in "The Gamester," he portrayed Beverly.

305. Howe, *Proceedings*, 1915–1916 [FN 479-1]. Stephen Woolls, acting in "The Padlock."

306. Probably the young Elizabeth Morris (1753–1826), actress. Known on stage as Mrs. Owen Morris; regarded once as the greatest attraction on the American stage. See *Dictionary of American Biography*, XIII, 206.

[*174 continued*]

friend to the morals and happiness of society I should
strive hard against the admission and much
more the Establishment of a Playhouse

[175]

1773
May 12

_____

in any state of which I was a
member.

Spent the morning in writing and
roving.
Dined with Col. William Bayard[307] at his
seat on North River. His seat,
table, and all around him in
the highest elegance and taste.
His daughter, Mrs. Johnson sung
3 or 4 songs with more voice,
judgment, and execution than I ever heard
any lady. Several of the Company
who heard the best singers in
London said she surpassed
them: All agreed she equaled
the celebrated Mrs. Brent,[308] but
Dr. Middleton[309] said his complais-

307. William Bayard (1729–1804). Prominent and opulent merchant of New York City, where he was born; died at Southampton, England; resided at Castle Pointe, Hoboken, New Jersey, and, although he joined the Sons of Liberty, his estate was confiscated because his principles would not permit him to aid the movement for independence. USGenNet, *American History and Genealogy Project*, 2000–2002.

308. Charlotte Brent (d. 1802), singer. Toured with her husband, Thomas Pinto, in Scotland and Ireland, 1770–80. See *Dictionary of National Biography*, VI, 261.

309. Peter Middleton (d. 1781), physician. Practiced in New York City after 1752. A founder of the Medical School of King's College (Columbia), 1767; also one of the incorporators of New York Hospital, 1771. See *Dictionary of American Biography*, XII, 602.

[*175 continued*]

ance[310] did not lead him to say

310. I.e., "civility." See Johnson, *Dictionary*, *supra*, n.p. "complaisance."

[176]

————

he had never heard better singing
in England, but he had met
with nothing like it in America.

Was this day invited to dine on the
morrow with David Vanhorne,
Esq.[311] and Mr. [blank] Broom[312] the husband of the late Miss Rebecca Lloyd[313], but
declined them both expecting on
the morrow to go through the sound
to Rhode Island.
Drank tea with Mr. Broom and lady;
she appeared in her usual good-
ness; he is endowed with much civility, understanding and politeness.

[PAGE 177 SKIPPED NUMERICALLY (NOT TORN OUT)]

311. Possibly General David Van Horne (1746–1801).
312. Howe, *Proceedings*, 1915–1916 [FN 479-2]. John Broome, merchant. "[M]arried Rebecca Lloyd of Long Island, a niece of Dr. James Lloyd of Boston. She was engaged to Edmund Quincy, brother of the writer, at the time of his death in 1768. *Memoir of Josiah Quincy, Jr.*, 109 n."
313. Rebecca Lloyd (b. January 2, 1746 or 1747); married John Broome in 1769.

[178]

1773
May 12th

———

Attended a Public Concert,
which was very full. The Musick
indifferent; the room intole-
rable. The ladies sprightly,
loquacious, familiar and
beautiful: the men not
so richly or elegantly dressed
as I expected, nor so gallant
as the incitements of the Night
seemed to justifie.
Miss Hallam[314] & Miss Storer[315]
(two actresses) sung several
times well, but the melody
was much injured by the instru-
mental musick. Indeed it is
not uncommon to hear vocal
musick frequently thus
destroyed and every softer beauty of it lost.

314. Miss Sarah Hallam, cousin to Lewis Hallam, "queen of the American stage." Returned to Williamsburg to conduct a dancing school which she opened in August of 1775; she lived until at least 1839. *Williamsburg and Its Theatres*, Department of Research and Education, Colonial Williamsburg, Inc., 1937.

315. Howe, *Proceedings*, 1915–1916 [FN 479-5]. Maria Storer. See George Overcash Seilhamer, *History of the American Theatre before the Revolution* (Philadelphia, 2005), 350.

[179]

1773
May 13th

———

Spent the day in riding & rambling,
and the Evening at the Playhouse.
The Tempest of the Shakespear,[316] the Masque
of Neptune, and Amphetrite,[317] and the Honest
Yorkshireman[318] was performed.
The scenery of the Tempest was far beyond what I tho[ugh]t practicable.
The players excel in comedy; are
but indifferent in tragedy.

14th

Preparing for departure and con-
gratulatory and complementary
trifles consumed the day.

———

316. William Shakespeare (1564–1616); *The Tempest* was first performed at court in Novem-ber 1611. See Drabble, *supra*, 890. Quincy possessed *The Beauties of Shakespear* at his death. See Quincy, Estate Catalogue, *supra*, item 203.

317. Amphitrite was the wife of Poseidon or Neptune, God of the Sea, with whom she had a son, Triton. See Howatson, *supra*, p. 458. A masque would have involved both dramatic and musical components. See *Concise Oxford Dictionary*, *supra*, 729. For example, William Dav-enant, John Dryden, and Thomas Shadwell added "a grand fifth-act masque of Neptune and Amphitrite," to Shakespeare's *The Tempest*, which was produced in London at the Theatre Royal in 1712 by John Weldon. Perhaps what Quincy saw was an adaptation of Weldon's pro-duction. See John Weldon, *The Tempest*, semi-Opera, to a text by William Davenant, John Dryden, and Thomas Shadwell after William Shakespeare, London, 1712. My thanks for this reference to Mark Sullivan, reference librarian beyond compare.

318. Howe, *Proceedings*, 1915–1916 [FN 480-1]. A ballet-opera, by Henry Carey.

[179 continued]

Paid Mr. Rivington[319] for his paper for
one year from the first publication;
which he is to send me free of further
expense.

319. James Rivington (1724–1802), bookseller, printer, journalist. Put out first regular issue of *Rivington's New-York Gazetteer* on April 22, 1773. Howe, *Proceedings,* 1915–1916 [FN 480-2]. The paper became so offensive to the Sons of Liberty, because of its neutrality, that a party of patriots destroyed Rivington's printing plant in November 1775. See *Dictionary of American Biography,* XV, 637.

ILLUSTRATION 21. Newport, R.I., in 1730. On stone by J. P. Newall, tinted lithograph, K. H. Bufford's Lith., 1864. Courtesy, Boston Athenaeum.

[180]

1773
May 15

———

By the desire of Col. Oliver and some
other polite company took passage
down the Sound for Newport.[320]
Was the rather induced to this tour by
water than thro' Connecticut,
having before gone thro' that Colony and my horses being so fatigued
with their journey as to render
it doubtful whether they could
reach home by Land.

17th May
[left margin, l. 14]

———

'Baring one storm which occasioned
our laying at Anchor one day
our passage was pleasant; and we
reach Newport safely this day
about noon.

320. Contained about 1000 houses; 75 miles SW by S of Boston. Jedidiah Morse, D.D., *The American Gazetteer*. Printed in Boston, 1797. See *Illustration 21*.

[181]

———

The Equestrian Statue of his Majesty near the Fort, is a very great
ornament to the City New York.
The Statue of Mr. Pitt[321] has all the
defects of that at Charlestown (I
before mentioned) with the addition-
nal one of being of the Pedestral
kind instead of the Colossal.

The general character of the Inhabitants of this City is much tinctured
with gayety & dissipation.
But having now got so near the
place of my birth & residence, my
sentiments and opinions may be
presumed to be too much
affected by former im-
pression and byases [biases] to make me
an impartial judge or wholly
indifferent relator. I therefore

321. William Pitt, 1st Earl of Chatham (1708–1778). Chatham, known as the "Great Commoner," was very popular in the colonies. He was a leader of the Whigs, and an advocate of conciliation. His son was William Pitt "the Younger" (1759–1806). Quincy greatly admired
Chatham, whom he described as "like Marcellus—'Viros Supereminet Omnes'." See The London Journal, Quincy Papers, vol. 1, pp. 252–257. There was also a "Colossal statue" of Pitt in
Charleston. See page 218 [90] supra.

[182]

_____

wave a detail of my observations and judgment upon the
two Colonies of New York and Rhode
Island for the same reason.

Thus (<u>Currente Calamo</u>[322]) have I given
some idea of the impressions made
upon my own mind in this
agreeable town. Opinions and sentiments formed in haste and
(as Lord Bacon says) upon the spur of
the occasion are liable to many
exceptions; and may probably be
erroneous.[323] However they are
evidences of my own judgment;
may serve of valueable purpose

322. Translation: With the pen running (i.e., in a hurried fashion).
323. "Sir Amice Pawlet, when he saw too much haste in any matter, was wont to say, 'Stay a while, that we may make an end the sooner.'" Francis Bacon, *Apothegms* (1624), No. 54. Quincy owned Bacon's *Works* at his death, and the posthumous portrait of Quincy by Gilbert Stuart shows a volume of Bacon's *Works* behind Quincy. See Quincy, Estate Catalogue, *supra*, Item 42. See note 295, *supra*, and see also *Quincy Papers*, vol. 1, pp. xxxv.

[183]

———

of bringing past scenes into present
and future view, and be a landmark
of our own errors. Some of the
most durable pleasures are of the
retrospective kind: some of the
best preservatives from present
mistakes are written transcripts
of past errors.

What I have set down will be
chiefly useful to myself: (it cannot be profitable or en-
tertaining to the uninterested reader
who may chance to cast his eye
on this hasty production. If he
throw it down with the gesture
of contempt—let him remember it was not intended to please
or instruct him.)—[324]

———

324. Ironically, this passage indicates at least some expectation by Quincy that others would
see the *Southern Journal.* How pleased and surprised he would be with the *Journal*'s current historical value.

[184]

———

A Bird of passage may easily
collect—peradventure bear
away—food for itself; but can
transport on his fleeting tour very little, if anything of sufficient solidity for the nourishment or
(regale) of others.

Where I to lament anything, it
would be the prevalent and extended
ignorance of one colony of the
concerns of another.—

Where I to hazard an excentric conjecture
it would be, that the Pen. [Penn], Baltimore or Fairfax familys will
hereafter contend for the dominion—and one of them perhaps attain the
sovereignty—of North America.[325]

325. Quincy's "excentric conjecture" has, quite fortunately, not come to pass. But the influence of these three families was immense, and their names now are reflected in those of great states, cities, and counties. The following helpful notes have been prepared by my research assistant, Nicole Scimone.

Penn Family: See the *Compact Edition of the Dictionary of National Biography* (Oxford, 1975), pp. 1630–1631. The Penn family is the founding family of Pennsylvania. The family can trace its American roots back to the 1682 arrival of William Penn, a Quaker, from England. King Charles II of England owed a debt to Penn as repayment of a loan from Penn's father, an Admiral, and the King, in turn, gave Penn land in what is now Pennsylvania and Maryland. Penn's first stay in America lasted only a year and ten months, but during this time, he was very productive in contributing to the development of the colony. He created a government for this territory which he entitled a "Holy Experiment" and which included an elective council and assembly, and guarantees of the fundamental liberties of the individual. Also, he superintended

ILLUSTRATION 22. Frederic Calvert, Lord Baltimore (1731–1771). Engraving, published in Horace Walpole, *Catalog of the royal and noble authors of England, Scotland, and Ireland* (London, 1806), vol. 5, p. 278. Courtesy, Boston Athenaeum. See p. 347, *Southern Journal*, p. 184.

the laying out of Philadelphia and built his own house several miles up the Delaware River. He then left and returned to England again in late 1701 to deal with a proposal in the English Parliament to annex all proprietary colonies of the crown. Penn died in 1718, and his wife died in 1727. After her death, the proprietorship of Pennsylvania passed to his surviving sons John, Thomas, and Richard Penn. The Penns, together with the Quaker establishment, opposed the American Revolution. John Penn was arrested in 1777 on charges of acting against the Patriots. Although the Penns received major compensation for losses during the Revolution in 1779, their influence in the state waned. Quincy comments at page 165 that the "family lost much of their Provincial influence by renouncing the Religion of their Ancestors and the Colony in general [Quakerism] for that of the Episcopacy." Quincy also observed that the powerful influence of the Penns' "proprietary" party in Pennsylvania's politics was limited by "a lineal successive defeat of capacity, want of policy, glaring avarice, and oppressive measures in the Penn-family." See p. 322 [165], *supra*.

Fairfax Family: See the *Compact Edition of the Dictionary of National Biography* (Oxford, 1975), vol. 1, p. 657. The Fairfax family was the leading Virginian family at the time of Quincy's visit. Thomas Fairfax, also known as sixth Lord Fairfax of Cameron, was the first Fairfax to exert influence in Virginia. Thomas traces his ties to Virginia to his mother, Catherine, who was heiress to the original colonizers of Virginia, the Culpeper family, who had been in Virginia for over four generations. The Culpepers' property had originally been part of a grant from Charles II to a group of Cavaliers. Thomas's great-grandfather was one of the grantees, and his son later purchased all the land from the other grantees. However, there was resentment within the colony to the Culpepers' ownership, and in 1733, when his family's Virginian property came under attack, a forty-year-old Thomas came over to America from England to help protect his inheritance. In 1747, Thomas decided to set up permanent residence in America, settling in the Shenandoah Valley. His life in America is marked as one of the utmost simplicity, lacking in the finer things that Quincy had admired in others during his tour of the South, such as fine wines, latest fashions, and a showy library. Thomas was a bachelor, who remained neutral during the Revolution. After his death in 1782, and ten years of lawsuits, the Commonwealth of Virginia acquired title to much of his land, and a real estate syndicate bought the rest from his heirs.

Baltimore Family: See the *Compact Edition of the Dictionary of National Biography* (Oxford, 1975), vol. 1, p. 291. The Baltimore family to which Quincy refers is the Calvert family, which obtained a charter for what is now Maryland in 1632, in part to provide a haven for Catholics. The first Lord Baltimore was George Calvert, who was born in 1580 in England. Having won the confidence of King James while acting as principal secretary of state and controller of the King's policy, he was later knighted in 1617. In 1625, George resigned from his appointment and the King created a new position for him—Baron of Baltimore in the Kingdom of Ireland. He had already developed an interest in America at that point, having been granted the entirety of Newfoundland in 1622, which was later restricted to cover only the peninsula of Avalon. After moving there with his second wife and all but one of his children in 1628, he complained to the king about the severe weather and asked for a land grant in a warmer climate. George Calvert died in 1632 shortly before receiving the Maryland charter, and, instead, it was issued to his eldest son, Cecil. Cecil's half brother, Leonard, was named Governor, and set out, with "twenty other gentlemen" and two Jesuit priests, to settle the new colony in 1633. Throughout the rest of the seventeenth century, George Calvert's heirs attempted to dominate control of the Maryland government, but their attempts were eventually quashed due to internal incompetence, and in 1692, a royal government was established in Maryland. Frederick Calvert (1731–1771), the sixth Lord Baltimore, died in Naples on Sept. 14, 1771, shortly after Quincy's trip. He inherited the

[185]
———

And where I to breathe a wish—
it would be, that the numerous and
surprisingly increasing inhabitants[326]
of this extensive, fertile and amazing
Continent may be thoro'ly attentive and suitably actuated by the
blessings of Providence—the
dangers which surround them—
and the duties they owe to GOD,
themselves and posterity.[327]

———

proprietorship of Maryland from his father. He was indicted at Kingston in 1768 for an assault on a female. Following his acquittal, he lived on the continent. Rather than fulfilling Quincy's prophecy of an American aristocracy, Calvert's greatest achievement was his account of a voyage "to the East," with many classical references. It was just the sort of thing Quincy would have loved, but it was not in his library catalogue. See Frederick Calvert, Lord Baltimore, *A Tour to the East in the Years 1763 and 1764* . . . (London, 1767). See *Illustration 22.*

326. Quincy was certainly prophetic here. The population increase of the United States from 1780 to 1869 was eleven-fold, 2,781,000 to 31,443,321. See James Willard Hurst, *Law and the Conditions of Freedom in the Nineteenth Century United States* (Madison, Wis., 1956), 71.

327. In retrospect, even Quincy, a demanding observer of himself and others, would credit these inhabitants with meeting their "duties" to "posterity" by creating a new nation!

INDEX

Note: Page references in italics refer to illustrations.
All locations are in Massachusetts unless otherwise indicated
(or well known, such as Philadelphia).
JQ refers to Josiah Quincy Jr.

THIS VOLUME HAS BEEN DESIGNED,
TYPESET IN CASLON TYPES, AND PRINTED AT
THE STINEHOUR PRESS, LUNENBURG, VERMONT

BOUND AT ACME BOOKBINDING,
CHARLESTOWN, MASSACHUSETTS